Commercial and Cyber Fraud

A Legal Guide to Justice for Businesses

Commercial and Cyber Fraud

A Legal Guide to Justice for Businesses

Second Edition

Ian Smith

LLB (Birmingham), Barrister, 33 Chancery Lane, London

Dr David Shepherd PhD

Senior Lecturer, University of Portsmouth

Bloomsbury Professional

LONDON • DUBLIN • EDINBURGH • NEW YORK • NEW DELHI • SYDNEY

BLOOMSBURY PROFESSIONAL
Bloomsbury Publishing Plc 41–43 Boltro Road, Haywards Heath, RH16 1BJ, UK

British Library Cataloguing-in-Publication Data

A catalogue record for this book is available from the British Library.

ISBN:	PB	978 1 52650 914 7
	ePDF	978 1 52650 916 1
	ePub	978 1 52650 915 4

Typeset by Evolution Design and Digital Ltd (Kent)

Preface

This guide arose from experiences of striving for justice for victims of fraud, both exhilarating and frustrating: Ian Smith's work as a lawyer, and David Shepherd's experiences as a fraud victim.

The authors' overriding objective is to arm businesses with information that will enable them to make confident and wise choices in their pursuit of justice. Some of those businesses will be large businesses with substantial resources at their disposal. Others will include the millions of businesses which do not have the resources and experiences of the largest corporations.

This is not a definitive guide and can never be so, because the law is an ever-changing labyrinth, people are complex and unpredictable, and greed and other motives inspire innovative but dishonest ways of making quick money.

Nevertheless, this guide is, we think, unique in bringing together different aspects of the fraud experience so that decision-makers in business, in-house lawyers, non-specialist lawyers and law-enforcers might gain a more rounded and fuller view of a victim's options. It is unique in providing and integrated and full picture of both the civil justice and criminal justice options for victims.

This guide does, in places, criticise the legal systems of England and Wales. These criticisms are not directed at those striving for justice for victims and the wider society. It is, nevertheless, important to shine a light where fault lies so that victims can appreciate not just the options and opportunities they have but also the serious obstacles they may face.

The main difficulties with the legal systems stem from their inherent unsuitability for dealing with serious and complex commercial fraud. The parallel systems of justice developed on their separate tracks long before the fiendishly complex frauds of today emerged. Whilst both the criminal and civil justice systems have evolved and continue to adapt to the innovations of fraudsters, serious legacy problems remain.

Distressed fraud victims with scant knowledge of the law must first find a way to access the legal systems in England and Wales. They must then make profound choices with serious implications for their lives: to sue, to punish, seek both or do nothing. Finally, they have to navigate their way around complex bureaucracies with the help of strangers.

This is a seriously challenging task. The criminal system can be very slow and does not prioritise compensation for victims. The civil system is faster and focused on asset recovery for victims but it is very expensive to access. It should not be beyond the wit of the legislators and the judiciary to develop a more coherent pathway to justice for victims of financial crimes. In the meantime, these are the systems that victims and their advisors have to negotiate. Our sincere hope is that this guide will help them to do so.

Preface

This guide sets out to be victim-centred. We have tried at all times to think of victims' concerns and interests ahead of others. We have endeavoured to explain, with as much objectivity as we are capable of, the various options and their respective merits. Whether we have succeeded or not is up to you the reader.

The authors would greatly welcome any criticisms and observations from any reader. We regard this guide as an on-going, evolving project and will produce revisions from time-to-time to incorporate readers' comments or criticisms and to reflect any developments in the justice systems. We are very keen to hear from and collect the stories of businesses, lawyers, investigators and police officers. Please do get in touch.

Ian Smith
is@33cllaw.com
Chambers of Andrew Mitchell QC
33 Chancery Lane
London
WC2A 1EN

About the authors

Ian Smith

Ian is a barrister (England and Wales) who specialises in representing victims of fraud. Ian works in both the civil courts and criminal courts, focusing on obtaining compensation for victims. He advises businesses and individuals on their justice options and their opportunities for recoveries in both domestic and international cases. Ian is a founding member of VOCAL (Victims of crime Association of lawyers), an association which aims to improve awareness of the legal needs and rights of victims of crime in Europe. Ian is also an expert in anti-financial crime for other professionals and businesses.

Dr David Shepherd

David's engineering business was a victim of fraud. He successfully sought justice through both the criminal and civil courts. The fraudsters were jailed for over six years and David's business obtained compensation through the civil courts. The experience inspired David to undertake postgraduate research into fraud and complete a doctoral degree. David has switched career and is now a Senior Lecturer at the University of Portsmouth specialising in fraud and corruption.

Acknowledgements

The authors have many people to thank.

The authors would like to thank the anonymous victims whose stories bring many of the pages of this book to life. All have been generous with their time and generous with their thoughts for others. It is not always easy to recount and reflect on bad experiences but sharing those stories provides a rich learning opportunity for others.

The authors are grateful to the following lawyers and others, some of whom gave feedback on drafts of this guide and some of whom gave the insights that appear as quotes from lawyers: Martin Adams, Ned Beale, Benjamin Borsodi, Graham Brown, Mark Button, Anthony Cole, William Christopher, Caoive Collins, Simon Cowie, Thom Dieben, Olivier Gutkès, Stewart Hey, Andrew Horrocks, Robert Hunter, Dominique Inchauspé, Han Jahae, Serafina Lee, Mehmet Karagoz, Trevor Mascarenhas, Igor Novakovic, Clara Poglia, Michael Potts, Anthony Riem, Sylvain Savolainen, Elizabeth Seborg, Alan Sheeley, Mark Thomson, Richard Trainer, Simone Trombetti, Sean Upson, Lee White, Mary Young and a senior Quantitative Analyst who preferred to remain anonymous.

Lastly, the authors wish to acknowledge all those who offered valuable insights or kindly lent an ear to discussions of the themes in this guide.

Contents

Directors' Handbook Series

Titles available from Bloomsbury Professional in the Directors' Handbook Series:

Bribery: A Compliance Handbook
Raj Chada, Christopher Sallon QC and Sam Tate
ISBN: 978 1 78043 328 8

Chambers' Corporate Governance Handbook (7th Edition)
Andrew Chambers
ISBN: 978 1 78451 444 0

Commercial and Cyber Fraud: A Legal Guide to Justice for Businesses
Ian Smith
ISBN: 978 1 52650 914 7

Company Law Handbook 2017
Saleem Sheikh
ISBN: 978 1 78451 436 5

Directors' Remuneration Handbook (2nd Edition)
Cliff Weight
ISBN: 978 1 78043 331 8

Rights and Duties of Directors 2018/19 (17th Edition)
Martha Bruce
ISBN: 978 1 52650 668 9

For more information on any of the above titles please visit www.bloomsburyprofessional.com/uk/law/company-law.

The Directors' Handbook Series are also available as part of Bloomsbury Professional's Company and Commercial online service. For more information or for a free trial, please call 01444 416119 or email customerservices@bloomsburyprofessional.com.

List of figures

About this guide

The guide's narrative deliberately speaks directly to businesses and requires little or no prior legal experience to read. It is aimed at all decision-makers in business, including in-house lawyers, who have to react to and decide what to do after the discovery of fraud on the business. The authors also have in mind non-specialist lawyers, non-UK lawyers and those law enforcement and legal professionals who are unfamiliar with one or other of the principal legal systems in England and Wales. The guide provides the police and prosecutors with an introduction to the civil regime.

The authors have used straightforward English but occasionally do use lawyerly language to familiarise lay persons with legal terms they are likely to encounter. It can be so difficult for victims to process a lawyer's advice whilst trying to untangle what, at first utterance, appear to be obscure phrases. The reality is that these words do not hold some kind of deep mystery which is only perceptible to learned students of law. They are ordinary words that, as in any occupation, whether in engineering, in science or in services, have particular meanings.

The guide is laid out thematically in an approximately chronological order, from discovery of the crime (⊳ *Section 1*) and consideration of options (⊳ *Section 2*), through engaging lawyers (⊳ *Section 3*), early interventions to secure assets in the hands of fraudsters (⊳ *Section 4*) and culminating in sections on legal rights and processes, including civil court trials (⊳ *Section 5*) and criminal justice (⊳ *Section 6*). The final chapter, *Section 7*, is an introduction to cross-border cases and is mainly aimed at lawyers dealing with international frauds. For that reason, it does include citations of the main international law and UK legislation that apply.

Cross-references are placed throughout the guide to assist you to navigate the guide. They are signified by the symbol ⊳. The cross-references allow you to dip into any section of the book and connect with other relevant sections. Having said that, if you are a victim, you are strongly urged to read *Sections 1 to 3* in sequence and in their entirety. Text boxes are placed throughout the guide to remind you of certain points and to emphasise their importance; those headed "Signpost" alert you to relevant material in another section. Quotes from real victims are included to lend their voices to the narrative and to let you know you are not alone. Others have been there too. Finally, quotes from fraud lawyers are set out in shaded boxes.

Fraud is a massive problem (⊳ *Section 1.4*). The Crime Survey for England and Wales estimates that 3,239,000 adults experienced fraud in the year to September 2017.[1] Recent research has also estimated the total annual losses to fraud in the UK at £190 billion.[2] The losses suffered by individuals is £7 billion, whilst organisations

1 ONS (2018). *Crime in England and Wales: year ending September 2017*. Available at: www.ons.gov.uk/peoplepopulationandcommunity/crimeandjustice/articles/overviewoffraudandcomputermisusestatisticsforenglandandwales/2018-01-25.

2 University of Portsmouth (2017). *Annual fraud indicator 2017*. London: Experian and PKF. Available at: www.crowe.com/uk/croweuk/news/annual-fraud-indicator-2017.

lose £183 billion per year. These figures show that fraud in its many guises causes far more financial harm than all other crimes put together. The stand-out point is that you, your business or your employer have been or are very likely to become a victim of fraud. Understanding how to deal with fraud cases is a necessity for businesses.

There are numerous practitioner publications which advise on fraud prevention, a scattering of official guides on how to avoid becoming a victim, and weighty law books which are virtually impenetrable to all but lawyers and academics. But there's very little which sets out in sufficient depth the justice options for victims and their relative merits, the hurdles that might have to be overcome and the strategic implications. This guide sets out to do those things.

The English and Welsh legal systems contain extensive powers which can be brought to bear against wrongdoers on behalf of victims and *can* deliver righteous justice. The emphasis on "can" is deliberate, as too often access to justice is denied because of the high costs of civil litigation and by the limited capacity of the law enforcement agencies.

One source of frustration is the apparent incoherence between the two main justice routes – criminal and civil. *Figure A* at the end of this section contains simplified flow diagrams of the main English and Welsh justice regimes, the civil and criminal systems, laid out side-by-side. The regulatory justice systems in the UK are omitted from the diagram: they are beyond the scope of this guide as they vary considerably, are heavily focused on professional compliance and are less concerned with justice for victims of fraud.

In principle, the civil and criminal regimes are not mutually exclusive, but the practical reality is that they often are immiscible because they have different objectives (▷ *Section 2*), they run on separate timetables, in separate courts and because almost all professionals dealing with fraud cases specialise in one route or the other, very rarely in both (▷ *Section 3.6*). The inevitable consequence is that victims struggle to obtain a neutral view of their justice options from those specialising in one jurisdiction or the other. "Parallel" cases which smoothly combine both routes are rare. This book aims to provide a balanced, in-depth guide to both the civil and criminal law options. It is, we think, unique in doing so.

Figure A illustrates the typical sequence of case events. However, cases rarely proceed with such mechanical precision. Stages usually overlap and activities invariably loop back, most notably as a result of investigations. Steps are frequently omitted or are less salient because, for instance, the defendant admits his wrongdoing early in the process, or the freezing of assets is unnecessary as the defendant is a large, stable corporation. Sometimes the sequence may be adjusted according to the circumstances and requirements of particular cases. At other times, and all too often, civil litigants and prosecutors delay freezing and restraining defendants' assets until later in the process. Such delays can severely damage the victims' chances of recovering their money: they allow the fraudsters and those assisting them to dissipate their assets, moving them beyond the practical reach of victims and prosecutors.

The most obvious point to take away from your first reading of *Figure A* is the similarity between the justice systems. Fraud victims often question why there are separate options and processes in England and Wales in fraud cases. This is a good question. The quick answer is that the justice systems have evolved along divergent paths, due to their distinct objectives, long before the emergence of serious and complex fraud as we know it today, and certainly way before the term "cyber fraud" was coined. The criminal regime is designed to determine guilt or innocence and impose punishment on behalf of society. The civil regime is designed to determine liability and quantify the amount of compensation for the claimant. This guide will explain how this separation can cause considerable anxiety and problems for fraud victims.

This guide also addresses a second source of frustration: the knowledge, language and communication gap between victims and the legal profession. The great majority of victims have had no prior experience of lawyers and the legal systems other than for conveyancing, some debt collection and minor motoring infractions. Victims need to know that they have options (▷*Section 2*). They need to be aware of the advantages and possible pitfalls of the options. They need to be armed with sufficient knowledge to have meaningful discussions with professionals so that they can make informed choices quickly and with confidence. A victim may want to see the fraudster imprisoned, thinking that our society is better served by sending a prolific offender to prison. More often, victims want to focus on recovering their losses. Sometimes victims want both (▷*Section 2.11*).

Dealing with fraud cases can be very complex and challenging. Fraudsters cover their tracks and deliberately launder their (or your!) money, often with other people and in other countries. Cyber fraud compounds these complexities (▷*Section 1.4*), adding technological and legal challenges for investigators as well as for claimants and prosecutors (▷*Section 6.6*). Fraud cases throw up multiple choices and dilemmas: what and whom to believe, whether to report the fraud to the police, whom to sue and whether to bring civil proceedings or do nothing at all. The fraudsters present moving targets and options need to be considered at speed. These circumstances and choices are unlike any other that business people or non-specialist lawyers are used to making in ordinary business life or even in ordinary commercial litigation.

It should be pretty obvious to the reader of this guide that we (the authors) have tried to present a realistic picture of the justice options open to victims and the costs of accessing these options. Criminal justice is, in theory, free to all victims of crime. The reality is, however, that there are very serious restrictions on the numbers of cases taken on by the police and prosecutors (▷*Section 6*). For its part, civil justice (▷*Sections 4 and 5*) can provide excellent routes to justice for victims. You have the right to bring civil claims if you have suffered losses and can identify legal claims against a wrongdoer. But accessing civil justice is expensive and sometimes very expensive (▷*Section 3*).

All litigation is uncertain. In the civil courts this uncertainty, together with the high costs of litigating, tends to ensure that the parties often do settle their differences without going to trial. We spend a considerable amount of time dealing with suggested approaches to out-of-court settlement of civil claims (▷*Section 5.15, Compromising claims*). This includes methods for valuing rational settlements in examples that we examine. It's crucial that you value your case realistically and that you continue to be realistic as your case progresses.

If you come away from this guide with just one thing, it should be this: when it comes to fraud, the law is not like a trusty vehicle breakdown service which, with lights flashing, always comes to the rescue, is routine, predictable and low cost. The police may or may not take up a case irrespective of its merits; civil litigation is expensive;

and both are likely to demand a considerable amount of your time, resources and patience. Lawyers are always happy to advise and represent victims, but is it worth the cost (▷ *Section 5.4*)? Will the under-resourced police have another priority (▷ *Section 6.10*)? How can you judge risks when justice is such an unpredictable process? Sometimes, with a compliant, remorseful defendant, it is easy and cheap. More often it is difficult, hard work, costly and uncertain. We (the authors) hope that this book helps you to take control and make confident and wise choices, which together with good advice from fraud lawyers will enable you to secure justice.

Figure A: Flow diagram through civil and criminal regimes

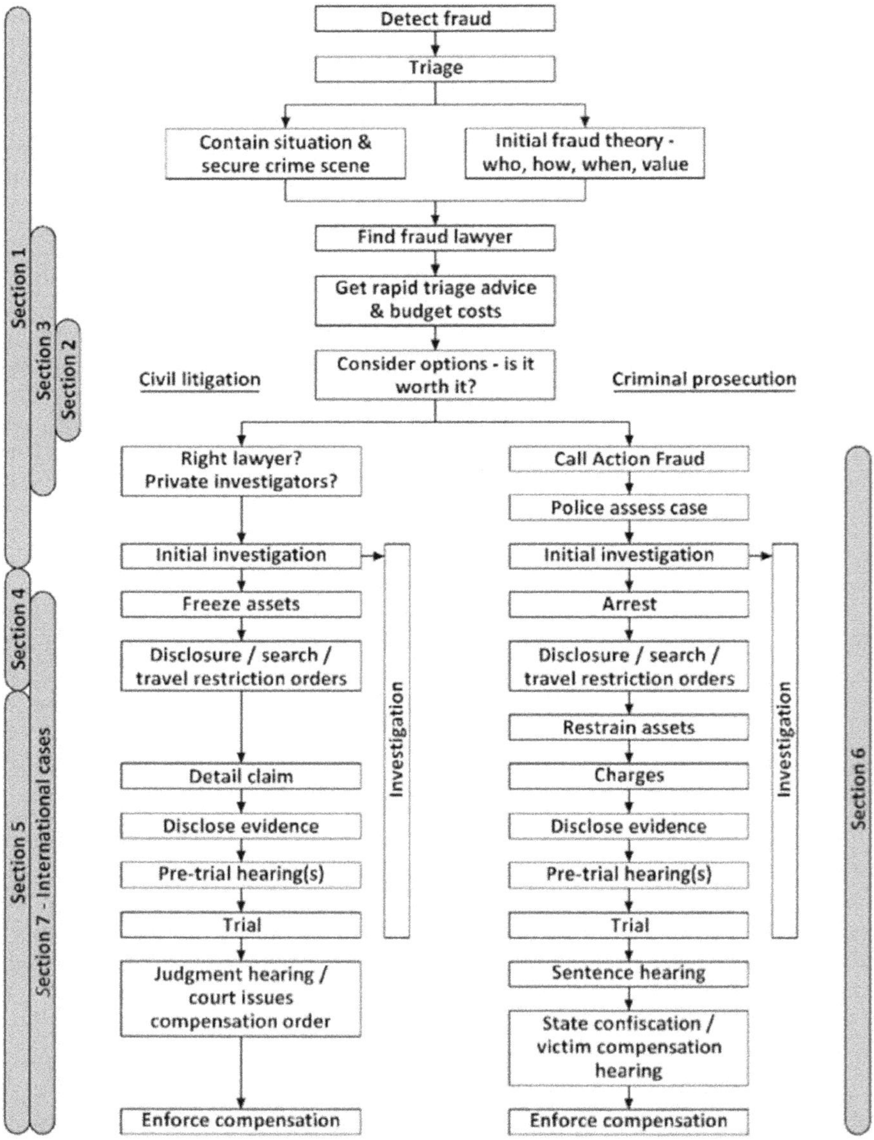

Discovery, first reactions and investigations

1.1 In this section

- The realisation that you have been defrauded
- The nature of fraud
- Who to trust in your investigation
- Evidence and evidence gathering
- Proving the fraud

1.2 Discovery

You receive a telephone call. It's anonymous, "Your Buying Director's got his hands in the till. He's doing deals with your supplier, bumping the prices and splitting the uplift." Is this real or does the caller just have a grievance? He says it's been going on for years. How much would that be worth?

Your accountant shows you three invoices and payments to an engineering company for "maintenance services". Plausible services, but £120,000 over six months is very unusual. Who are they, who authorised it?

You have spent £1.5 million acquiring an established business as part of a modest expansion strategy. Six weeks later the turnover is lower than expected. Debtors are disputing sales invoices. Creditors are demanding settlement of six-month-old invoices despite the completion accounts showing nothing older than three months. Despite all that due diligence, did you misunderstand something?

A new customer returned £7,000 of supplies. You refunded him with a BACS transfer. It then transpired that goods were bought with a stolen credit card. This is the third time in four months. Is it the same customer? Is there an insider involved?

More and more of your employees are leaving and some of them are going to a competitor and you discover that customer lists and other commercial information has been emailed to employees' personal email addresses.

You sense something is wrong with the cash flow, but you can't put your finger on the cause. You have to put off paying some suppliers. Why?

1.3 The slowly rotated dimmer switch …

The first reaction to such events can be an instant light-bulb moment. More often it is a slowly rotated dimmer switch. It starts with confusion, then a search for alternative explanations followed by a dawning realisation. Your emotions turn from bewilderment to horror then to fear and anger.

You do not know what to do. You are embarrassed. You do not want to tell anyone. You are afraid of the consequences if employees, suppliers and customers find out.

You spend valuable time trying to understand it, doubting yourself and silencing the inner voice. You feel it is your fault and you have let others down. Eventually you realise that you have to tell someone.

> **Signpost**
>
> You need rapid advice from a specialist lawyer with a deep knowledge of the relevant law. Speed is of the essence because action may need to be taken very quickly to contain your situation, to freeze the fraudster's assets, to prevent further losses or to impress the police with the need for urgency. ⊳ *Section 3*

You confide in a colleague and they run the same range of emotional responses, first doubting your findings and seeking alternative rational explanations before accepting reality. You cannot yet see how much you have lost. It could be catastrophic. You debate what to do next and come to the conclusion that you really have to call for outside help. Who? What for?

You may be thinking, "What will happen to us?". Even senior management in large multinational companies experience a range of emotional responses when discovering fraud:

> "Members of the Corporate Team involved in what should have been a routine reconciliation exercise to close out the financials on a high capital value project were initially puzzled as to why they could not balance the accounts. This was followed by a sense of frustration as to why the usual exercises required to achieve close out were not working when it seemed that they should. Feelings of puzzlement and frustration were then displaced by a sense of disbelief when it became clear that the only explanation for the 'hole in the accounts' was a fraud. Disbelief was quickly overtaken by alarm and a gearing-up into 'crisis mode' when evidence pointed to a near certainty that one, possibly more, members or former members of the Finance Team were involved in the perpetration of the fraud."

Being conned can be a longer, more emotional experience than, say a burglary. A burglary is visible and obvious. You are quickly into the anger phase, you call the police and your insurer deals with it.

A fraud often means someone you trusted has let you down. It might be a supplier you know very little about, nevertheless you trusted them. Worse, it might be an employee or business associate you have worked with for years.

> A fraud lawyer: "Discovering a fraud can be extremely distressing, particularly if it looks like it was an inside job. Part of a good lawyer's role at the start of a case is to offer reassurance and support as well as damage limitation in terms of reputation and morale."

Once you have accepted the reality, the first step is to drop the guilt: they did it not you. This frees you to get a grip and start thinking, "What should I do to them?"

A chaotic journey is entirely normal for those who have not previously experienced fraud. David knows, because he was a victim, was slow to accept he had been defrauded and subsequently thrashed around looking for a solution. Ian knows because he has seen it many times in the legal system where victims, like David, spend too much time wrestling with the problem and the emerging realisation of its implications before seeking legal advice from a fraud lawyer.

With the benefit of hindsight, David would have done things differently. He believes that he would have been far better served if he had stopped to take a very deep breath and engaged in constructive activity.

> **Signpost**
>
> Fortunately for victims, the civil courts have strong powers to help victims to identify wrongdoers and trace assets. A key power is the ability of the court to make a "Norwich Pharmacal Order". ▷ *Section 4*

Organising your thoughts and observations is the best thing you can do. It calms the destructive emotional chaos, allows you to test and confirm your initial suspicions, and prepares you for your next steps. Importantly it assists you in developing your priorities (▷ *Section 2, Objectives and options*) and most of all prepares you for efficient and effective discussions with lawyers (▷ *Section 3.7, How to get the most from lawyers*) and police officers (▷ *Section 6.9, Making a criminal complaint*).

1.4 What is fraud?

Before proceeding further, we briefly need to consider what fraud is. Fraud is by its nature a secret, silent crime committed by stealth and guile. These characteristics make fraud crimes difficult to investigate. There are no gunshots, shattering windows or screeching getaway cars. There is no bloodied victim, and never in the history of policing has an officer raised alarm by shouting, "Stop, fraudster!" This means it is often not detected at all and, when it is detected, the victim companies often discover that it has been going on for some time, even years: the average duration of a fraud scheme is 18 months.[1] Once an offender has learnt how to commit a fraud and got away with it, they feel secure and do it again and again and again. Without intervention, the opportunistic offender turns into an habitual fraudster. Unfortunately this means a detected fraud is often just the tip of an iceberg. If there is an upside to this, it is that fraudsters often become complacent, leaving more and more evidence in their wake.

1.4.1 Definition of fraud

We need to briefly set out what the law thinks fraud is. *Section 6.4* goes into further detail with respect to the criminal law definition of fraud based on the Fraud Act 2006. *Section 5.13.7* deals with the most closely related civil law definition, the tort of deceit. For present purposes, both the criminal and civil regimes recognise fraud as an intentionally dishonest misrepresentation that causes victims to hand over money or other property to offenders. Many frauds look very much like theft. It is theft, for

1 Association of Certified Fraud Examiners (2016). *Report to the Nations*. Retrieved from: www.acfe.com/rttn2016.aspx.

example, when a sales manager raids the petty cash box. But it also becomes fraud when he takes the money and leaves a falsified expense receipt in the box. Similarly, it is also a fraud when a warehouse worker takes stock and adjusts the computerised inventory records.

In other cases of fraud, the dishonest representations actually cause the victims to pay away moneys or part with property. These dishonest communications can be of any type, including verbal, hand-written, typed, word-processed, or by way of a false entry into a database. They can involve genuine forms, such as purchase orders, invoices or expense claims, except that the information entered onto these forms is dishonest.

1.4.2 Types of fraud

There are many ways that a business can be defrauded by directors, employees, suppliers, contractors, customers and partners. The following list is by no means exhaustive as fraudsters are often very innovative, but it gives you an idea of the types of fraud threats that your business may face.[2] This typology is useful when considering your fraud theory (⊳ *Section 1.6, The fraud theory*).

Account redirection or mandate fraud

A fraudster impersonates a genuine supplier and instructs the customer to pay money owed to the supplier into an account set up by the fraudster.

Account takeover or facility takeover fraud

A fraudster impersonates a genuine customer of a bank to gain control of the customer's account and then make unauthorised transactions. This usually involves identity theft.

Application fraud

A fraudster provides dishonest information or stolen identities when applying for a job or credit account, or other services such as bank accounts, loans, mortgages, insurance cover and insurance claims.

CEO fraud

A fraudster impersonates a senior member of staff and instructs a junior member of the accounts department to make an urgent electronic payment into an account set up by the fraudster.

Employee fraud

Account redirection – Employee changes the payee on a cheque or electronic payment to their own name, their secret company or another party.

Accounting fraud – Employee falsifies the accounts to hide the theft of money by cheques, money transfers or other means.

---

2 Adapted from: Button, M. and Gee, J. (2013). *Countering Fraud for Competitive Advantage*. Chichester: Wiley, and from Action Fraud (www.actionfraud.police.uk).

Asset fraud – Employee falsely writes off equipment as obsolete and then acquires it below its real value.

Cash-in expenses fraud – Employee claims for first / business class travel, cashes the ticket in for economy class and pockets the difference.

Conflict of interest – Employee conducts private work or has other interests that conflict with the interests of the company, for example he secretly owns a supplier company or has a secret interest in a competitor.

Credit card fraud – Employee uses the company's credit card to order supplies for her personal use.

Expenses fraud – Employee submits a fictional, inflated or duplicate expense claim, or changes the details of expenses that do not comply with the company's rules.

Identity fraud – Employee sells or uses banking details of clients for fraudulent purchases.

Inventory fraud – Employee steals products and falsely adjusts the inventory system.

Job application fraud – Prospective employee falsely declares or falsifies qualifications, experience, references, criminal record or immigration status.

Money transfers – Employee moves money into a personal bank account.

Payroll fraud – "ghost employees" – Fraudsters add non-existent employees to the payroll.

Payroll fraud – salary fraud – salary increments, overtime or allowances are falsely added to an employee's pay.

Procurement fraud – "ghost suppliers" – Employee sets up a fictitious supplier on the purchasing system and submits invoices for non-existent supplies.

Procurement fraud – personal purchases – Employee uses the purchasing system to order supplies for his personal use.

Resource fraud – Employee uses the company's resources for private interests without approval.

Sick pay fraud – Employee claims sick pay when not sick.

Identity fraud

Identity theft and fraud – Identity theft is when a company's identity credentials (e.g. banking details) are stolen. Identity fraud occurs when a fraudster uses the stolen credentials to impersonate a company and causes money to be paid into their accounts, paid out as cash, or used for purchases.

Intellectual property fraud

Intellectual property fraud occurs when a fraudster portrays that a product or service is sourced from a genuine supplier when it is a copy or facsimile that breaches patent, copyright, design or trademark rights.

Investment fraud

False accounting fraud – Company falsifies its accounts to boost its balance sheet value or share price.

Insider information – Staff or others use insider information to make advantageous share purchases or sales.

Litigation fraud

Legal claim fraud – An entirely fictitious or falsely exaggerated claim is brought against the company by employees, customers, suppliers or others.

Professional advisor fraud

A professional advisor, such as lawyers and accountants deceive their clients by providing dishonest advice or information or by withholding information in order to secure a gain to themselves or others. It is also a fraud if the professional advisor deceives others who are not clients, but to whom they nevertheless owe a duty, for example lenders. Professional advisors are also liable if they knowingly assist fraudsters, even if they do not make a gain for themselves.

Sales fraud

Accounting fraud – Customer falsifies its accounts to boost its credit rating in order to secure supplier credit and then defaults on payment (see also credit fraud).

Bribery – Customer demands a bribe or an employee offers a bribe to secure a contract.

Card-not-present fraud – This is a form of identity fraud in which the fraudster impersonates a legitimate customer and the victim is the supplier. The fraudulent customer uses a stolen credit card or stolen details of a credit card to order supplies.

Credit fraud – Customer secures a legitimate credit account with a supplier and orders supplies, but without any intention of paying.

Credit application fraud – Customer secures a credit account with a supplier by providing dishonest details or using the stolen details of a genuine business.

Product returns fraud – This is usually perpetrated with an employee. A customer purports to return goods, when he has not, and receives a false refund. Sometimes goods are actually returned, but the refund is at the list price rather than the original discount price.

Supplier fraud

Advance fee fraud – Provider promises a service in return for an advance fee, but has no intention of delivering the service, for example, business directory and domain name scams.

Bribery – Supplier offers a bribe or an employee demands a bribe for a contract or for inside information.

Business directory fraud – This is a form of advance fee fraud. Fraudster offers free advertising in a business directory, but the small print commits the victim company to paying a fee. The directory is non-existent or has very low circulation.

Duplicate invoice fraud – Supplier invoices for the same services more than once.

Fictional invoice fraud – Supplier submits a fictional invoice for services not provided.

Inflated invoice fraud – Supplier submits a falsely inflated invoice.

Sub-standard goods fraud – Supplier invoices for high quality goods but supplies low quality or counterfeit alternatives.

1.4.3 Cyber-fraud

Those with a keen eye will be wondering why the above list excludes the term "cyber-fraud". We will explain. There are essentially two type of cyber-crimes:

- Cyber-dependent crimes are offences that can only be committed via computer technology, for example hacking for vandalism purposes or to steal information, ransomware and distributed denial-of-service (DDoS) attacks.
- Cyber-enabled crimes are traditional crimes, but the fraudsters use computers and the Internet to assist them with their offending.

Most, if not all, so-called cyber-frauds are actually cyber-enabled frauds, i.e. traditional frauds with a significant cyber component. It is important to understand that fraudsters have always exploited the emergence of new communication technologies. The advent of postal services and then telephony both extended the range and speed of frauds. Digital technologies, especially the Internet, have hugely expanded the scale, reach, speed and efficiency of fraud. With companies now relying on the expedience of computerised business systems and electronic payments, it is highly likely that frauds against businesses involve a digital component.

The cyber components of these "modern" frauds has placed considerable demands on businesses to implement new prevention methods, such as firewalls, anti-virus software, digital security protocols and vigilance training. However, as the essence of these cyber-enabled frauds are the same as for purely analogue based frauds – a false communication – the methods and options for accessing justice are very similar if not the same in most cases.

The list below sets out the most common technology based methods that enable fraud. They are all used for fraud-enabling identity theft. The key message here is that these cyber elements are very often precursors to the main event of modern-day frauds. Therefore securing the evidence of these bogus communications can be crucial to subsequent investigations.

The methods are organised into two groups: hacking and entrapment. In the hacking group, victims are completely unaware of the existence or activities of the fraudsters: computers or networks are broken into either to gain control over the systems in order to perpetrate purchasing or account take-over type frauds, or to steal identity information. In the entrapment group, victims are enticed into revealing their identity information, login details and authorisation credentials.

1.4.3 *Discovery, first reactions and investigations*

Hacking

Adaption of PIN entry devices – Fraudsters modify PIN entry devices to record card payment details. These identity credentials are then used to fraudulently obtain money or supplies. The card details are often sold through black market networks into countries that do not use chip and PIN.

Call or text diversion – Fraudsters harvest personal information about an individual through public information or phishing. They then use this information to persuade the victim's mobile phone provider to issue a new SIM, claiming that the handset has been damaged, lost or stolen. The fraudsters can then perpetrate an account takeover fraud by accessing the victim's online banking system.

Computer hacking – Hackers break into computers or networks to steal identity information. They also take control of systems in order to perpetrate other opportunistic crimes, such as purchasing, accounting or account takeover frauds.

Malware and viruses – These are used to collect identifying information and logon credentials, or to take control over a computer or network in order to perpetrate a fraud.

Entrapment

Botnets – A botnet is a network of computers that pretend to be human beings, i.e. robots. Most spam email originates from botnets. They are used to mass market fraudulent offerings in order to entice victims into revealing their personal details or to entrap victims in a scam.

Computer services frauds – A bogus supplier who purports to represent a technology company, e.g. Microsoft or Apple, offers to make emergency repairs in return for a fee or to gain access to a computer or server for other fraudulent purposes.

Pharming – Emails, social media or websites are used to direct victims to fake websites that collect identity information.

Phishing and Spear phishing – Fraudsters send emails or text messages that purport to be from legitimate, trusted organisations. They direct victims to bogus websites that collect identifying information and logon credentials.

Smishing – Fraudsters use text messaging to lure victims into revealing identity information.

Sniffing – Identifying information and logon credentials are collected as data is sent across Wi-Fi networks. Criminals also set up "evil access points", public Wi-Fi connections that capture any transmitted data.

Spear phishing – A more direct form of phishing which targets specific individuals, making an email appear to be from someone known to the recipient. Businesses are particularly susceptible to spear phishing attacks which claim to have specific, critical knowledge of a business.

Romance scams – A method of fraud where the perpetrators create and use fake identities and profiles (the process is sometimes called catfishing), usually on social media platforms, to lure a person into a romantic online relationship, sometimes supported by phone contact. The risks to businesses comes from the fact that some perpetrators of these scams target directors or employees of businesses persuading them to misappropriate monies or confidential information from businesses in which they work.

Tab napping – A type of phishing attack that targets people who keep multiple tabs open in their browsers. The fraudsters use JavaScript to change the contents of an open but inactive tab to mimic the logon screen of a bank, email provider or online store. They sometimes include the sort of session time-out message typical of banks. When victims click back onto the tab, they assume they have been logged out and re-enter their user information, which is sent to the fraudsters.

Vishing – Fraudsters obtain identifying information by phone, often claiming to be a representative of a legitimate organisation.

1.4.4 Extent of fraud

Unless you are a self-sufficient hermit, it is highly likely that you have been or will be a victim of fraud, either personally or through your business. You will not be alone because it is a massive problem. Nobody knows the true extent, but in financial terms fraud losses in the UK are certainly many times that of all other crimes put together. Like all acquisitive crimes, it is predominantly motivated by need or greed. However, unlike "street" crimes such as burglary, mugging and extortion, fraud is very often committed by ordinary, respectable people – doctors, lawyers, accountants, police officers, teachers, football coaches, managers, employees, contractors, suppliers and customers. Professionals and persons of high social status are just as likely to commit fraud as anyone else.

- The Crime Survey for England and Wales (CSEW) estimated that 3,239,000 adults were victims of fraud in the year to September 2017.[3] The true victim rate is far higher as this excludes frauds against businesses.
- The CSEW also estimated that 1,503,000 adults were victims of computer misuse and 541,000 of these had personal information stolen.
- The Association of Certified Fraud Examiners (ACFE) in America reckons that businesses typically lose the equivalent of 5% of turnover to fraud.[4]
- Recent research in the UK has estimated the total annual losses to fraud in the UK at £190 billion.[5] The losses suffered by individuals is £7 billion, whilst organisations lose £183 billion per year. Private sector businesses lose £141 billion per year, mainly through purchasing and payroll frauds: the majority of these frauds are perpetrated by or involve employees.

---

3 ONS (2018). *Crime in England and Wales: year ending September 2017*. Available at: www.ons.gov.uk/peoplepopulationandcommunity/crimeandjustice/articles/overviewoffraudandcomputermisusestatisticsforenglandandwales/2018-01-25.

4 ACFE (2018). *Report to the Nations*. Available at: www.acfe.com/report-to-the-nations/2018/.

5 University of Portsmouth (2017). *Annual fraud indicator 2017*. London: Experian and PKF. Available at: www.croweclarkwhitehill.co.uk/wp-content/uploads/sites/2/2017/11/Annual-fraud-indicator-2017.pdf.

The attrition rate through the justice systems is extremely high. In 2017 the police recorded just 662,519 offences from three sources:[6]

Action Fraud	272,980
Cifas	301,764
UK Finance	87,775
Total	662,519

Only 11,482 proven offenders were processed through the criminal justice system in 2017.[7] Of these, a mere 2,086 received custodial sentences and 74 were ordered to pay compensation. Cautions and convictions for cyber-dependent crimes under the Computer Misuse Act 1990 are included in these fraud figures because the justice system counts computer crimes as a type of fraud. However, as prosecutions are based on the intended, underlying offences under the Fraud Act 2006 or the Theft Act 1968, proceedings for these hacking type offences are very rare: 35 persons were found guilty in 2017 and just 7 were imprisoned. It is extremely unlikely that you would get justice by way of a prosecution under these hacking laws (⊳ *Section 6.6, Cyber crimes*).

The overall attrition rate from well over 3.2 million victims to 2,086 custodial sentences and 74 compensation orders indicates that victims, whether individuals or businesses, are very unlikely be satisfied with the criminal justice process.

The level of cyber-crimes against businesses is just as startling. According to the Department for Digital, Culture, Media & Sport (DCMS), 43% of UK businesses experienced cyber security breaches or attacks in 2017[8] – that's nearly 2.5 million firms. Larger firms are more likely to be victimised – the rate for medium-sized firms is 64% and it is 72% for large firms. Security failures included fraudulent e-communications (32%), impersonation by others (12%), unauthorised access (6%) and hacking of bank accounts (3%). 3% of businesses lost money due to cyber-crimes at an average direct cost of £695. When compared to the total estimated fraud losses of businesses (£141 billion), it is clear that businesses are still far more vulnerable to traditional frauds, particularly those involving employees, purchasing processes and the payroll.

1.5 Investigating fraud – some things you should know

Fraud is by its nature a secret crime committed by stealth and guile: no smoking gun, broken windows or empty driveway. This means it is often not detected at all and when it is detected the victim company discovers that it has unknowingly been

6 ONS (2018). *Crime in England and Wales: year ending September 2017*. Available at: www.ons.gov.uk/peoplepopulationandcommunity/crimeandjustice/articles/overviewoffraudandcomputermisusestatisticsforenglandandwales/2018-01-25.

7 MoJ (2018). Criminal Justice Statistics – Quarterly update: the year ending September 2017. Available at: www.gov.uk/government/statistics/criminal-justice-system-statistics-quarterly-september-2017.

8 DCLMS (2018). *Cyber Security Breaches Survey 2018*. Available at: www.gov.uk/government/statistics/cyber-security-breaches-survey-2018.

a victim for some time, perhaps even years. For the same reasons, it can be difficult to investigate.

There is no magic formula for investigating fraud. Some fraud investigations are easy and some are complex. This section does not set out to teach you how to conduct a fraud investigation, rather it reviews some principles, what might be involved and your options at the investigative stage.

Frauds tend to involve repeated events. Once an offender has learnt how to commit a fraud and got away with it, they do it again, often accelerating their offending. Without intervention, the opportunistic offender turns into a habitual fraudster. Unfortunately this means a detected fraud is often just the tip of an iceberg.

Signpost

When gathering information for your lawyers, be as accurate and ordered as possible. It can damage your case if you have to correct a series of mistakes in narratives passed to the other side. ⊳ *Section 3*

Fraud investigations in businesses require the assistance of management. Lawyers and professional investigators, whether from the police or private sector, need management to explain and guide them through the business systems, company procedures, forms, responsibilities and normal ways of working. It requires commitment and can be time consuming.

Investigating a fraud is often a bit like peeling an onion: until you start peeling you do not know how many layers there are. It is certainly going to make you question the integrity and competence of a number of people whether they are your fellow directors and employees, sub-contractors.

Was it a fraud or was it a mistake, negligence or a misunderstanding? These are important questions you will need to bottom out. Labelling conduct as fraud is not easy. It is also unwise unless you have good evidence to back it up. But if you have concerns or suspicions then you really should act on them. The alternative, not investigating, could expose your business to more fraud and losses.

Just how much have you lost? This is a central question but often difficult to answer. Some frauds involving just a few transactions are easily diagnosed and quantified, but most are complex and hidden with an average duration of 16 months.[9] Identifying the perpetrator and any conspirators can be challenging enough, but following the money to work out where it has gone and how it has been used can be a daunting prospect.

Signpost

Stretched law enforcement resources mean there is a glaring gap between what public bodies could achieve and what they do achieve for victims of fraud. But resources are not the only problems. The value of confiscation orders (for the benefit of the state) are out-pacing the value of compensation orders (for the

9 ACFE (2018). *Report to the Nations*. Available at: www.acfe.com/report-to-the-nations/2018.

benefit of victims). Whatever the reasons may be, the disparity looks wrong. ▻ *Section 6*

To build a picture of what has happened you need to be curious, open-minded, creative, patient and determined. Even after a full investigation, there is likely to be lingering uncertainties about who was involved and how much was lost, but you cannot go on forever, you need to know when to stop.

Investigating fraud is not about 100% certainties. It is only in rare cases that all the damning documentation has been preserved and the wrongdoers confess their guilt. Fortunately, that level of certainty is not necessary in order for you to protect your business and to bring action against wrongdoers.

But you do need clear and cogent evidence of wrongdoing that is illegal, not just immoral or unscrupulous. You need evidence that builds a compelling picture of the fraud, its perpetrators and beneficiaries. Evidence that rules out both innocent explanations and the bogus explanations given by suspects. Evidence which the police, a judge or jury will believe.

And finally a word about you. You must remain professional. Whatever the temptations, you must maintain your integrity and honesty. Any lack of probity will be exposed and undermine your case. A prosecutor will be far less likely to proceed with the case. The civil courts may dismiss your claim and make you pay the defendant's costs.

1.6 The fraud theory

The first thing to do is to write down what you think has happened. This is what investigators call the fraud theory. Subsequent investigations test the theory to prove it, disprove it or adjust it. Do not analyse everything to death because that will take too long. Do your best to describe your interpretation of events and the context of those events.

- What alerted you to the fraud – whistleblower, document, accounts?
- Has a business process been manipulated and abused?
- Which business process and how has it been manipulated?
- Is it an internal fraud by an employee or an external fraud?
- Who is involved – employee, supplier, customer, names, positions?
- Does it involve a cyber component?
- Where are they or how can they be found?
- Could others be doing the same thing?
- Characteristics of suspects?
- How much money?
- Where has the money or other assets gone?
- When detected?
- One-off event or repeated?
- Is it happening now?
- Could it happen again?
- How long has it been going on?
- Is the crime scene secure?

Setting out your fraud theory in writing helps to clarify your thoughts and prepares you for effective discussions with professional advisors or the police. Obtaining the right legal advice is likely to be pivotal to how you decide to proceed with your case. Your options are set out in *Section 2, Objectives and options* and selecting the right lawyer is discussed at length in *Section 3, Choosing, using and paying for lawyers*. You may also need to call on the services of professional investigators. The following section introduces the types of investigator commonly used in fraud cases.

1.7 Professional investigators

The three types of investigator encountered in fraud investigations are observational investigators, computer forensic analysts and forensic accountants. The distinction between them is somewhat blurred. Police detectives, for example, conduct surveillance, interview offenders and witnesses, and examine computer transactions and documents. They call in computer and accountancy specialists when the case demands greater expertise.

> **Signpost**
>
> A payment to a director, employee or agent of a company is presumed to be made with a corrupt motive if the company is unaware of that payment. The same is true when a partner in a partnership receives a secret payment. ⊳ *Section 5*

1.7.1 The police

If you do call in the police, do remember at all times that they do not work for you, they work for the state. Prosecuting fraud is not a state priority and their official case acceptance criteria are set out so that they can with some legal legitimacy reject virtually any case (⊳ *Section 6.9, Making a criminal complaint*). You should also be aware that if the police do investigate your complaint and they find evidence of other criminality in your organisation, they may pursue unexpected lines of enquiry which could cause you significant embarrassment.

1.7.2 Private investigators

On the other hand private investigators work for you. Anyone can be a private fraud investigator, computer analysts or forensic accountant. The traditional image of an ex-policeman with hat pulled down, rooting around in a dustbin still holds true today for the surveillance and covert operation investigator.

The Security Industry Authority (SIA)[10] is trying to raise standards through training and licensing but, currently, only physical guarding activities require licenses. The SIA does offer private investigator licenses on a voluntary basis. These licenses require an investment of about £550 for a home-study qualification and a 3 year license. It is not yet clear what these licenses say about the quality or ethics of investigators.

---

10 www.sia.homeoffice.gov.uk/Pages/home.aspx.

The private investigation industry appears to be polarised between self-employed fraud investigators and large security and financial audit organisations which offer investigation services, such as PWC, KPMG, Control Risks and Kroll.

Signpost

Bribery (often referred to as "corruption") is a key feature of many cases affecting business. This is because fraud is often an "inside job" in which an outsider will have corrupted the insider (or vice versa) to carry out the fraud on the business. ▷ *Section 6*

Some investigators are "accredited" whilst others are not. Certified Fraud Examiners (CFE) receive their training and accreditations from the Association of Certified Fraud Examiners (ACFE),[11] which has about 75,000 members worldwide, mainly in America. The Accredited Counter Fraud Specialist (ACFS) is a UK based qualification. About 13,000 investigators have received this accreditation[12] and are registered on the Professional Register of Counter Fraud Specialists (PRCFS) by the Counter Fraud Professional Accreditation Board (CFPAB).[13]

Good fraud lawyers know capable investigators, both accredited and non-accredited. They will be able to "instruct" investigators for you. If you are thinking of choosing or hiring investigators yourself, make sure you also do your own checks on the competence and integrity of the investigators you have in mind.

1.7.3 Forensic accountants

You may well require forensic accountants. Forensic accountants mainly emanate from the accountancy profession and are usually members of one of the accountancy bodies such as the Institute of Chartered Accountants in England and Wales (ICAEW)[14] or the Association of Certified Chartered Accountants (ACCA).[15] They may also hold further accreditations with ACFE or the PRCFS.

Good forensic accountants can be worth their weight in gold as they are able to quickly cut through a mass of data to pinpoint the fraud and present the evidence to lawyers in a simple, cogent manner. Poor forensic accountants can chew through fees, busily doing nothing useful.

1.7.4 Computer examiners

Computer examiners are unregulated technical types who conserve data, image hard drives and interrogate systems to recover data: accounts and purchasing systems, work reports, e-mails and internet activity. They are more interested in the readable quality of data files and how systems were accessed and manipulated by wrongdoers and less concerned with the content of data files and their meaning except where that

11 www.acfeuk.co.uk.
12 Button, M. and Gee, J. (2013). *Countering Fraud for Competitive Advantage*. Chichester: Wiley.
13 www.port.ac.uk/centre-for-counter-fraud-studies/counter-fraud-professional-accreditation-board/.
14 www.icaew.com.
15 www.accaglobal.com/uk/en.html.

content and meaning is important to their enquiry. They are also far more focused on the technical elements of the fraud rather than the human story of betrayals, despair, greed, dysfunctional personalities and so on. Your lawyers are best placed to recommend and then instruct good computer examiners if they are needed.

> **Signpost**
>
> If you make it really easy for the police then you have a greater chance of having your case investigated. But if your case looks tricky, time consuming and uncertain, it will not be prioritised. ⊳ *Section 6*

1.7.5 Other specialists

In addition to factual evidence, specialist expert evidence is sometimes also necessary. Document examiners, for example, are sometimes useful in fraud cases to spot forgeries and altered documents. Others are engaged to contextualise the evidence and to provide opinions on a range of matters, such as trade or industry practice, accountancy practice, valuations, banking practices and foreign law. If you need expert evidence in your case, this ought to be highlighted to you by your lawyers and they are best placed to recommend experts and to instruct them on your behalf.

1.8 Do you need specialist investigators?

> A fraud lawyer: "It is vital for fraud investigation teams to avoid being seen as a cost centre. They should work with management to develop and implement effective fraud prevention and detection systems. In the event of the detection of a fraud, swift and firm action should be taken against the perpetrators, in order to maximise chances of recovery and to discourage any further such conduct."

If you elect to go down the criminal route and are lucky enough to attract the interest of the police or the Serious Fraud Office, there will be no choice, detectives will arrive. For civil proceedings, you have the choice – do it yourself or seek assistance. You must ask yourself whether you have the time and the skills.

If it is a straightforward case, perhaps involving an employee, simple transactions and readily accessible evidence, you may not need investigators. One CEO, whose company was defrauded of £430,000 by an employee, found his own investigation an exciting stage. Fortunately, he also had direct access to a helpful accountant:

> "I found this part extremely interesting, on my part having a wife as an accountant was hugely beneficial, it was a sort of jigsaw in looking how the accounts were pieced together by the fraud, and us dismantling it piece at a time, finding the pieces that didn't fit and adding these up to over £430,000 of theft. Also, working closely with our lawyers the breakdown of where he may have 'used' the stolen money was actually a real learning experience, houses, cars, jewellery and foreign property."

If it is a more complex case involving external parties and deliberately disguised transactions, you will need specialist assistance of one form or another. Sometimes managers become consumed by the justice motive and apply themselves too vigorously to investigations. The business then suffers and the damage caused by the fraud is further compounded.

Fraud investigations need to be conducted quickly and speed calls for both specific business knowledge and experienced investigators. This means the right solution is a co-operative investigation between the management team and external specialists.

The police generally welcome the assistance of management in their investigations. Indeed they may be delighted to take on and pursue a case when the victim presents them with substantial, well ordered accurate and persuasive evidence (▷ *Section 6.10.1, Higher priority cases*): it allows them to take on investigations and win cases without draining their limited resources.

1.9 Working with specialist investigators

Experienced investigators know how to work with lawyers. They can summarise the information and present it in a way which makes the lawyer's job easier, more efficient and at lower cost. You should also assume that investigators will be called as witnesses so that they can be cross-examined by the defendant's barrister. Do-it-yourself investigators can be great witnesses because they know far more than anyone else about the business and how the fraud worked but it is a daunting prospect which requires robust individuals.

> **Signpost**
>
> When thinking about your own objectives, you should consider what you know about the wrongdoer. Was she an employee, a sub-contractor, an outsider? What message do you want to send by your actions and how is the wrongdoer likely to respond to those actions. ▷ *Section 2*

Whatever the pressures and motivations may be, investigations must be conducted in an ethical manner. There can be nothing more frustrating than having strong evidence but then finding it is unusable in the criminal or civil courts due to the way it was obtained or handled. You do not want to damage your credibility as a witness and victim. You certainly do not want to do things which give the police or the prosecutors any reason to drop your case on the grounds that evidence is inadmissible.

Finally, we need to say that private investigations are most efficient and effective when guided by a fraud lawyer. CPS lawyers guide the police. Your own lawyer guides private investigations by focusing the investigators' efforts on the type of evidence required to prove the allegations and in the proper way in which it should be obtained.

It is also important to be forewarned that investigations often require the support, protection and powers afforded by and supervised by the courts. Lawyers are, by far, the people best placed to obtain the freezing, search, production and disclosure orders which may be necessary to make investigations effective (▷ *Section 4, Tracing and securing assets in the civil courts*). Without appropriate legal supervision of the orders and the investigators, the valuable evidence gathered may be compromised and even become inadmissible in court proceedings, wasting much time and money.

1.10 Who in your business should be involved in the investigation?

A fraud lawyer: "It's often a good idea to have a small number of people authorised to undertake any internal investigation. It usually means decisions can be made more quickly than if a company's whole board was involved, and any information discovered can be shared on a need to know basis."

This can be difficult. Who can you trust? Even if the police or other professional investigators are engaged, someone needs to be appointed to lead and represent the interests of the company on a day-to-day basis, though final decisions should still be taken by the chief executive of the company. Who should be the company's representative if not you?

If you have a legal department, its head should probably lead the enquiry. The next best alternative is usually the Finance Director. When employees are suspected, companies sometimes default to the human resources department. Think carefully before allowing this. Whilst HR can and often should be involved in the team dealing with the consequences of fraud, they are not usually best placed to take the lead or dictate strategy because employment factors are usually secondary to the main issues.

If there is no-one else, it's you!

Signpost

If a major objective is compensation or the recovery of assets and you have the means to make the running with a case then you ought to be thinking of bringing your own civil proceedings. ⊳ *Section 2*

At the outset, few people will know of the incident and the investigation. The number will expand but you must be in control of that expansion. You should only invite colleagues to assist in the investigation when you are absolutely sure you can trust them. You must then remind them of their duties to the company and the need for confidentiality.

As more employees are drawn into the investigation as witnesses or to assist, you need to make it clear that it is a strictly confidential matter and any breach of confidentiality will be subject to disciplinary action. Managing confidentiality becomes increasingly difficult when third parties are brought into the enquiry.

Your professional service providers – lawyers, accountants, banks, insurers and so on – have a duty to you to keep your information confidential and any unauthorised disclosures by them are likely to have serious repercussions for them. However, you have limited control over other persons or organisations whom you approach as you follow potential lines of enquiry.

If you use lawyers, then you will have the advantage of being able to communicate with them under the cover of legal professional privilege (▷ *Section 3.3, Why use lawyers?*).

1.11 Overt or covert investigations?

Investigations typically begin shrouded in secrecy. Some are abandoned without confronting anyone and remain a hidden history. Those that do proceed need to be carefully managed to avoid alerting the suspects prematurely.

Key points you should consider are:

- company reputation;
- whether observational (surveillance) evidence is required;
- destruction of evidence; and
- dissipation of the money (or other assets).

If you are concerned about your company's reputation or causing disquiet amongst your staff then you are not alone. This is a common concern expressed by directors and owners of businesses. And it is a reason why some do nothing at all in response to fraud. However, there is very little evidence, if any at all, of adverse reputational repercussions from revelations of fraud. Nevertheless, it is wise to manage disclosures to show that you are in control, to show that your actions are considered and deliberate.

If the suspect is an employee, your instinct may be to suspend him immediately. Stop, think and seek advice because this is often unwise. It may be necessary to commence an investigation with covert surveillance, either physically or through computer activity so that you can prove an allegation.

Signpost

In nearly all cases of fraud, the court will accept that it would be undesirable to alert a wrongdoer to the fact that you are seeking to establish his or her identity and to trace monies which have been fraudulently extracted from you. ▷ *Section 4*

To run a successful covert phase, you will find that you will have to give plausible reasons for unexpected activities – examining computers, producing data reports, unusual meetings and the appearance of strangers. Maintaining plausible explanations for your activities becomes increasingly difficult as time goes by. Employees begin to speculate as to the true reasons, causing greater disquiet, insecurity and speculative rumour-mongering than the disclosure of the fraud itself. Because of this, the covert phase must be completed as quickly as possible.

The challenges raised by running a covert investigation were well expressed by one victim:

> "Speed and secrecy were of the essence … These imperatives necessarily imposed constraints on communications from and between members of the crisis management team. The need to avoid alerting others to the unfolding situation

and to ensure that findings reported to people who 'needed to know' were based on accurate information required that this information be obtained in roundabout ways or after-hours. This added to the burden of the work to be done and the timeframe for the assessment and reporting onwards."

You must also avoid alerting the suspect fraudster until you are confident that you have secured the "crime scene" and where necessary and possible obtained a court order to prevent the fraudster from dissipating his assets. Expert lawyers can arrange freezing injunctions within a short number of days (⊳ *Section 4.8, Freezing injunctions*).

1.12 Document everything

You will not know at the outset what might become vital to the investigation in your case. Something disregarded early on, may become relevant later. Record everything which may become relevant from the moment you begin to have concerns and keep going with that until the conclusion of the case.

Label every item you collect with a unique reference number. Create an indexed database or spreadsheet of all the data you gather with dates and times, brief descriptions, how and where it was obtained.

If you are concerned about losing evidence, make copies or scan documents into a computer, and then back-up to a secondary device. But do remember that original records and documents are best evidence and that your back-up copies are just that.

You should keep a diary in which you write down everything that happens and is relevant to the case. Do this even if you engage external investigators or the police. Write down what happens each and every day, what you examine, all conversations, telephone calls and e-mails. Continue with this discipline all the way to trial. Make sure that you tell your lawyer about the diary and be aware that your diary may have to be disclosed to the other side, so be polite.

One other advantage of keeping a diary of the time you spend investigating is that it may be possible for you to claim, from the wrongdoer, financial compensation for the management time spent in investigating.

1.13 Stages of investigation

There are essentially four interlinked stages to an investigation, the last overlapping with the court processes (⊳ *Figure A*):

- triage and containment;
- proving the fraud;
- litigation support; and
- court witness.

Although the majority of cases do not go to trial, you should firmly have in mind from the outset that your case will, otherwise mistakes could be made which would prejudice your case in the event that it does go all the way.

1.14 Stage 1 – triage and containment

The first stage aims to determine whether the fraud is real and to characterise its nature. This can be quite an intense stage and follows on from the development of your initial fraud theory (⊳ *Section 1.6, The fraud theory*). It does not require proof to a standard required to win a court case (that comes later). It requires rational suspicions so that you can make early decisions on how to progress the case (⊳ *Section 2, Objectives and options*).

> **Signpost**
>
> Freezing injunctions (often called freezing orders) are the most commonly used of the court's "nuclear weapons". They are an essential power against fraudsters and others who launder or even just wrongfully receive the proceeds of fraud. ⊳ *Section 4*

If you decide to progress a civil claim, you would need rapid legal advice on what evidence and information is required to seek a freezing injunction (⊳ *Section 4.8, Freezing injunctions*). It would involve tracing the defendant's assets, and because freezing injunctions require advocates to represent you at court, you would be best served with advice from a barrister.

If you rely on the police, they will take control and advise you. Not following their advice may give them reason to withdraw from the case. Whichever way you decide to proceed, it is important to work as efficiently and quickly as possible. One victim business set up a crisis management team to address multiple issues simultaneously:

> "The immediate issues faced by the 'crisis management team' once the method of perpetration and the potential suspects had been identified were to quantify the scale of the fraud, to analyse whether the technique adopted by the fraudster could be or might have been deployed elsewhere in the Group, to see how to address this and to confirm that there were no further suspects."

1.14.1 Secure the crime scene

You should consider your business as a crime scene. Freezing a crime scene to secure it and prevent contamination, though ideal, is impractical as you need to continue trading. However you need to be conscious of the need to disturb as little as possible. If documents are relocated for security purposes, record their original location. Similarly, if any computer files have to be moved, record their original location.

Securing the crime scene involves four elements: immediate containment, risks to investigation, securing evidence and preventing access by the suspects.

1.14.2 Immediate containment

Firstly, contain the situation to prevent further damage:

- Is immediate intervention required to prevent further frauds?
- Can any suspect transactions be stopped?

Unless advised otherwise by your lawyer, you will want to intervene whenever possible to prevent further losses and halt any suspect transactions. This could entail preventing an internal transaction, such as a purchase order or expense payment, or contacting your bank or other financial institution to stop a payment.

Exceptionally, if the suspect transactions are of low value, you may be prepared to allow them to complete to gather the further evidence, but we suggest that you should only do this on the advice of a lawyer.

1.14.3 Risks to the investigation

Consider the risks to the investigation. Write down what these risks might be. Doing so alerts you to immediate actions you may need to take. It also provides valuable information for lawyers.

- Is there a risk of loss of evidence?
- Has anyone else been told?
- Can they be trusted?
- Might the suspect think their position has already been compromised?
- Would launching an overt investigation alert them?
- Might they run?
- Are systems backed-up and secure?
- Are paper systems secure?
- Is remote access secure?
- Do they take work home?
- Is a whistleblower scared or anxious?
- How to protect the whistleblower?

1.14.4 Secure evidence

> A fraud lawyer: "So much of our day-to-day life is undertaken online or electronically, that it's often necessary, as part of investigations into a fraud, to get specialist help from IT experts. This can involve someone making sure that a copy is taken of a company's server on a particular day to preserve evidence, or it could involve imaging smart phones or obtaining copies of email accounts. This is not a job for a lawyer, this is a job for a forensic IT specialist who could also appear before a Court to explain how the information was imaged or preserved. Vital evidence can be obtained in this way."

Secure all data so that it represents the "frozen" condition of the evidence at the time you became aware of the fraud:

- secure paper documents;
- image hard drives; and
- back-up computers, network systems and e-mails.

If you suspect certain individuals, write down their names and any other information you may have so that they can be found and contacted: home addresses, places of work, telephone numbers, emails and so on. Preserve any relevant information which might assist in tracing where the money has gone, such as bank account details, building society memberships and online gambling accounts. It is easy to forget to secure these details early in a case, but they may prove critical in not only proving the fraud but also in ensuring you can recover your losses.

It is very important to realise that all computer files and electronic communications include embedded metadata – data about data. Metadata can be far more important to an enquiry than the actual contents as it can include information about who originated a file, when and where it was generated. The metadata may not provide actual names and physical addresses, but it will often include Uniform Resource Identifier (URI) information, including Uniform Resource Locator (URL) and Internet Protocol (IP) addresses that can lead investigations to wrongdoers. This type of information can be crucial to investigations.

You should be very careful how you secure computers. Even opening e-mails, documents and other files may change a document or alter its metadata and thereby disturb relevant evidence. This is why computer forensic investigators image a computer hard drive and then examine that rather than directly examining the hard drive itself.

1.14.5 Prevent suspect access

Preventing suspect access avoids further fraud events and secures evidence. However it also alerts the suspects. If the immediate risk of further damage to your business and loss of evidence is high, these actions should be undertaken without delay. You should seek the advice of a specialist fraud lawyer before alerting the suspect.

- Suspend suspected employees (on legal advice).
- Suspend their expenditure authorisations.
- Change access rights – computers, banking, payroll, purchasing, remote access.
- Change physical access security – door entry codes, change locks.
- Retrieve door, safe, filing cabinet keys.
- Retrieve laptop, storage devices and phone – treat as evidence.
- Retrieve work documents from possession of suspects – treat as evidence.

1.15 Stage 2 – proving the fraud

The second stage is to test your fraud theory by generating evidence to prove the allegations against the identified wrongdoers: who did what, where, how much was lost. The emerging data may require that your theory is adjusted, completely revised or dismissed altogether. The final theory becomes the allegation which lawyers particularise into the claims presented to the wrongdoers and to the court.

1.15.1 Types of evidence

There are a number of kinds of factual evidence in fraud cases:

- *Testimonial evidence* – from victims, witnesses and suspects.
- *Documentary evidence* – including electronically stored evidence, such as purchase orders, payroll, cheques, bank statements, audits.

- *Computer evidence* – log-on times, accounts and passwords used, documents deleted, records of documents altered and documents printed, information downloaded or uploaded, URI addresses of remote computers, communication and file metadata.
- *Physical evidence* – keys to cupboards and cars, CCTV footage, photographs of scenes, measurements of weight and size.
- *Observations of investigator* – logs, evolving analysis, surveillance and covert operations after the initial discovery of a potential fraud.

The evidence can also be classified as direct or circumstantial. Direct evidence, such as the witness statement of someone who observed the fraud or a cheque made payable to the fraudster, is the strongest proof. However, circumstantial evidence is frequently a critical element of fraud investigations and is equally powerful provided it is relevant and cumulatively connects circumstances, events and wrongdoers. For example, a single unusual payment to a supplier is not proof of fraud. But if this happens regularly then the circumstantial evidence starts to accumulate.

In one case that led to a successful civil suit, a company's Engineering Manager raised bogus purchase orders on a supplier every month for at least two years. The manager and the supplier's directors denied fraud. However, receipts into the manager's bank account appeared within days of the payments to the supplier, there was no physical evidence of any supplies, the supplier's factory supervisor had no knowledge of the supplies and the conspirators could not offer a plausible explanation.

The cumulative build-up of evidence is precisely what the courts expect to see in a fraud case, slowly but surely building a case into one which leads to a powerful inference that the accused person must have been knowingly involved in the wrongdoing.

The most important evidence in a fraud case is often documentary and computer evidence. Witness evidence is also important because it gives voice and meaning to the documentary and computer evidence; sometimes it is crucial.

Signpost

Think about details but always remember the big picture as well. You must be accurate with facts and figures, dates and times and so on. But you should also remain objective and able to see the bigger picture so that you can make good judgments about your options and prospects of success. ▷ *Section 3*

Surveillance operations, occasionally mounted by large commercial organisations, the police and other state agencies, are rare in smaller fraud cases. Nevertheless they may be used when it is necessary, for example, to physically associate an employee with an ongoing transaction at a particular place and time or to catch an employee red-handed. Surveillance may also be required when tracing assets to identify property such as houses and cars.

A final point needs to be brought to your attention in this section. It relates to personal information and data protection laws. Judges in courts can query whether the evidence gathered during the course of investigations has breached the Data Protection Act 1998 (DPA) by accessing personal information held in the victim organisation's physical or digital filing system. You should be forewarned about this possibility rather than overly concerned because the DPA allows organisations to access and share personal information for the purposes of preventing crime and in support of both criminal and civil legal proceedings.[16] Your advisors should be aware of any DPA implications so that, if any issues arise, they can be comfortably and easily addressed.

1.15.2 Witness co-operation

Investigations are straightforward when the documentary evidence is to hand, and the suspects and witnesses co-operate. Other than the suspect, there are essentially three types of witness: the expert witness discussed earlier, the crime scene witness who has observed the fraud or is intimate with the context of the crime and the third party witness, for example a bank which has been used by the fraudster.

The willingness of witnesses to co-operate is highly variable. The reputation and social purpose of the police is usually sufficient to generate co-operation from individuals. But banks and other businesses are typically more hesitant, worried about being drawn into legal proceedings and about breaching customer confidentiality and data protection. Even when the police are involved, banks and others will often only fully co-operate when forced to do so by court orders.

Third party organisations tend to resist private enquiries. Sometimes they have legitimate concerns about being sucked into a legal case, about customer privacy and so on; but other times they just can't be bothered. Resistant organisations have to be pressed by legal means. In *Section 4.7, Norwich Pharmacal orders*, we set out the kinds of information you can force organisations to provide to assist you with your investigations and asset tracing.

Private investigations often require more empathetic social skills to nurture witnesses. Participating in interviews with management representatives or private investigators is entirely voluntary.

Employees are usually co-operative. It can be made a disciplinary matter if employees, whether witnesses or suspects, refuse to co-operate with management: fraud aware companies include co-operation with enquiries as a term in their employment contracts. Refusal to co-operate is then easier to discourage and to deal with.

1.15.3 Interviewing suspects

You can interview suspects yourself, but interviewing is a specialist skill which requires great care so as not to compromise your case, especially if you are considering a criminal prosecution.

You should assume that unfairly or illegally obtained interview evidence would be inadmissible as evidence in court. You can't, for example, unfairly coerce or threaten suspects and if they are not fluent in English you may need an interpreter. It is strongly recommended that you seek legal advice before interviewing suspects.

---

16 The Data Protection Act 1998 was replaced by the EU General Data Protection Regulation (GDPR) in 2018. The access and sharing exemptions will be carried forward into the GDPR.

A fraud lawyer: "Moving quickly without trampling all over the scene of the crime is essential. Some of the hardest cases in terms of recovery of assets are ones in which the victim has started trying to undertake their own investigations. I've acted on cases where the corporate victim thought it would be a good idea to interview the suspected fraudster without taking any advice first. It wasn't a good idea."

If the suspect is an employee, you will be entitled to require his or her attendance at an interview in your offices, which you can record. It is not normal for employers to allow employees to be accompanied by a lawyer but you may be required to allow another person or a union representative to accompany the employee.[17]

The police use the so-called "PEACE" framework for interviewing[18] and, if you are going to interview suspects, you may find it helpful to have a similar plan:

- Planning and preparation;
- Engage and explain;
- Account, clarification and challenge;
- Closure; and
- Evaluation.

Signpost

Thinking about tracing and securing the assets of the wrongdoer at the outset is crucial otherwise a successful judgment in your favour may turn out to be a pyrrhic victory. The courts are there to help victims but obtaining the various orders is a complex business which requires the assistance of experienced lawyers. ⊳ *Section 4*

1.15.4 Interviewing witnesses

Interviewing witnesses is less onerous, but must still be handled with care. They must not be unfairly coerced either by threats or rewards. Sometimes witnesses are reluctant to speak up because they are afraid of the suspect or are unnecessarily worried that they will be somehow blamed. They must be protected and assured.

You must also be cautious about what people say. Sometimes witnesses offer statements of fact which are not based on the witness's own direct knowledge. Occasionally, witnesses are overly eager to assist and speculate about events and suspects, or say what the interviewer wants to hear. It is important to find out *how* witnesses know what they are saying and *how* they obtained the knowledge.

Records of witness interviews can be kept confidential. You, or more likely your lawyers, should notify a witness that the interview record is confidential and protected

17 This depends on the terms of your employment contracts and is a matter of employment law, beyond the scope of this guide.

18 National Police Improvement Agency (2009). *National Investigative Interviewing Strategy*. Available at: http://library.college.police.uk/docs/npia/BP-Nat-Investigative-Interviewing-Strategy-2009.pdf.

by litigation privilege from revelation to other persons without your company's permission. Witnesses are not normally given the opportunity to record interviews or consult with their own independent lawyers during interviews. You should take advice on privilege matters relating to compiling and using interview records so as to preserve litigation privilege.

1.15.5 Chain of evidence

The credibility of evidence is not just based on what it is, but also on how and by who it was obtained. Maintaining the reliability and integrity of evidence is essential. Here are some guiding rules:

- Maintain a good filing system.
- Protect original documents in files or envelopes.
- Label the files or envelopes with unique reference numbers and record them on the database.
- Do not handle original documents excessively. Make copies for review purposes.
- Never modify or otherwise interfere with original documents.
- Never make notes on original documents.
- Record on the indexed evidence database how evidence is gathered, when it was obtained, exactly where it came from, who provided it, who obtained it, where it is stored and who subsequently handles it.

1.15.6 Prove the value of losses

Proving the scale of losses can take as much if not more effort than proving that the fraud took place.

The police and prosecutors focus on the offenders with the aim of obtaining the minimum evidence required to first secure guilty verdicts and then proportionate sentences, all at the lowest cost. Their main interest in the damage caused to the victim is limited to these ends; it is not to fully quantify victims' losses.

If you are considering bringing civil claims, the court will expect to see proper, evidential proof of the amount you claim to have lost.

Whichever route you choose to bring your case to court, you need to use the same kind of rigour when investigating the extent of your losses as you do investigating the fraud itself. And often the two things will be linked, as showing how much went to the wrongdoers helps you prove not only who was involved but how much you lost.

Signpost

In order to succeed in a civil claim, you have to prove your claim to the civil standard, the balance of probabilities. You must be able to show that it was more likely than not that the alleged wrongdoer committed the wrong. This is a considerably lower standard of proof than the criminal one. Nevertheless the claim still needs a proper investigation. ▷ *Section 2*

1.16 Stage 3 – litigation support

The third stage involves supporting your lawyers as they prepare the case, correspond with the other side and set out your case to the court. Inconsistencies in the evidence may emerge which need to be examined and explained. Further investigations may be required when a wrongdoer denies aspects of the case and offers alternative explanations for all or parts of it.

1.17 Stage 4 – court witness

Finally, investigators are likely to be called as witnesses to be cross-examined at court (▷ *Section 5.17, Civil trial* and ▷ *Section 6.19, Criminal trial*). It can be a daunting prospect for an experienced witness, never mind for a victim. The burden is greater if you do not employ expert witnesses and in effect act as your own expert witness. It requires robust preparation because you will not know what questions you may face.

It is important to note that your lawyers can only offer limited assistance in preparing you for court: the convention is that lawyers may familiarise their witnesses with the process of giving evidence but, unlike in television courtroom dramas, they cannot coach them on its content.

You should also be aware that whilst giving your evidence orally to the court (which may last a few days) you are in "purdah" which means you cannot speak with anyone about the case, including your own lawyers during court adjournments, whether lunch breaks or overnight.

1.18 Conclusions

The following summarises the key points from this section:

- Investigations should be supervised and guided by a fraud lawyer.
- Be ethical and remain legal, whilst tenaciously pursuing lines of inquiry.
- Strike a balance between being curious and open-minded and being decisive.
- Specialist investigators may be required for speed and when dealing with complexity.
- Management must be involved, and the greater their contribution, the lower the costs.
- Limit your losses.
- Act quickly to secure the crime scene and evidence.
- Obtain a freezing injunction quickly to secure your assets/ the fraudster's assets.
- If the police are involved, you have no control over the investigation.
- The police limit their investigations to proving guilt and securing proportionate sentences, not to fully quantifying your losses.
- Investigations should proceed on the assumption that the case will go to trial.
- Handle witnesses carefully and with respect.
- Always analyse whether the evidence supports your case.
- Always discriminate between belief or speculation and facts.
- Record everything.

Objectives and options

2.1 In this section

- Going to the police
- Making civil claims
- Insurance claims
- Regulatory routes

2.2 What do you want? And how can you get it?

This section provides an overview of the options available to businesses who are victims of fraud – whether commercial or cyber fraud.

It is critical that you are aware of and that you evaluate all your choices as early as possible. A failure in this regard is often not the fault of the victim but it is frequently the biggest cause of problems and regret later.

"We want our money back!" "They have to go to prison for this!"

These are the typical sentiments that fraud investigators and lawyers hear time and time again. Theoretically you can have both and it does happen, but very rarely. Often recovering losses and punishment are mutually exclusive. You will be faced with tough choices and those choices will depend on your aims, resources and risk evaluations.

At the start, you may not be clear about your aims because you do not have sufficient information about the options, costs and risks. However, it is a good idea to imagine you cannot have everything and think about your initial priorities.

After the initial shock has worn off and you learn more about the options and costs, your priorities may change and your list of objectives may become shorter. In no way are we saying you must limit your choices; we are just saying that you need to prioritise things.

Signpost

Have, or at least be prepared to develop, strong ideas of what you consider to be good and acceptable outcomes to your case and discuss these with your lawyer, so that he or she is clear about what you want to achieve. You should also work out what would be an unacceptable outcome to your case and discuss this too. ▷ *Section 3*

As part of your thinking about your own objectives, you should also consider what you know about the wrongdoer. Was she or he an employee, a sub-contractor, an outsider? What message do you want to send by your actions and how is the wrongdoer likely to respond to those actions?

To a large extent, your options will be dependent on your resources and means: do you wish to spend the time and money pursuing a legal case and, if so, how much of this will you want to leave to others to control and carry out?

2.3 The victim merry-go-round

It is an unfortunate fact that very many, if not the majority of victims of fraud, end up on a sort of merry-go-round[1] in their search for advice and help in how to respond to a case of fraud. The first problem which presents itself to a victim of fraud is who to turn to for advice and help.

Even experienced company directors and business partners may have limited experience of significant fraud and will usually have little or no experience of fraud cases in the civil and criminal courts. They will know of lawyers and accountants who help them in their business and personal affairs but those advisers may not have the expertise to help in the case of a fraud.

In *Section 3, Choosing, using and paying for lawyers,* we give more guidance on this important topic. In this section, it suffices to say that a great many victims do not end up getting specialist expert advice from the outset and this can restrict their options and cause them serious difficulties with any case that they pursue.

The situation for victims is particularly confusing because of the split legal regimes which they have to consider. We are talking here about the fact that there is a civil-court system of law and a criminal-court system of law, each with its own structures, complexities and legal language (⊳ *Figure A*). And on top of that, victims may also be advised to look to regulators for help.

Signpost

Frauds tend to involve repeated events. Once an offender has learnt how to commit a fraud and got away with it, they do it again, often accelerating their offending. Without intervention, the opportunistic offender turns into a habitual fraudster. Unfortunately this means the detected fraud is often just the tip of an iceberg. ⊳ *Section 1*

In *Section 6* we describe in detail the process for reporting fraud to the police (if you choose to do so). You need to be aware that most reports by victims do not end up as fully-fledged police investigations, let alone prosecutions. You also need to be aware that reporting to police and then waiting for them to respond can eat into very valuable time.

Let's now take a look at your choices in a bit more detail.

1 A phrase commonly used to describe victims' experiences. See www.gov.uk/government/uploads/system/uploads/attachment_data/file/118468/better-deal-for-fraud-victims.pdf.

2.4 Do nothing

You are always free to do nothing at all.

Maybe you have more money than you could ever spend and will not notice the loss. Maybe you just cannot face having to confront the possible embarrassing publicity and hassle of having to do something about your loss. Maybe you think that there is more value in focusing energy and resources on, for example, generating new business rather than pursuing the losses. Managing an investigation and court case is time consuming, as one in-house lawyer, whose company did bring civil proceedings, put it:

> "The time input required of senior management and specialist resources had a knock-on effect on operations generally as the investigations and follow up measures required took from the time available for normal management activities."

If you decide to do little or nothing, you would not be the first victim to make that choice after learning of a fraud. But for many, if not most victims, doing nothing is both unpalatable and unwise.

Most directors and business owners do feel the loss when their companies become victims of fraud. They either need the money that they have lost or can imagine what they could have done with the money. Their plans may have been disrupted and they think about what they would be able to do if they could get the money back.

Directors also know that failing to deal with cases of fraud increases their vulnerability to further incidents and to other damaging consequences.

> "A substantial manufacturing company, P, recruited a new Project Manager, Adam, to oversee some time-critical engineering projects. Shortly after arriving Adam introduced a new contractor, F, with whom he had had a long relationship. Within weeks he entered into a pre-arranged corrupt scheme whereby he awarded F contracts worth £250,000 and received 2% in kickbacks. Halfway through the programme P's management discovered the corruption but reasoned that confronting the problem would cause damaging delays. By the end of the programme, Adam had further committed P to £150,000 of unjustified contract variations. P's management paid the money to avoid the embarrassment and distraction of litigation. Adam was dismissed for incompetence, not gross misconduct. It subsequently transpired that the engineering was sub-standard which meant engaging another contractor to rectify the work. P's long-standing suppliers, aware of the circumstances, had walked away. P was forced to engage a new supplier and fork out another £50,000 at premium rates. Overall P lost £200,000, damaged its reputation, lost the support of key contractors and suffered the feared delays, all because it did nothing."

If you are thinking of doing nothing, there is just one thing you must do. That is, make sure that you consider whether you need to disclose the fraud and the company's losses to your shareholders and secure their agreement to your proposed inaction. It would be sensible to take legal advice on this. Without that agreement from your shareholders you may put yourself at risk, not only of being dismissed from your directorship but also at risk of being sued by your company for breaching your duties owed to the company – in this case, duties to help the company recover stolen assets. The same is true for partners, who should disclose their discovery of fraud and losses to other partners.

2.5 Getting your money back from your bank or the receiving bank

If you can get money back from your bank quickly and easily, then that may stem all of your losses. The bank will then end up out of pocket having to decide whether it will pursue the wrongdoer.

Whether your bank will reimburse you / re-credit your account depends on the terms and conditions that you have in place with your bank (which you will need to read very carefully) and on your rights under the Payment Services Regulations 2017.[2]

Under the Payment Services Regulations 2017, banks are obliged to re-credit business customer's accounts[3] if they make payments out that were not authorised by you or where the bank makes payments that are defective, i.e. not in accordance with your payment instructions. There are some qualifications to these general propositions.

The most important qualifications[4] are that the Bank is not required to reimburse you / re-credit your account:

- If there has been "undue delay" in your notification of the problem transaction to the bank or if, in any event, you fail to notify the bank within 13 months of the problem transaction.
- If you intentionally or with gross negligence failed to keep secure bank cards, personalised security information or other payment instruments and/or failed to notify the bank that cards or other payment instruments and personalised security information had been misappropriated or used without your authority.

It is harder to seek reimbursement from a receiving bank, i.e. not your bank but the one to which your money was sent as a result of the fraud.[5] But you should check for latest news and legal updates as the Financial Conduct Authority is pressing banks to take more responsibility for their receipts of money in cases of fraud.[6]

2.6 Make an insurance claim

If you have insurance in place which covers your losses from the fraud, then you are highly likely to want to make a claim. Some companies take out so-called "fidelity" insurance cover to insure against fraudulent loss of money and other company property as well as covering the costs of investigating fraud and bringing claims against wrongdoers. Broadly speaking there are two types of anti-fraud insurance available to a company:

---

2 Which implements the European Union's Second Payment Services Directive, Directive (EU) 2015/2366 of the European Parliament and of the Council of 25 November 2015 on payment services in the internal market.

3 We address here only the most important protections for business customers. Protections for consumers are wider still.

4 Banks are also entitled to refuse to re-credit accounts and reimburse customers where the customers have themselves behaved fraudulently.

5 There are kinds of legal claims which victims may be able to bring against receiving banks but they are outside the scope of this guide.

6 See www.fca.org.uk/news/press-releases/fca-introduces-new-rules-handling-complaints-about-authorised-push-payment-fraud.

- "internal" fraud insurance; which covers losses caused by fraud or theft by directors and employees of the company; and
- "external" fraud insurance; which covers losses caused by fraud or theft by persons from outside the insured company.

If you have insurance, you will almost certainly need to notify your insurer as soon as possible and in any event within a specified time of your discovery of the fraud and failure to do so may mean that you will not be covered in respect of the losses you have suffered.

> **Signpost**
>
> When lawyers and courts talk about the value of a claim, they mean the financial value, not the emotional or reputational issues surrounding the bringing or defending of a case. ▷ *Section 5*

When making an insurance claim, you will need to carefully consider the terms of your insurance policy. In particular, you will need to consider whether any excess you have to pay will limit the amount you can expect to receive from the insurer.

Insurance excess amounts may become a serious problem for you if, for example, you have suffered a large number of small thefts of money or company property. This is because your insurer may be entitled to treat each incident of wrongdoing as a separate event giving rise to a separate claim and therefore apply the excess to each and every one of those incidents. In an extreme example, this could wipe out all insurance cover.

You can make an insurance claim simultaneously with complaints to the police and with bringing your own court proceedings. However, you should first check your insurance policy and talk to your insurer about your proposed actions as they may have a right to intervene and ask you to take one course or another. They may decide to reject your claim, insist that you report the matter to the police, pay your claim with no further action or pursue civil litigation at their cost.

If your insurers do ask you to report the fraud to the police, do think very carefully about whether this fits your main objectives/ strategies in the case. If not, then be prepared to argue with the insurer about whether it really is important to the insurer or whether it is just one of their standard requests.

2.7 Complain to the police

You are free to choose whether to report a fraud to the police.[7]

The police, for the most part, no longer accept complaints directly from victims of fraud, including cyber fraud. Reports are now handled by a central call centre,

7 There are a few exceptions to this general position (for example, insurer insistence or regulatory obligations), and those are beyond the scope of this guide.

Action Fraud and passed on to the National Fraud Intelligence Bureau (NFIB) which then channels cases deemed to be "viable" for investigation to the relevant police constabulary (⊳ *Section 6.11, Reporting a fraud to Action Fraud*).

One advantage of engaging the police and the Crown Prosecution Service (CPS) is the cost of the investigation and prosecution is borne by the state. There may be a cost to you in management time and other incidentals, including obtaining your own legal advice, otherwise it is free. Another potential advantage is that, after convictions have been secured, the CPS can seek compensation and restitution orders against the offenders on behalf of the victims (⊳ *Section 6.7, Compensation orders and restitution orders*).

Unfortunately, fraud is not a priority for the police and furthermore your fraud case may not be a priority amongst the cases that are filtered through to the police. (⊳ *Section 6.9, Making a criminal complaint*).

> A fraud lawyer: "Clients are often keen to report the matter to the police, which is completely understandable because in many situations a crime has been committed. I often spend time talking through what they hope to achieve with a police report and reminding clients that the police won't be looking to get their money back for them, which may well be the Client's main priority."

You also need to consider who controls the case if you go to the police. Although you will be involved in making the complaint and the police will need your help to build a case against the fraudsters, you will have very limited rights of participation in the criminal investigation process and the police will volunteer to you very few details about their investigations. You will also have very limited rights in relation to the criminal prosecution process which would be conducted by lawyers in the CPS or perhaps the Serious Fraud Office.

What this means is that you will relinquish control of the case and you will become dependent on the police and prosecutors to do a good job in their investigations, securing convictions in court and obtaining a compensation or restitution order for you (⊳ *Section 6.7, Compensation orders and restitution orders*). It also means that you cannot stop the investigation and prosecution should you find that it comes into conflict with another of your objectives such as obtaining compensation directly from the wrongdoers.

One company's deliberations over whether to report a fraud to the police was well expressed:

> "The question of whether to report the fraud to the police, once it was established that there was no legal obligation to do so, weighed considerably on the minds of several members of the senior management team. The natural instinct of several members was to report wrong-doing to the police to save others from potentially becoming victims of the fraudster. They faced a dilemma when advised that a well-intended public-spirited action could in fact hamper the company in the recovery of its assets, which could in turn have had implications for board members in terms of their accountability to shareholders to act in the best interests of the company."

When things work well with the police and the CPS, the results can be excellent. Both organisations have substantial state-funded resources and both have very strong legal powers which are rightly feared by wrongdoers. They can:

- arrest people and hold them on remand in prison if they pose a danger to the public or there is a risk of flight;
- ensure the accused do not dissipate their assets by imposing restraint orders;
- seize assets;
- interview the accused and witnesses, search people and property and demand materials from banks and other organisations; and
- pursue others who assisted or handled the proceeds of the crimes in the same way.

> **Signpost**
>
> Complaining to the police or the Serious Fraud Office (SFO) is cost free. However your chances of having your case investigated and prosecuted will improve if you have lawyers helping you in preparing your evidence and in liaising with the police and prosecutors. ⊳ *Section 6*

The civil regime has many of the same powers, but not all of them, and there are differences (⊳ *Figure A* and *Figure 2.2, Comparison of characteristics of justice routes*).

Although you can turn to and feel supported by the police, you do need to know that the criminal regime is focused more on the accused than the victim. As one fraud officer commented:

> "Sure the victim matters, we are human. But first of all we're policemen, we want to leap hedges and catch the bad guys, that's what gets us up, that's what we're for."

The criminal justice system is designed to catch the bad guys, determine their guilt, attach a criminal record and impose a sanction, whether a warning, community orders, fines or ultimately loss of freedom. And at the same time, the police and the prosecutors must comply with onerous rules governing their investigations and prosecutions to ensure the accused are fairly treated and to avoid miscarriages of justice.

The burden of proof rests entirely with the prosecutor who must disclose evidence and other relevant materials in a prescribed manner even when doing so harms the prosecutor's case and assists the accused person's case. By contrast, the accused is not obliged to produce any evidence or relevant materials, except if he intends to rely on them and even then he can for the most part just deploy his evidence at the trial stage.

One consequence of the disclosure rules that apply to criminal cases, is that the police may gather materials which you regard as both confidential and irrelevant and deliver copies to the accused. The sensitive information may also be revealed to the public through the course of the criminal trial.

In order to succeed the prosecutor must prove to the jury trying the case that the accused person is guilty to the criminal standard of proof, beyond all reasonable doubt. This is a high standard of proof and to satisfy it the prosecutor must have clear and cogent evidence. This can be circumstantial evidence but, if so, it must be powerful and the wrongdoer must lack a credible explanation for his or her actions.

> **Signpost**
>
> It does appear wrong that the state's coffers are benefiting more than the victims. There may be reasons for this but it is hard to imagine that they are good reasons. And it is hard to see why victims should be encouraged by these figures. ⊳ *Section 6*

The combination of the burden of proof, the standard of proof and the procedural rules, especially the disclosure rules to be followed by crime prosecutors mean that investigations and the preparation of evidence for criminal cases can take many months, if not years. It also means that criminal trials, especially fraud trials can be complex and lengthy, sometimes lasting many months. Trials have to proceed at a speed which juries are able to cope with. One victim found the criminal process to be an intensely frustrating experience:

> "I have found the criminal side rather difficult. I cannot believe the amount of work the police must do for a case that is really quite simple (which they admit is quite simple) given the amount of clear and indisputable evidence. I share the frustrations of the police officers who are passionate about getting the right result. It seems the [Crown Prosecution Service] are terrified to charge without destroying an area of Amazonian Forest just for the extra copies of evidence for this case. We have had four different case officers on this to date, and told that this isn't unusual! It may not be unusual but surely is a real waste of resource."

Victims frequently are unaware that the criminal courts can order convicted offenders to pay them compensation or restitution (⊳ *Section 6.7, Compensation orders and restitution orders*). Here's an introduction to these kinds of financial reparation for victims.

2.7.1 Criminal compensation orders

Criminal compensation orders require offenders to pay victims for their losses. The orthodox understanding of the relevant case law is that they can and should only be dealt with in "... simple straightforward cases".[8] As we explain later (⊳ *Section 6.7, Compensation orders and restitution orders*) there may now be a shift in the approach of the courts towards dealing with the more complex cases but criminal courts are still unlikely to deal with very complex calculations of loss, including, for example, victims' indirect losses, particularly if the offender does not agree to the compensation award.

Victims have no right to address a court, either themselves or through a lawyer, and no right to appeal or seek a judicial review of a court's refusal to make a compensation order.

8 www.cps.gov.uk/legal/s_to_u/sentencing_and_ancillary_orders_applications/#a01.

You should bear in mind that the police and prosecutors focus their efforts on gathering sufficient evidence to secure guilty verdicts, not on your compensation rights let alone the quantification of your losses. You are unlikely to receive any detailed advice from police or prosecutors about compensation and if you do then this may come late into any case.

> **Signpost**
>
> The Magistrates' Court's strongest enforcement tool – the threat of imprisonment for failure to pay a compensation order – is a double-edged sword. A person who serves such a sentence would no longer have to pay the compensation order. ⊳ *Section 6*

2.7.2 Criminal restitution orders

Restitution orders focus on restoring property to victims. Historically, the courts have only made restitution orders in "the plainest cases"[9] but, just as with compensation orders, this may also be set to change so as to allow more complex cases to be determined by the criminal courts. Property can be specific items of property belonging to the victim (except land) or property which was clearly acquired using the victim's money. So, if a fraudster uses the proceeds of a fraud to buy shares he can be ordered to hand over those investments to the victim. Unlike the situation with compensation orders, victims do have the right to address the court when seeking a restitution order. As is the case with compensation, the police and prosecutors will not, at an early stage, be concerned with your restitution rights and you may receive little or no detailed information about them at any stage of the case.

> **Signpost**
>
> If you are pinning your hopes on a criminal court compensation order, you will need to strike a balance between being ambitious about the amount you can and should claim for your losses, and being realistic and trying to keep the explanation and calculation of your losses as simple as possible. ⊳ *Section 6*

2.7.3 Police and prosecution mistakes

Like other organisations, the police and the public prosecutors do make mistakes and it is important to understand that they have limited accountability to victims for their errors. Sometimes these errors cause cases to fail:

> "A builders' merchant was defrauded of £850,000 by one of its Directors conspiring with four suppliers. The company reported it to the police and it was then taken up by the CPS. The defence lawyers complained to the judge at a pre-trial hearing that the prosecution had failed to properly disclose all the evidence to them. The judge gave the CPS the opportunity to rectify the failure. The CPS

9 www.cps.gov.uk/legal/s_to_u/sentencing_and_ancillary_orders_applications/#a01.

appointed a new team of barristers and re-presented the evidence to the defence team. Immediately prior to the reconvened pre-trial hearing the defence team advised the CPS of errors in the disclosure process. The prosecutor then arose and advised the judge that the prosecutor would not offer any evidence against the defendants, and the case was dismissed. It is fortunate that the company managed to prove its civil case and recover its losses in full."

Most victims do not seek help from lawyers when making complaints to the police. But some do and in fraud cases this can make a big difference to the likely outcome, particularly in relation to criminal court awards of compensation or restitution. An experienced lawyer will understand how to help you manage your relationship with the police and prosecutor and will be able to prompt timely actions and court interventions by those agencies that help ensure, for example, that evidence is gathered, that wrongdoers cannot dissipate their (or your!) assets and that your claims for compensation or restitution are properly pursued and supported by the police and CPS.

Signpost

In some cases, either wrong or inadequate criminal charges are brought leaving victims little or no hope of appropriate levels of compensation (if any) through the criminal courts even if persons are convicted. ⊳ *Section 6*

2.8 Private prosecutions

You have the right to bring a private prosecution if you consider that you are the victim of a fraud. That right is not widely known or taken up by victims of fraud. This is not surprising since bringing a criminal case before the criminal courts is generally seen as a state function. It is also not surprising, therefore, that the Director of Public Prosecutions, who heads up the Crown Prosecution Service (CPS), has the power to take over the conduct of a private prosecution to continue it and then has the power to stop the case from continuing.

Signpost

If you want to bring a private prosecution, you would have to know a lot more than is in this guide because of the heavy responsibilities which are placed on private prosecutors. ⊳ *Section 6*

Private prosecutions require a good deal of expertise and resources.[10] To win, you must comply with the same procedural and evidential laws rules, and ethical requirements that govern the conduct of the police and public prosecutors. You must

10 Thousands of private prosecutions are conducted each year by specialist organisations; the aims of the overwhelming majority are punishment, to deter others and put a stop to harm. The RSPCA, for example, secured 744 convictions in 2016 through private prosecutions for mistreatment of animals (https://view.pagetiger.com/RSPCAProsecutionsAnnualreport2016). A small number of private proceedings are brought each year by organisations such as the Federation Against Copyright Theft (FACT) and broadcasters seeking to stop abuse of intellectual property rights.

also prove your case to the criminal standard of proof. You may not have the same resources which the state can muster to investigate and prosecute a fraud; nor will you have all of its powers.

You would not have the police's powers of arrest, nor would you be entitled to carry out any raids for evidence. You would be entitled to ask the court to issue a restraint order to freeze assets held by a wrongdoer but only after you have commenced the prosecution of the wrongdoer. By contrast, the CPS can obtain asset restraints during the investigation stage of a case.

Why do people bring private prosecutions? There are three main reasons: lack of police interest, for more control of the case and a quicker result. Although private prosecutions for fraud are rare, they are becoming a little more frequent and there are lawyers who specialise in this area.

In *Section 3, Choosing, using and paying for lawyers*, we provide an overview of the costs of paying for lawyers. Significantly, victims who bring a private prosecution are, generally, able to recover reasonable legal costs associated with the prosecution from the state. However, the Court of Appeal gave stiff warnings in a case in 2014. Costs recovery is uncertain, can be quite limited and is certainly not a free-for-all.

Signpost

As a victim, you have every right to expect the police to make themselves aware of your needs and wishes for financial reparation. They ought to know whether you intend to bring civil proceedings to run in parallel with their criminal case, and whether you intend asking the criminal court to award you compensation or restitution. ⊳ *Section 6*

2.9 Civil court claims

The civil courts decide on responsibility and financial liability of wrongdoers, not criminal guilt, or indeed moral culpability. The civil law in England and Wales caters pretty well for victims in its potential coverage and in its strength but, as we explain below and later in this guide (⊳ *Section 3*, *Choosing, using and paying for lawyers*), it is expensive to access.

There are a number of different kinds of claims which victims can bring against wrongdoers. In *Section 5, Civil court claims* you will find a guide to the kinds of civil claims which you can bring against fraudsters and what you need to be able to prove to win those claims. That section also provides a guide to some of the procedural aspects of bringing a claim.

For you to succeed in a civil claim, you have to prove your claim to the civil standard. That standard is the balance of probabilities. What this means is that to win, you must be able to show that it was more likely than not that the alleged wrongdoer committed the wrong. This is a lower standard of proof than the criminal one. Considerably lower. Nevertheless, the claim still needs proper investigation and proof. Court's expect victims who allege fraud to present clear and cogent evidence.

2.9 *Objectives and options*

There are three key aspects to the investigation prior to a civil claim: assembling sufficient evidence, demonstrating the value of your loss, and identifying your money or other assets in the defendant's possession (▷ *Section 4, Tracing and securing assets in the civil courts*).

Proper preparation of a fraud claim is essential. This is not just because the price of failure in a claim can be very high – if unsuccessful, you would, generally, be ordered to pay the costs of those you have sued – but because without proper preparation you can lose even if you win your case. What we mean by this is that a judgment against an impecunious person can turn out to be a very expensive, pyrrhic victory.

The civil courts are able to empower claimants by making orders which assist investigations and the preparation of cases. These orders cover investigating the identity of the fraudsters and what has become of the money or other property you have lost, enabling you to obtain evidence from other parties such as banks, internet service providers and telecommunications companies (▷ *Section 4.7, Norwich Pharmacal orders*).

The civil courts can also give you protective measures whilst you wait for the outcome of your civil claim, including freezing injunctions (▷ *Section 4.8, Freezing injunctions* and ▷ *Section 4.9, Proprietary injunctions*). These then ring-fence the wrongdoer's assets so that they cannot be fraudulently dissipated before the trial and before you can enforce any judgment against the wrongdoer. These injunctions can also coerce wrongdoers to reveal what has become of monies and other assets that they have stolen and the extent of the wrongdoers' asset holdings.

Freezing injunctions made by civil courts are often designed to be international in their reach. They can freeze assets held by, or for the wrongdoer, wherever those assets are located in the world. An English-court freezing order can be combined with similar orders in other countries to put a total freeze on assets in a number of locations (▷ *Section 7, International cases and enforcement*).

If arranged properly, with the help of lawyers in other countries, it is possible to stage-manage a total freeze of a number of assets located all over the world, but as you can probably imagine this sort of coordinated activity using lawyers in different countries can be very expensive.

> **Signpost**
>
> When considering litigation, you should regard the fraud loss as a sunk cost. You then view the claim as a possible gain. Even if you desperately need to recover the property or money, it helps to think of litigation in this hard-headed way. ▷ *Section 5*

The legal system in England and Wales itself can be expensive to access. In *Section 3, Choosing, using and paying for lawyers*, we set out the options which you have in that regard. Because it can be expensive to hire and use lawyers, many businesses are rightly cautious about bringing civil claims in the courts, even in the case of fraud. This is especially so in the case of modest-value fraud cases, where the amount lost does not easily justify substantial expenditure on legal costs.

The directors of a large business debated its options rationally on pure economic grounds, before committing to and ultimately succeeding in complex, international litigation:

> "The dilemma of whether it was in the best interests of the company to pursue recovery of the monies was less of a moral one and more of a financial and operational one, but it was nonetheless a dilemma. This is because it had the potential to be very costly, time-consuming and rather long drawn out, due to the fact that the monies were traced into assets which were located in more than one jurisdiction, including a jurisdiction which does not recognise orders of an English court and had been dissipated in a variety of ways, requiring different recovery strategies."

The victim-claimant, the defendant and their respective legal teams have to comply with the Civil Procedure Rules. The obligations on the opposing parties in the courts are much more equal than in the criminal courts. All parties in civil proceedings must disclose all documents which they wish to rely on in their case as well as all documents which adversely affect their own case or that of another party to the case.

You may not win. This may be down to the fact that you were wrong in accusing the defendant of fraud, or because you did not have enough evidence, or because your lawyers were not good enough.

If you lose you are liable to pay the defendant's costs (▷ *Section 3.12, Adverse costs in civil cases*), which can be considerable, in addition to your own costs. The only consolation for you here is that the same court rules apply to the defendant's costs as to the claimant's, so that even if he wins the case, the defendant will have to pay a portion of his costs out of his own pocket.

The costs of participating in civil-court claims persuade most claimants and defendants to settle matters or even abandon their claims or defences before cases get to trial (▷ *Section 5.15, Compromising claims*).

Signpost

A disclosure order can be a powerful tool for gathering information about the assets of a wrongdoer. When combined with the information the victim may already have, a detailed picture can emerge of the assets to be frozen. ▷ *Section 4*

2.10 What do you know about the wrongdoer?

The position of the wrongdoer is very relevant:

- If the wrongdoer is a director and / or an employee, you are going to need to pay close attention to the impact on your business whether you do or don't take action. If you do wish to take action, this may inform what kind of action you choose to take. This is because the insider-wrongdoer is likely to have access to confidential business information and to still have friends in your business.
- If the wrongdoer has done and / or continues to do business with your organisation, you will want to consider the business impact of taking or not taking action and what kind of action is most appropriate.

What about the character of fraudsters? Can you try to determine how they will react to action which you take? What legitimate pressure can you put the wrongdoer under, whilst avoiding any suggestion that you are "blackmailing" him or her into submission? Sometimes, the mere possibility of proceedings is enough to make a fraudster admit liability and pay up:

> "We had a telephone call on a Friday afternoon. The Chief Exec had suspected that the FD was messing about with the funds. So we sent in one of our investigators and one of our forensic accountants when he wasn't in, on a Friday. We literally just stopped everything and looked at everything. It was such an easy one to spot because we just went straight into his internet activity and he was doing online bingo, constantly. He spent over £700,000 of the company's money on online bingo at work. By the Sunday afternoon we had actually got his house signed over [to the company]."

In another case, the wrongdoer confessed immediately when confronted:

> "William was a very quiet unassuming and very likeable man; he was studying to become a qualified accountant and worked well with the team. The problem was he couldn't ever explain the accounts to me and that is why I started to have doubts. When we discovered the theft and fraud, I called William in to suspend him on suspicion of theft and an investigation would take place. He sat staring at me in silence for at least 5 minutes, then he removed his glasses without looking away from me, and for a split-second I thought he was going to attack me. He fell on to his knees and pleaded that I should think about his children. While he was suspended, he emailed me for a job reference to take another bookkeeping role, which of course I refused, he then sent me an email saying that I was a terrible person."

However, even if you think that you have caught the fraudster red-handed, you may find that he or she digs in for a fight. This is particularly so in cases where victims involve the police and the wrongdoer's liberty is at stake. Even persons who confess in the early stages sometimes try to retract those confessions or otherwise raise defences when the full ramifications are known to them. It is for this reason that it is often better, from a strategic point of view, not to report a wrongdoer to the police if your priority is the recovery of money or assets from the wrongdoer.

In many other cases, even when you have won your case, it is not the end of the road. The final step is enforcing the court order to actually get you your money. With compliant defendants with sufficient assets this is straightforward: they pay up. With others, depending on their obstinacy and available assets, enforcing the orders can be hard work and take time (▷ *Section 5.18, Enforcing court orders*).

Signpost

Good police officers and prosecutors understand the need for victims to bring their own civil claims alongside criminal action. This should neither put them off prosecuting a case and managed well the parallel proceedings may even offer some advantages to the public authorities. ▷ *Section 6*

2.11 Criminal and civil cases in parallel

You can combine complaining to the police (or indeed a private prosecution) with a civil-court claim. The advantages are two-fold. Firstly, there is the prospect of both civil recovery and criminal punishment – instead of just one of these results. Secondly, evidence can be shared. However, you should bear in the mind the following:

- The civil and criminal cases are brought independently of each other in separate courts which have different functions and outcomes. It is very unlikely that the two cases will proceed at the same pace.
- There will be restrictions on what information and documents originating in one investigation and proceedings can be used in the other investigation and set of proceedings. You will, in some cases, need to obtain a court's permission to use restricted information.
- It is not legitimate to deliberately use criminal investigation and prosecution to put pressure on the wrongdoer to reach a financial settlement with you. If you threaten or bring a prosecution that must be for sound reasons you must be prepared to see that through to the end.
- The very fact that you have brought criminal proceedings may make the wrongdoer and his associates fight harder than they would had you just brought a civil claim. The wrongdoer, threatened with prison for himself and others (for example, a spouse) has every incentive to think creatively to come up with a defence and little incentive to capitulate or reach a compromise with you.
- The police and prosecutor will not be able to advise you on or help you with your civil-court claim. Helping you to get financial reparations before the civil courts is not part of their job description or public duties.
- The police and prosecutor will not readily understand your civil court claim. They have expertise in the criminal court process but are much more focused on the potential criminal liability of the wrongdoer than on your desire for compensation. In addition, they are unlikely to have any significant experience of civil-court claims against wrongdoers. That said, they should at least understand why you may be interested in bringing a civil claim.
- The police or prosecutor may try to dissuade you from mounting a civil claim or at least ask you to wait until they have finished investigating or prosecuting the criminal case. If you have already begun civil proceedings, they may ask you to stay (suspend) those proceedings until the conclusion of the criminal investigation and case. In most cases, this is not good advice. It stems from ignorance and from attitudes which are well meaning but often wrong.
- If you find there is a conflict between your civil case and the Crown's prosecution you will not be able to stop or suspend the prosecution but the prosecutor may – in exceptional circumstances – be able to persuade the civil court to suspend your civil case pending the outcome of the criminal case.
- There is the risk that the police and prosecutor and indeed the criminal court may be obliged to seek a financial order payable to the state rather than payable to you (either a confiscation order, forfeiture order or costs order) and which may end up being paid by the fraudster ahead of making a compensation payment to you (▷ *Section 6.7.3, Seeking compensation and restitution*).
- The defendant's resources may be consumed in defending the criminal allegation, leaving you less or nothing to recover at the conclusion of your civil claim. Whether the defendant will be free to spend assets on legal fees

depends on the particulars of the case and whether the defendant is prosecuted in England and Wales or elsewhere.

2.12 Timing issues

Time is of the essence: Justice delayed is justice denied. This is particularly true in fraud cases – fraudsters do not hang around when they have obtained their ill-gotten gains, your money. In cyber fraud cases, time-frames can be even faster, as cyber fraudsters work fast to try and spirit away your money!

Lawyers despair when victims of fraud come to see them with good claims that are rendered worthless by the passage of time. There is also a legal reason why time matters. Civil claims can become time barred. So whatever you choose to do, do it now.

2.13 Regulatory options

Complaining to regulators is an option pursued by some victims, either on its own or in parallel with the criminal or civil routes. Regulators can provide a level of satisfaction to victims by imposing sanctions on lawyers, accountants and other professionals.

However the sanction menu available to most regulators is limited, the maximum being to remove their licence to practice. In some cases, such as where the professional has fraudulently overcharged a client, the regulator can order the offender to return the money.

Regulators are not, however, generally empowered to award compensation to victims of fraud. Some sector regulators such as the Financial Conduct Authority (FCA) can order individual firms to compensate victims.

If you do not have the appetite for criminal or civil proceedings, the regulatory route is a cost-free alternative which has a positive social value in ensuring professionals cannot repeat their offences and harm others. Reporting to the regulators assists them to keep their professions clean and helps to strengthen their deterrence strategies.

It is important for victims to understand that they may be able to complain to regulators. But because of the limited opportunities for obtaining compensation through regulators, we do not devote any more space in this guide to regulatory action.

2.14 Conclusions

In this guide, we think it would be inappropriate to give prescriptive recommendations as to which route you should take when seeking justice. *Figure 2.2* provides a snapshot comparison of the justice routes. As we said at the start of this section, much will depend on your objectives, your resources and the value of your case. We can, however, offer some general observations and suggestions:

- If you can afford to seek help from a lawyer then do so as soon as possible and seek help from a lawyer who specialises in advising and representing victims of fraud; ideally one who understands both civil and criminal fraud proceedings (▷ *Section 3, Choosing, using and paying for lawyers*).
- If you can get money back from your bank quickly and easily, then that may stem all or most of your losses. The bank will end up out of pocket having to decide whether it will pursue the wrongdoers.
- If a major objective is compensation or the recovery of assets and you have the means to make the running with a case against a wrongdoer then you ought to be thinking of bringing your own civil proceedings (▷ *Section 5, Civil court claims*).
- The sooner you bring a civil claim the better, and commencement of a case should, if at all possible, be coupled with seeking court freezing orders or other protective measures against the wrongdoers right at the start of your case.
- Civil proceedings are usually faster and, given the lower standard of proof, are easier to win than criminal cases brought by the state, but they are far more expensive.
- If you do not have the means to mount your own civil court proceedings and you cannot find lawyers willing to take on your case on an alternative fee basis or with the support of a litigation funder then you will probably have to entrust your case to the police.
- If you are less concerned about obtaining compensation or asset recovery but are really interested in seeing the police investigate with the possibility that the wrongdoer will be prosecuted, found guilty and then punished, then you may be happy with simply making a complaint to the police and seeing to it that your complaint is properly investigated (▷ *Section 6.9, Making a criminal complaint*).
- If criminal prosecution is your priority and you want to have more control of the criminal prosecution and have the financial means to hire lawyers to mount a criminal case then consider the possibility of bringing a private prosecution (▷ *Section 6.3, Private prosecutions*).
- You can bring legal proceedings yourself without the help of lawyers, but pursuing a fraud claim as a litigant in person would be an extremely challenging proposition with a number of risks, including adverse costs risks in the event of failure (▷ *Section 3.12, Adverse costs in civil cases*).
- It may be possible to bring a civil claim in parallel with a criminal prosecution (either brought by a public prosecutor or by you as a private prosecutor). There are practical and strategic advantages and disadvantages to parallel civil and criminal investigations and litigation.

> **Signpost**
>
> Given the complexity of the law, it is important that you do not have too many fixed ideas about what kind of case you can or cannot bring before you receive expert help in formulating claims that are most likely to succeed. ▷ *Section 5*

Finally, we need to emphasise that your practical options for accessing justice through either of the dominant state criminal or private civil routes is driven to a great extent by your resources and the value of your case. Low value cases are less likely to be of interest to the police and prosecutors. And if you have low levels of resources to put into pursuing justice, then this may severely hamper your access to civil justice. This simple view of accessibility of the justice systems is illustrated in *Figure 2.1*.

- Low case value with low levels of resources – you are unlikely to be able to access either route.
- Low value case with sufficient resources – the most realistic option is the civil route.
- High value case with limited resources – it's likely that the criminal route is the only option unless you are able to access lawyers using alternative fee arrangements (▷ *Section 3.16, Alternative fee arrangements*).
- If your case is high value with sufficient resources, then you have the option to pursue either or both routes.

Figure 2.1: Simple view of accessibility of criminal and civil justice

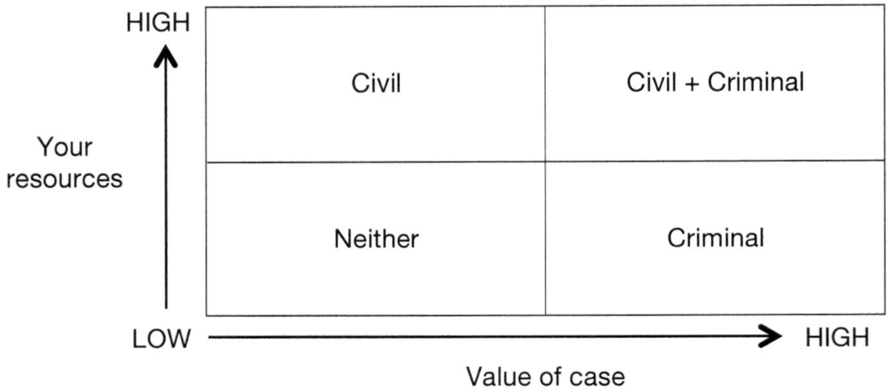

Figure 2.2: Comparison of characteristics of justice routes

	Criminal Prosecution	**Private Prosecution**	**Civil Litigation**	**Regulatory**
Focus	Offender focused	Offender focused	Victim focused	Offender focused
Purpose	Conviction of offender	Conviction of offender	Recovery of losses	Improve conduct or exclusion
Claim value	All values	All values	All values	Usually limited
Compensation and restitution	Simple, direct losses and restitution only	Simple, direct losses and restitution only	More complex direct and consequential losses	Some regulators may order limited compensation
Trial	Jury	Jury	Judge	Some with tribunal panel, some without hearings
Standard of proof	Beyond reasonable doubt	Beyond reasonable doubt	Balance of probabilities	Balance of probability except criminal standard for lawyers
Investigation powers	Strong investigation powers	Weaker powers, require support of courts	Weaker powers, require support of courts	Strong powers
Disclosure	Prosecutor disclosure only, defendant may disclose	Prosecutor disclosure only, defendant may disclose	Claimant and defendant disclosure required	Variable requirements
Timescale	Slowest investigation, long trial	Slow investigation, long trial	Fastest investigation, shorter trial	Variable investigation speed, shorter or no hearing
Victim's control	No control	Limited control; may be taken over by CPS	Victim has control	No control
Legal expense costs to victim	No cost (unless victim wants support of lawyers)	Low to high cost (majority can be recovered from state win or lose)	Low to high cost (majority can be recovered from the fraudster if win)	No cost

Choosing, using and paying for lawyers

3.1 In this section

- Why using lawyers is a good idea
- The differences between barristers and solicitors
- Choosing lawyers
- Getting the most from lawyers
- The options for paying for lawyers
- Litigation funding
- Recovering legal costs
- The risk of adverse costs

3.2 Introduction

We think that choosing the right lawyers and working out the best way to use and pay for them is so important that it deserves a whole section to itself. We set out what we see as the most important things you will need to know and think about when choosing, using and paying for lawyers. Get it right and you are likely to have an excellent experience that maximises your chance of success in your case. Get it wrong and you will regret your experience with the law.

Before getting further with this section, it is important to remind you that speed is almost always vital in fraud cases in order to contain the situation, prevent further losses and stop the fraudster from dissipating your money. You don't want to be in a position where you can prove your case but can't recover your losses. Choosing lawyers under these pressured circumstances can lead to costly mistakes. Time pressures are not helpful but if you are going to use a lawyer, it is important to find the right one quickly.

When it comes to choosing a lawyer, there are good sources of information and advice you can turn to. There are directories in which lawyers are recommended according to their specialisms (more on these below). You may also find valuable information on the websites of the professional associations which represent the interests of barristers and solicitors in England and Wales: The Bar Council[1] and the Law Society.[2]

Many victims of fraud ask themselves: do I really need lawyers to advise me or represent me? A few decide they can manage without lawyers, mainly due to cost pressures, but the vast majority decide that they do need lawyers.

---

1 www.barcouncil.org.uk.
2 www.lawsociety.org.uk.

3.3 Why use lawyers?

Fraud cases are often complicated, usually much more complicated than other kinds of legal cases. You may also find yourself up against a wrongdoer who knows his way around the law and who may have lawyers who are expert in defending him against your allegations. You may not even be able to identify the wrongdoer initially. To go it alone should be your last resort.

Fraud cases are complicated for a number of reasons and court action is difficult for persons who are not legally represented. Take, for example, civil claims.

- Firstly, they are factually complex. Wrongdoers need to be identified and then layers of misconduct need to be recognised, unravelled and explained to a court.
- Secondly, the law itself can be labyrinthine. This is particularly so where a number of distinct but overlapping kinds of claims can and often must be "pleaded" in a civil case (▷*Section 5.14, Overlapping and alternative claims*).[3]
- Thirdly, the civil courts have a number of very powerful "nuclear weapons" at their disposal to help victims of fraud to find, freeze and then recover assets but the courts will only release these weapons if they trust the person who wishes to use them and so it requires skill to obtain their use and to be allowed to continue their use over a period of time without making costly mistakes (▷*Section 4, Tracing and securing assets in the civil courts*).
- Fourthly, fraud cases often cross borders, thus requiring co-ordinated activity in different countries for investigations, to bring claims and to freeze and recover assets (▷*Section 7, International cases and enforcement*).

Getting rapid advice from good lawyers can make a big difference, even for the most experienced of company management teams, as one in-house lawyer observed:

> "The ability of the client's legal advisers to reassure even a relatively sophisticated client team by responding very quickly in the first instance with unequivocal guidance on a handful of 'preliminary' issues such as: Are we obliged to report to the police? Should we or should we not report to the police immediately and if so, how do we go about this and if not, why would we not do this given that it seems to be the logical thing to do? Can we go and confront the fraudster? And explaining the difference between prosecutions and civil actions (etc) is key."

One of the big advantages of using a registered lawyer[4] to help you in your case is that you are able to take advantage of legal professional privilege.[5] This means that, as a general rule, you are entitled to freely discuss your case and receive advice about it in a way that does not have to be revealed to your opponents or to the court. Although "litigation privilege"[6] can sometimes cover some of the work of accountants and private investigators, as a general rule your discussions with non-

---

3 Pleadings, officially called "Statements of Case", are the written claims and defences which set out the nature of a dispute prior to a trial.

4 Protection will only be afforded to you if you communicate with a registered member of a legal profession: barrister, solicitor, a chartered legal executive, or a registered foreign lawyer.

5 Legal professional privilege can be complex and is beyond the scope of this guide. The term "privilege" is an English and American term. In other systems, such as those on the continent of Europe, "secrecy" is more commonly used.

6 Litigation privilege is distinct from legal professional privilege. It is beyond the scope of this guide.

legal professionals are not protected under legal professional privilege, even if those non-legal professionals are qualified to give legal advice; just as your discussions with friends and colleagues would not be protected. Only lawyer-client discussions attract legal professional privilege.

3.4 Lawyers

Firstly, we need to clarify what we mean by "lawyers". The two principal types of English and Welsh qualified lawyers[7] are barristers and solicitors. Having a clear understanding of the two roles is vital to anyone seeking help from the law to avoid misunderstandings and unnecessary costs. Robert's story is real.

Like many people, Robert's only experience of lawyers involved house conveyancing and business contracts. So, when his small business was defrauded he engaged a local solicitor for advice on pursuing a civil claim. He furnished evidence of the crime and handed over £1,500. A week later, the solicitor advised Robert that he had a good claim but they needed to get the opinion of a barrister.

> "I was confused because it turns out that she was like a gatekeeper. She said, 'Barristers are experts in the law. We know how the law works, barristers know what it is.' So, I handed over another £3,000 so they could organise the papers and get his opinion on it."

A month later, without ever meeting the barrister, Robert was taken through the report, an elegantly presented treatise which summarised the fraud and concluded the claim had merits, but the barrister needed further instructions to assess the chances of success.

> "I felt I'd been hooked and sliced. I'd got nowhere except pick up weasel words like 'merits' which is meaningless and 'instructions' which means cash. I lost all trust in them and it set me back."

Despite five weeks and £4,500, Robert was still not able to make informed decisions: there was no advice about the way forward, options, costs, timescales, risks and likelihood of success and time was ticking away. Robert sought out new lawyers and started again. His story illustrates the naivety of many people when approaching the law and how relationships with lawyers can be soured unnecessarily at the outset. It also illustrates the different lawyerly roles.

Robert is far from being unique in his displeasure of lawyerly ways. One cyber fraud victim, who had a poor experience with the police was also unhappy with the structure of the law profession:

> "Once they find a competent lawyer, I believe victims are in good hands. They know what to do straight away and are good counsel … however, the English system of barristers and solicitors is misguiding and potentially ruinous for victims."

---

7 There are also so-called Registered European Lawyers qualified to practise in England and Wales. You can find out more about these at www.barstandardsboard.org.uk/regulatory-requirements/the-old-code-of-conduct/annexes-to-the-code/annexe-b-the-registered-european-lawyers-rules/ and at www.sra.org.uk/solicitors/code-of-conduct/guidance/The-Establishment-Directive-and-RELs.page. And there are Chartered Legal Executives, on which see https://cilexregulation.org.uk/chartered-legal-executives/.

Solicitors do much of the preparation and running around and can quickly assemble teams of other solicitors if necessary. Barristers usually have a better grasp of the detail of law and of how cases should be prepared and presented but they can also be somewhat distant from the client if they are not correctly engaged. Barristers can undertake much of the work of solicitors, but, typically, solicitors cannot or do not do the advocacy work of barristers.

3.4.1 Barristers

There are approximately 16,000 barristers in England and Wales. They are at their most visible in the higher courts as they sometimes wear wigs and gowns in civil courts and always wear them in the Crown Courts (where most serious crimes are dealt with). Their theatrical garments, obsession with polite protocol and verbal skills create much loved characters in television legal dramas. Barristers tend to spend more time than solicitors in court, advocating (or "pleading") cases on behalf of clients.

Though barristers have the right to represent clients in both criminal and civil courts, it is rare to find a barrister who is an expert in both civil and criminal fraud.

Criminal law barristers spend much of their time in court, prosecuting or defending criminal cases. Civil law barristers usually spend less of their time in court – because civil trials occur in only a small percentage of civil cases – and do spend much of their time reviewing evidence, advising, and preparing important case documents.

As a general rule, barristers tend to be less expensive than solicitors because they have lower overheads and because they get to keep all of the money you pay them (as opposed to seeing some of it go to other partners).

Signpost

Civil-court fraud cases are not about revenge. Nor should they be brought for the purpose of ruining an opponent's reputation. They are about money and other financial objectives. ⊳*Section 5*

3.4.2 Solicitors

Solicitors, as a general rule, spend less time in court and more time preparing client cases, interviewing the client, witnesses, corresponding with opponent lawyers and so on. They tend to specialise quite early on in their careers so it is unlikely that you will find a solicitor who is equally expert and at home in the civil and criminal courts.

Solicitors have always been allowed to appear as advocates in the lower courts, tribunals, magistrates and county courts but, historically, were excluded from advocacy in the higher courts. However, the rules changed in 1990 to allow a new breed of "solicitor advocates" with appropriate qualifications and experience to gain Higher Rights of Audience and then appear for clients in the Crown Court, High Court and the appeal courts. Of the 146,000 solicitors registered to practise in England and Wales, about 6,800 have Higher Rights of Audience, although only 21% of these are qualified to appear as such in both civil and criminal courts.[8]

Whilst the advent of the solicitor advocate is welcome it is not without its problems. A study of judicial perceptions of the quality of criminal court advocacy published in 2018[9] highlights some particular problems associated with solicitor-advocacy. 50 criminal court judges were interviewed for the study which reported that many of those judges think that independent barristers are better performing advocates than their solicitor counterparts. An earlier report commissioned by the Ministry of Justice[10] questioned the quality of some within the solicitor advocacy profession and was particularly critical of the then disparity in training: barristers completing 120 days of advocacy training, solicitors qualifying after just 22 hours. The lack of training is then compounded by lack of time spent in court: most solicitor advocates spend less time in court than their barrister counterparts.

3.5 Law firms and barristers' chambers

Law firms comprise mostly solicitors and support staff, although some firms have barristers as well. They are what they say they are: firms which provide legal services. Most modern law firms are limited liability partnerships[11] but a few are registered limited companies.

Whatever the organisational structure, law firms are people businesses. They tend to reflect the skills and desires of the partners or directors who run them. They can be very small (just one solicitor) or very big (thousands of lawyers). The law firms specialising in fraud work include both large multinationals and small firms with specialist niche practices.

Some barristers work alone as sole practitioners and a few are employed in law firms with solicitors; but their traditional habitat is within a set of "chambers". It is just a traditional term for a suite of offices where independent, self-employed barristers share facilities and administrative services. They share the running costs but they don't share their incomes. This mode of operating allows barristers from within the same chambers to act for different clients in the same case and this does happen on a regular basis.

The character of a chambers of barristers obviously reflects its members and their practice areas. In the field of fraud litigation, it is unusual to find a chambers which contains both expert civil fraud and criminal fraud litigators. Typically, they have one or the other.

---

8 Solicitors Regulation Authority: Regulated Population Statistics. Retrieved from: www.sra.org.uk/sra/how-we-work/reports/data/higher_rights_of_audience.page.

9 *Judicial Perceptions of the Quality of Criminal Advocacy* (June 2018), commissioned by the Solicitors Regulation Authority and the Bar Standards Board and carried out by researchers from the Institute for Criminal Policy Research, Birkbeck, University of London. Retrieved from: www.sra.org.uk/sra/how-we-work/reports/criminal-advocacy.page.

10 Jeffrey, B. (2014). *Independent criminal advocacy in England and Wales*. London: Ministry of Justice. Retrieved from: www.gov.uk/government/organisations/jeffrey-review.

11 But some are still unregistered partnerships with no limits on the liability of their partners.

For many years, the only way in which a business or member of the public could gain access to help and representation from a barrister was via solicitors. A change in the rules has diminished this gatekeeper role so that an increasing number of barristers will accept clients on a so-called "public access" basis, meaning that they can help and represent a client without a law firm intervening between the client and barrister. Nevertheless, the traditional path of solicitor then barrister remains the most common route.

If you are considering making direct contact with a barrister you should be aware that, unlike solicitors, they cannot handle client money.[12] This means that they will not ask for nor hold your money on account of their fees; and they will not agree to handle your money for the purposes of making payments to others in relation to your case. They will, of course still need to be paid and will usually insist that you pay them in advance of any work to be done on a stage by stage basis. Lastly, you should also check that the barrister you are thinking of approaching is registered with the Bar Standards Board for direct public access.[13]

Many generalisations of the past are now becoming just that: historic generalisations. The government has sought to increase access to justice by breaking down restrictive practices, increasing competitiveness, raising efficiency and reducing costs. More than ever before, barristers and solicitors are working in modern dynamic arrangements which reflect their clients' needs rather than some historic mode of operation. Yet, as we make clear later in this section, affordability remains a very real problem for many victims.

3.6 Which lawyers should you choose?

A fraud lawyer: "Specialist fraud litigators might not be the cheapest, but choosing on price can be a false economy. Where very large sums of money are at stake, the savings that can be made on legal fees pale into insignificance compared to the advantages that a specialist can bring: one bad judgment call can be the difference between winning and losing a case."

How can you avoid Robert's "two-step and start again" experience? Who should you turn to first, a barrister or a solicitor? How can you assess their expertise?

3.6.1 Seek out a true expert in fraud cases

Most business people will have come across and used lawyers at some point, when establishing a business, collecting debts or just buying a property. If you are dealing with a fraud case for the first time – and for your sake we hope it is a first time – then it is unlikely that you will have experience of lawyers specialising in fraud.

---

12 Bar Standards Board (February 2018). *The Public Access Scheme Guidance for Lay Clients*. Retrieved from: www.barstandardsboard.org.uk/media/1666529/2._the_public_access_scheme_guidance_for_lay_clients.pdf.

13 Check public access registration at www.directaccessportal.co.uk/search/1/barrister.

It is for the same reason that you ought to be a little wary of personal recommendations from friends or colleagues. These will be well meaning but unless the person giving the recommendation has a good understanding of the legal services market and has practical experience of a fraud case, they are unlikely to be able to offer more than general suggestions.

Even highly experienced in-house company lawyers can find the challenges of a fraud case novel and demanding, as one observed:

> "First and foremost, a corporate client faced with a corporate fraud needs clear direction from legal advisers as to what it should and equally what it should not do. Although a corporate client may be well-resourced in terms of having well-qualified and highly experienced personnel, fraud nonetheless presents specific technical challenges which may be new to even the most seasoned of financial, HR and legal professionals and which require a rapid response."

You need rapid advice from a specialist lawyer with many experiences of fraud cases and a deep knowledge of the relevant laws. Speed is of the essence because action may need to be taken very quickly to contain your situation, for example, to freeze the fraudster's assets, to prevent further losses or to engage law enforcement with a request for their immediate action.

The most balanced and neutral advice would be from a lawyer who has no competency bias towards the criminal or civil regimes, whether that is a barrister or a solicitor. This is easier said than it is to achieve. The numbers of lawyers who are true experts in both civil and criminal asset recovery law are very few in number.

The 146,000 solicitors and 16,000 barristers working in England and Wales possess varying degrees of skills and expertise in the various fields of law. A lawyer who thinks of himself as expert may not of course be as expert as another. Some concentrate on just one aspect of the law, whether conveyancing, immigration, family or fraud cases. Others advertise themselves as all things to all persons with a long list of skills.

The main point is that whatever competencies they claim, you don't want to be paying for a lawyer to learn how to conduct a fraud case, namely your fraud case. The lowest fee rate does not turn into the lowest cost if the lawyer is learning on the job, makes mistakes, is inefficient and causes delays which gives the fraudster time to hide or spend your money. One CEO emphasised the importance of having full confidence in lawyers:

> "I feel it is of the upmost importance that you trust implicitly your lawyer and their team. There are never any guarantees of any recovery given and the costs can be vast. This is where the litigation lawyers and barristers are King. They have the ability to completely dissect the fraud, and recognise who should be held responsible within a case where it seems only one person committed the fraud … Being the CEO of [a *company*] and in real terms 'gambling' with [the *company's*] money, the decision to go ahead was done with complete confidence, even if we made another loss … having confidence in your lawyer is critical."

> **Signpost**
>
> Successful litigation requires you to remain fully engaged at all times. If not, your case will drift and guess who will notice that? Your opponent. And after that, so too will the court. ⊳*Section 5*

Many fraud cases contain an international dimension. You may not think that your case is "international" but it may well turn out that it is; for example, the wrongdoer may have transferred your money abroad. It is for this reason that is often critically important to choose lawyers who are experienced in dealing with international fraud cases (⊳*Section 7, International cases and enforcement*).

3.6.2 Guides to lawyers

> A fraud lawyer: "Choosing lawyers can be extremely daunting if you've never done it before. Even knowing the right terminology to use can be a minefield. There's nothing wrong with using Google (other search engines are available). Legal directories (Chambers and Partners or Legal 500) compile lists of the people they rate as the best in the field. That said, if you're a company based in Wolverhampton, you might not want to instruct a central London firm."

Although there are no fraud-specific qualifications or accreditations for lawyers, there are some publications that help clients to locate recommended lawyers that are worth looking at. The two best known guides to lawyers in the UK are free to read on the internet at www.chambersandpartners.com and at www.legal500.com. Both of these provided segmented guides to fields of specialism in the law and provide lists of recommended barristers who practice in chambers and recommended lawyers working in law firms. Each provide lists of recommended lawyers in relation to fraud litigation, both civil and criminal.

The commercial publishers of these guides research the legal market and take references in order to make their judgments about who to recommend. You can read about the individual lawyers and see quotes from peers and clients. Just a quick word of warning about these guides: they are just that. Every lawyer knows very capable lawyers who don't get a listing. Also, be careful about the rankings: remember they are the work of publishers based on a relatively small number of interviews and quotes and are not based on formal rigorous skills assessments. With those caveats, there is probably no better way of getting an idea of who is working in and recommended in the fraud law fields.

3.6.3 A barrister first, or a solicitor first?

Which one you approach first is less important than making sure that the one you do approach is an expert in both civil and criminal fraud cases.

That said, knowing that you can directly approach barristers, it may be that they can handle all aspects of your case without the need for solicitors. Similarly, engaging the right solicitor advocate may mean you will not require a barrister to represent you in court.

Whichever lawyer you first meet may suggest that a team of lawyers will have to be assembled to work on your case. If the barrister recommends you should use the services of solicitors – and in many cases, this will be a good thing – the barrister can help you find the right solicitors and make recommendations. It can of course work the other way around too. If you approach a solicitor first, he or she will be able to recommend one or more barristers.

The choice will depend on your resources, your budget, your aims, the size of the fraud loss and the complexity of the case. Simpler cases may only require the services of a barrister. The most complex cases may need a team of barristers and solicitors supported by investigators and forensic accountants (▻*Section 1.7, Professional investigators*).

One issue you may encounter with solicitors firms is that your case may not be big enough for them to want to take you on as a client. Many firms now have lower limits on the scale of cases that they will take on and / or the scale of fees that they must expect to charge with any new case they take on.

These law firm limits could be very high. For example, some law firms will not want to take on cases where the damages to be claimed are worth less than £1 million (or even more) and others may not take your case unless, for example, they can expect to bill you £100,000 or more in the first 6 months of working for you.

Signpost

Very many, if not the majority of victims of fraud, end up on a sort of merry-go-round in their search for advice and help in how to respond to a case of fraud.
▻*Section 2*

Barristers, by tradition, take on all cases that they are experienced enough to take and which clients wish to pursue. Indeed, for some areas of work this is an ethical requirement. So you are unlikely to be rejected by a barrister on the basis that your case is not big enough.

One further point you need to know about is potential conflicts of interest. No lawyer can accept a new client and case if to do so may lead to a conflict of interest between the new client's needs and objectives and those of an existing client of the lawyer. In the case of law firms, the problem is magnified because a single lawyer in a firm must avoid taking a client whose needs will conflict with those of a client of another lawyer in the same firm.

3.6.4 The ideal fraud lawyer?

Is there an ideal fraud lawyer? A set of experiences and qualities that are just perfect for every conceivable fraud case? The answer to that is probably "no". But there are some characteristics that most if not all experienced and skilful fraud lawyers share. We'll summarise them (as we see them) here:

- *Deep and varied experiences.* As we have already said and will continue to say, a good fraud lawyer is one who not only has deep knowledge of the law but many and varied experiences of fraud cases in and out of the UK.
- *Good judgment and decisive.* A fraud case demands good judgment. Fraud lawyers have to work at speed under a great deal of pressure. They sometimes need to be able to be decisive and make good judgments late at night and early in the morning.
- *Calm and focused.* Things can get quite het up in a fraud case. Allegations and counter allegations abound and emotions run high for many of the people involved in the case. A good fraud lawyer will acknowledge the stresses of his or her client but will remain focussed on the big picture and the strategic imperatives of the case.
- *A strategist.* A good fraud lawyer will think deeply about the strategic alternatives and imperatives of the fraud case. Fraud cases present particular challenges because of the many and varied motives of the different parties involved in them and because so many cases are international.
- *A good listener.* Victims of fraud have many justifiable concerns and anxieties. A good fraud lawyer will always listen carefully to clients, witnesses (and the wrongdoers). It's a really important skill because clients (including, in the case of companies, their representatives) will often be very stressed and it can be difficult to get to the really important facts of the case.
- *Objective.* A good fraud lawyer will understand the outrage and disgust felt by a client but at the same time will remain level-headed and objective about the best options open to the client. He or she will, for example, be able to see the dangers of and warn the client against alleging fraud if the case is weak or against suing too many people if that would dilute the effectiveness of the case against the main wrongdoers.
- *Big picture thinker with an attention to detail.* Both! Quite a difficult feat. Even if you have a large team of lawyers working for you, each with their own characteristics, most of those lawyers will still need to be able to concentrate on large amounts of information and yet still see what is really important and what is not. If you have only one lawyer it's crucial that he or she has this ability.
- *Authoritative.* A good fraud lawyer displays the right balance between flexibility and decisiveness, and between being a good team player and an authoritative team leader. Although the client will be (and must be) in control of their decision-making in a case, the lawyer must lead that decision-making. For this, the lawyer needs to be authoritative. He or she also needs authority to gain the confidence of the court.
- *Articulate and persuasive.* Obviously, the good fraud lawyer is both articulate and persuasive. They need to be able to communicate complex ideas and legal issues to you as the client and they need to be able to do the same when it comes to explaining your case to the court. And with that they also need to be persuasive.

> A fraud lawyer: "If you've just discovered a fraud you'll need someone with experience in the area who knows what can and can't be done, and can give you a realistic assessment of your chances of recovering any of your assets. It also helps if they seem like someone you can get on with, as you might end up speaking to them a lot."

Here is how one victim described the necessary qualities of a fraud lawyer:

> "Fraud lawyers need to be firm and authoritative without being overbearing to make sure that a corporate client who may be somewhat panicked and who may make decisions by committee actually hears and takes in the advice given and understands the consequences and implications at a later stage of adopting or not adopting a particular course.
>
> As fraud is quite a technical area of law and finance/accounting, even when cybercrime is not involved, a fraud lawyer needs to demonstrate a mastery of the subject at a technical legal level, an understanding of usual and unusual 'patterns' of fraudulent activity and the 'psychology' of fraud and to map out the various paths that the asset recovery path could take at an early stage.
>
> A key attribute for a fraud lawyer is the ability to digest large amounts of financial and other data and to harness the skill sets of various corporate team members and advisers so as to convert complex data and information flows into a presentation, oral or written, that can be readily understood by an uninvolved third party such as a court."

A fraud lawyer: "Knowing how to reassure a client and shouldering the weight of some of the client's problems is essential and probably one of the most important aspects of being a lawyer. This takes more than just being a competent lawyer. Lawyers who do this for their clients really make a difference for their clients and stand out from their peers."

3.6.5 Some pointers on choosing a lawyer

Here are some points about choosing lawyers and some suggestions about what you should and should not do when meeting lawyers for the first time:

- You must first check that the barrister or solicitor would be able to take on your case in that he or she would not have a conflict of interest. The last thing you should be doing is providing a lot of confidential information to a prospective lawyer who already represents the wrongdoer in your case!
- When meeting lawyers you are thinking of hiring, it's best not to talk about your own case in any detail. Instead, you should spend time finding out about the lawyers themselves, their skills and knowledge, how they work, how much they charge. If you do get stuck into the detail of your case, you will end up just thinking about that rather than whether the lawyers are right for you. You will also be more likely to be influenced by predictions that relate to your case rather than trying to understand the lawyers' expertise.
- Be careful not to be seduced by grand predictions of likely victory when you are meeting a lawyer for the first time. It would be unwise for you to feel comforted by imprudent advice at such an early stage.
- Also, be careful not to be seduced by the fact that the lawyer tells you that he or she has won X number of cases or perhaps won the last case that resembled yours. All good lawyers win cases from time to time just as all good lawyers lose cases from time to time and it is impossible for any lawyer to be measured by win rates, let alone for any lawyer to be able to measure his own success

by that criteria. Instead focus on the skills, knowledge and experience of the lawyer.

- Ask a number of questions designed to test the knowledge and experience of the lawyers who will be working on your case. Although not easy to do, hopefully this guide will help you in that. You can certainly ask things about the practice profile of the relevant lawyers. For example, you could ask what percentage of their working time they spend claiming compensation for victims of fraud, how much of that is spent in the civil courts and how much of it in the criminal courts. You should also ask how much experience the lawyer have in dealing with international cases of fraud, as your case may well turn out to have an international dimension.
- Do ask which lawyer would handle the majority of the case work on your case on a day to day basis because it is that individual who will be advising and helping you. It would be unfortunate if you trust and like the person you first meet but then rarely see him or her again.
- Ask yourself whether you will be able to get along with the lawyer. It is important that you have a constructive relationship, but do not be swayed solely by likeability and demonstrative sympathy with your plight. As Colin found out to his cost. Colin was persuaded to engage a solicitor because the solicitor was angry about what had happened to Colin and his company:

  > "I liked him. He cursed him [the fraudster], saying it's not fair that they get away with it, how it was screwing up my life and the like. He was really energetic and got so angry he was nearly jumping on his desk. It was impressive, really on my side, so I gave him £2,500. But then he went on holiday, then was busy with something else. Then when he did get on it, it just became problems and obstacles, one after the other. He didn't know what he was doing so I said enough and found [another law firm] and they were on it like a rash."

- Although it is inevitable and important that you ask the lawyers about their charging rates and enter into discussions about budgeting for work that will be required going forward, beware that it is very difficult for lawyers to make predictions about costs at an initial discussion.
- Ask if the lawyer or lawyers offer alternative funding (⊳ *Section 3.16, Alternative fee arrangements*).

A fraud lawyer: "Most clients find litigation stressful in some way. They come to lawyers because they have a stressful situation that they need help with. Court cases generate anxiety and frustration. The role of a lawyer is, therefore, not only to provide legal services but also to help the client to remain composed and even to find some peace of mind. In order to achieve this goal, a lawyer has to be responsive, empathic and know her or his client's case intimately. A client has to be able to trust that his or her lawyer will deal seriously and diligently with his or her concerns."

3.7 How to get the most from lawyers

When you enter into a business relationship with a lawyer, or a group of lawyers, you will probably be entering into a relationship which will last for some time. Many fraud cases last at least two years if they go all the way to a trial and then enforcement of the judgment to recover your money.

Given that you will be in an enduring relationship with your lawyers, it is worth remembering that you will need to do your bit, just as they must, to ensure that the relationship succeeds to maximise the chances of success in your case.

Lawyers work on a commercial basis; like you, they have business costs and living costs to pay. But many of them are also values and results driven people who really want to see their clients succeed.

Here are a few tips on getting the most from your lawyers and keeping costs down:

- Remember that no lawyer can guarantee success and just angling to get your lawyer to tell you what you want to hear, or getting annoyed if they don't, is not the way forward. On the other hand, it is a good idea for you to probe and query the advice you receive from your lawyer.
- You should be able to develop a relationship of trust with your lawyer which will enable both you and your lawyer to speak freely and frankly about your case and for you to feel that you can rely on and follow your lawyer's advice and recommendations.
- Have, or at least be prepared to develop, strong ideas of what you consider to be good and acceptable outcomes to your case and discuss these with your lawyer, so that he or she is clear about what you want to achieve (▷*Section 2, Objectives and options*). It is important that you arrive at a realistic valuation of the worth of your claim (▷*Section 5.4, Valuing your claims*). You should also work out what would be an unacceptable outcome to your case and discuss this too. As your case progresses, you will need to keep in mind that compromise with the wrongdoer is something you should also work towards (▷*Section 5.15, Compromising claims*).
- Insist on a clear protocol as to which lawyers will work on your case for which pieces of work which are likely to arise. If you will be using a team of lawyers, insist on a protocol which minimises duplication of work (as this will keep costs lower) but does allow for some overlaps between lawyers (both inevitable and often a good thing). If using both barrister and solicitors, you can – to a very large degree – decide which of these does which pieces of work and choose which you think will provide best value for money for each piece of work.
- Establish a strong protocol for costs budgeting and management and how you will pay for those costs (▷*Section 3.9, Negotiating fees and paying lawyers*).
- Establish a clear method of communication from the start. Would you prefer to give information verbally to your lawyer at face-to-face meetings or would you prefer to write things down in private and send written narratives to your lawyer? Either is fine, but whichever method you choose, make sure you get a very clear idea from your lawyer about what information you need to gather and supply.
- When gathering information to give to your lawyers, be as accurate and ordered as possible. If you have to make a correction to the narratives which you have given or worse still you make a series of mistakes, this can really damage your case.
- Prepare an accurate and detailed chronology of events, which is cross-referenced to documents and other sources of information.

- When gathering documents, you will need to preserve their integrity as well as get them well ordered for presentation to your lawyer. This usually means keeping the original documents in the same state and order as you found them in your files and business records but then making copies and putting those copies into chronological order for your lawyer.
- When preparing a written narrative for the lawyer, always use sub-headings and sign-posts to give the clearest possible description and explanation of the events you are relating. Remember also that you are giving an explanation that has to be understood by somebody, ultimately a judge or jury member, who did not witness or live through the events you are describing; someone who has no prior knowledge of your business organisation and who may have only a limited understanding of the industry in which you work. The wrongdoer's culpability may be obvious to you, but may not be to them.
- Think about details but always remember the big picture as well. Fraud cases require some level of detailed analysis and explanation. For that reason, you must be able to be accurate with facts and figures, dates and times and so on. But you should also strive to remain objective and able to see the bigger picture so that you can make good judgments about your options and prospects of success in any court case you bring.

Signpost

International laws and their application are complex and present many strategic issues. It is essential to get advice from lawyers who routinely carry out international work. ⊳*Section 7*

3.8 Legal jargon

Lawyers sometimes speak another language.

Even without using Latin (now officially frowned on by the courts), lawyers still talk a lot of legalese. That is of course part of their job and you will expect them to be fluent in it when explaining your case to a judge (or as they may call it "putting" or "pleading" a case).

But in conversations with your lawyers, you need to be able to understand what they are saying and over-use of legal terms can make that difficult. What are the kinds of legal terms we are talking about?

Here is how a conversation can look like between a lawyer and client (only a little bit exaggerated):

> *Lawyer*: Before they can instigate their claims, claimants have to follow the CPR pre-action protocol.
>
> *Client*: What's that?
>
> *Lawyer*: Oh, it's a procedure that was introduced many years ago by the Woolf reforms. But don't worry, we won't actually be following the pre-action practice direction because we can go ex parte to a judge.
>
> *Client*: Sorry, ex what?

Lawyer: As I was explaining, you can go without notice rather than on notice to the court in a fraud case. The only downside is that, as the quid pro quo, you will have to give full and frank disclosure to the court.

Client: I'm not sure what you mean by full and frank disclosure.

Lawyer: Well, if you want the court to issue a freezing injunction – you may have heard about them, they used to be called Mareva orders – then you have to give the court draft particulars of claim and point out to the court what could be wrong with your case.

Client: I didn't think that there was anything wrong with my case.

Lawyer: There isn't but we have to insure you against an application by the other side to discharge your freezing injunction at the return date hearing.

Client: I didn't know that I needed insurance to bring a claim.

Lawyer: You don't but actually we could arrange ATE insurance in case your claim fails and you end up being liable for inter-partes costs.

Good lawyers avoid this kind of confusing conversation. They will speak to you in plain English. But even the best will still have to use some legal terms and explain these to you in digestible language.

If you do find yourself bewildered by the language your lawyer is using, just say so and ask for explanations in plain English.

3.9 Negotiating fees and paying lawyers

Soon after meeting lawyers you will need to get down to talking money. We are not talking here about how much money you can expect to win in your case but how much you are going to have to pay lawyers if you want their help. Money considerations may play a significant part in your choice of lawyers.

Since lawyers are well known to be expensive, you might be worried about this aspect of finding and using a lawyer. Don't be. Yes, lawyers can be expensive but if you choose well you will get the best deal possible. And if you are likely to struggle to afford the cost of taking a case all the way to trial and beyond then it may be possible to hire lawyers who are able to offer alternatives such as "no-win-no-fee" or "no-win-low-fee" arrangements (▷*Section 3.16, Alternative fee arrangements*). It may also be possible to obtain funding from companies which specialise in litigation funding.

There is no best way to pay for legal services; only what is best for you and your case. Before we take a look at the various options, we want to say a little about court fees and recoverability of costs.

3.10 Civil court fees

You will need to factor into your costs the court fees you will have to pay. The Ministry of Justice sets the fees. We'll not examine all the varying fees for all civil claims.[14] This is because there is little point in the context of a civil fraud claim to think about the fees applicable to the smallest kinds of claims and there is also little possibility of securing the slightly discounted fees for bringing online court claims.

Figure 3.1 sets out the relevant bands of court fees for issuing claims, depending on the value of your claim (including interest):

Figure 3.1: Court fees for issuing claims

Value of claim	***Court fee for issuing the claim****
£10,000–£200,000	5% of the claim value
£200,000 upwards	£10,000

(* In addition to fees calculated by reference to the monetary value of claims you are bringing, you will also need to pay fees to be allowed to bring any non-monetary claims, for example proprietary claims (⊳*Section 5.11, Proprietary claims*) you are making and this will add a further sum of money – up to an extra £528 – to the amount you have to pay to issue your claim.)

Although the courts do provide a high quality service, the court fees are not popular and are a factor when a business is deciding whether to bring civil proceedings. In the words of one company:

> "As a large, relatively well-resourced multi-national corporate, the court fee of £10,000 to file the civil claim against the suspected fraudster is an irritant (albeit a minor one), especially when compared to other established jurisdictions where filing fees are a fraction of this sum. For a smaller company, a fee of this magnitude on top of a substantial fraud might be sufficiently off-putting to dissuade the victim from pursuing the perpetrator."

Other fees you are likely to encounter are in relation to "applications" made in the lead up to the trial (*Figure 3.2*). Applications involve going to court with official forms and supporting documents and evidence for a short hearing to ask the judge for an injunction or court order. The cost depends on whether your application is made without notice to your opponent (i.e. secretly) or on notice to your opponent – for an explanation of these different types of application see *Section 4, Tracing and securing assets in the civil courts*. If your case goes to trial, you will also have to pay a fee for the trial itself.

Figure 3.2: Court fees for hearings

Nature of hearing	***Court fee***
Without notice application	£100
On notice application	£255
Trial	£1,090

14 You can view them at: https://assets.publishing.service.gov.uk/government/uploads/system/uploads/attachment_data/file/728133/ex50-eng.pdf.

Lastly, you may have to pay court fees at the time of recovering costs from your opponent, as these may have to be determined by the court. The minimum fee payable is £369 (for determination of costs bills of up to £15,000) and the maximum payable is £6,160 (for costs bills in excess of £500,000).

3.11 Recoverability of costs in civil claims

It is possible to recover all your legal costs if your opponent agrees to pay them and it is included in an out-of-court settlement (⊳*Section 5.15, Compromising claims*). However, If your case goes to trial and you win, not only will the court decide on the amount of compensation for the harm caused, it will also order the wrongdoer to pay you an amount for your legal costs expenditure. How much can you recover in the way of costs? Here are some general principles:

- The maximum you can recover in respect of your costs is limited by the amount that you have paid or have to pay to your lawyers and for court and other expenses in a case. To put it another way, the wrongdoer cannot be ordered to pay more than you actually pay in legal costs.
- If you win an application, you can expect to recover the court fee you paid in respect of that application. If you win your case outright at trial, you can expect to recover the whole of the court fee you paid for the issue of your claim as well as the court fee for the trial itself. But if you win only part of an application or part of your claim at trial, you would probably recover only a portion of these fees.
- In relation to the fees you will have to pay to your lawyers, the court will not order the wrongdoer in a fraud case to pay any success fee or damages-based sharing fee (see below in relation to CFAs and DBAs) and you will have to pay these yourself if you choose to fund your case in this way.
- The court will use so-called Guideline Hourly Rates for lawyers in law firms (⊳*Section 3.14, Paying by the hour*).
- You cannot recover from the wrongdoer the VAT element of the legal bills you have to pay if you are VAT registered and able to recover that VAT as an input tax.[15]
- In most cases, the court will order the wrongdoer to pay your expenditure on "reasonable" legal costs which is known as a costs award on a "standard" basis. On this basis, it is extremely unlikely, if not impossible, to recover all of what you have paid to your lawyers. As a guide, it is likely that the costs order will be between 60% and 80% of the amount you pay to your lawyers.[16]
- In exceptional cases, the court will order the wrongdoer to pay costs on an "indemnity" basis, which would mean that you would be entitled to recover

15 All discussions of cost amounts in this guide are net of VAT.

16 This is a deliberately wide band and in fact could be said to be wider. It is notoriously difficult to predict the percentage of recoverable costs in a case because the court which determines the recoverable amount looks at a very wide range of factors. The orthodox advice given by lawyers to clients used to be that they should, in the event of outright success, expect to obtain a costs order of between two-thirds and three-quarters of the costs incurred and paid by the winning party. But there are definitely cases when the court awards less and some in which it awards more. So, after much discussion and debate with other lawyers, we have plumped for the wider 60%–80% range.

nearly all of the amounts that you have paid to your lawyers and in respect of other case-related expenses.

- On either the standard or indemnity basis you are very unlikely to recover all your legal costs, so that you will pay the difference, usually out of the damages awarded.

This last point is a frustrating aspect of the civil regime for victims. The law talks about "putting claimants back in the position had the wrong not taken place". Imagine you have lost £500,000 to a fraud and spent £200,000 on litigation. You win the case and are awarded the full £500,000. The court then makes out a cost order in your favour for £140,000 (70% of your expenditure on legal costs). Even if you can and do recover £640,000 from the wrongdoer, your net loss on the whole experience will be £60,000. Using lawyer-speak, you have not been put back in the position you would have been had the fraud not taken place.

Signpost

You will not recover all your costs, it is more likely to be between 60% and 80% that you recover. ▷*Section 3.11*

Be wary of lawyers who tell you, with real certainty, that they can recover nearly all of your legal costs expenditure from the defendant. Also, be wary if they do not voluntarily explain the difference between "own lawyer" costs and "recoverable" costs at the outset. At best, it can damage the client's relationship with lawyers, at worst it could mean pursuing a fruitless claim. Gregory's company spent £30,000 to win a £45,000 claim against an employee, but his assumption that he would recover all his costs left a sour taste:

> "We had no idea until the end of the trial that we weren't getting all our costs back when they started talking and arguing about it in court. We looked at each other, 'What's this about?' We ended up agreeing about £20,000 costs or we faced more costs arguing about costs … We had a right to do with them [the lawyers] because they'd put us in this place [where] we had to make this quick decision and we had no idea it was coming. It made us feel we'd done the whole thing for them, not us … If they'd told us at the start, would we have done it [litigated]? Probably, but I say that now because we got 35 and that's better than nothing."

3.12 Adverse costs in civil cases

The flip-side of the possibility that you can recover some of your costs spent pursuing a successful case against an opponent is, of course, that you can end up having to pay some of the costs incurred by your opponent if you lose your case (or lose part of it). Lawyers and the courts call these "adverse" costs.

When deciding whether to bring a case in the courts you need to factor in the potential costs you would have to pay to your opponent in the event of losing your case (or losing part of your case). Just how much those costs would be is difficult to predict at the outset of a case but you should probably assume that they would be at least as high as your own legal costs expenditure.

You can incur partial losses in the steps leading up to trial because you may lose in particular discrete pre-trial "applications" you make against the wrongdoer. If this is the case, you may end up having to pay certain amounts to the wrongdoer at the pre-trial stage. Your lawyers will need to keep you informed about the pre-trial costs risks.

> **Signpost**
>
> Proper preparation means careful cost budgeting at the start and throughout your case, so that you have enough money to pay your lawyers at each stage of the case and do not end up stalling and causing delays and do not get outgunned by the wrongdoer who may also be using and paying for lawyers. ⊳*Section 5*

As a case progresses, each party is required to prepare and disclose to each other and the court costs budgets for the various stages of a case. This should give you a degree of information about the likely adverse costs you face.

You will need to think about the possibility that your claim may result in a partial victory for you and a partial victory for your opponent. In such a case it would be safe to assume that your award for costs will be lower.

> **Signpost**
>
> Civil-court fraud cases are not about revenge. Nor should they be brought for the purpose of ruining an opponent's reputation. They are about money and other financial objectives. ⊳*Section 5*

Your lawyers should advise you about the risks of a mixed-result outcome at trial, just as they will need to advise you about your chances of an outright win or loss at trial. This will feature in any negotiations you have to settle a claim (⊳*Section 5.15, Compromising claims*).

If you wish to insure against the possibility of having to pay adverse costs then your lawyer may be able to help you find an insurance company whose premium you are content to pay. This kind of insurance is known as after-the-event insurance (ATE insurance).

3.13 Recoverability of costs in private prosecutions

Victims who bring a private criminal prosecution are, generally, able to recover reasonable legal costs associated with the prosecution from the state.[17]

However, the Court of Appeal gave stiff warnings in a case in 2014 and only allowed the victim to recover a small fraction of the amount it had actually spent pursuing the case. Costs reimbursement is certainly not a free-for-all and, indeed, can be quite limited. Here's a summary of relevant principles:

---

17 Prosecution of Offences Act 1985, s 17.

- In order to prevent vexatious prosecutions, the court will not award costs to complainants if the proceedings were brought without good cause.
- In deciding whether to award costs and what amount to award, the court must consider whether the victim attempted to complain to and support the police and public prosecution efforts (whose costs would have been borne more cheaply by those organisations rather than the victim).
- The recovery of costs is limited to the costs incurred "in the proceedings" and so the recovery of investigation costs in particular is very uncertain.
- The court will only award reimbursement of an amount of costs which it considers "just and reasonable". Victims are expected to obtain competitive quotes from solicitors and barristers before engaging those lawyers. In addition, guideline hourly rates are used as a benchmark, the same rates as applied in civil-court cases (⊳*Section 3.14, Paying by the hour*).
- The rates can and will be higher than those payable by public prosecutors but the total costs will be limited to the kinds of costs which would be incurred in a public prosecution. So for example, solicitors costs will usually be limited to managing a case and instructing barristers to prosecute the case in court and would not be allowed for things such as considering the law and preparing submissions to the court. Further deductions would also apply because you would not recover costs for all work done but only for "reasonable" numbers of hours of work (similar to the 60% to 80% recoverability of costs in civil claims) (⊳*Section 3.11, Recoverability of costs in civil claims*).
- Victims cannot claim for any costs from the state up-front, which means spending the money first and then at best recovering it in stages as the case goes or at worst just recovering it at the conclusion of the case. Given the length of criminal case, that can be a very expensive and extended outlay indeed.
- You cannot recover from the wrongdoer the VAT element of the legal bills you have to pay if you are VAT registered and able to recover that VAT as an input tax.[18]

3.14 Paying by the hour

> A fraud lawyer: "It's really hard to give an estimate of costs at the start of a fraud case. Until you've started working on the documents it's difficult to understand what will need to be done and how long that will take. Most law firms charge on an hourly rate basis, with estimates of costs given so the client knows the sort of fees they'll have to pay. When an urgent case comes in, it's sometimes necessary to have a team of people all working on it all-day, every-day. A team of three working for a full day could easily run up fees of £10,000+ per day."

All lawyers are prepared to work if paid an hourly rate for the work they carry out. This has become the most prevalent method by which lawyers charge their fees. Many lawyers' working lives are time-sheeted so that they log and bill every six minutes of time spent working on a client case. Rates vary enormously.

---

18 All discussions of cost amounts in this guide are net of VAT.

Big multinational City firms hired by FTSE 100 companies charge eye-watering rates whereas firms based well away from London and other big cities charge much lower rates. However, before you get carried away thinking that you will find a lawyer in a town as far away from London as possible, do bear in mind that lawyers specialising in fraud cases tend to work in the big cities and many of the specialists are indeed in London.

Civil courts up and down the country apply so-called Guideline Hourly Rates (GHRs) for lawyers in law firms (not independent barristers) when making costs orders (more about costs orders below).[19]

> **Signpost**
>
> Civil courts expect claimants to be very cautious in making serious allegations. Fraud claims must be based on credible material which establishes a "prima facie" case with clear and cogent evidence. Improperly made fraud allegations can and do backfire spectacularly. ▷*Section 5*

The GHRs are used by the courts to assess the reasonableness of law firms' bills. They are a good starting point for you when considering fee proposals from law firms.

The recommended GHRs are broken down both for seniority of solicitors and between inner London (EC1–EC4), central London, outer London and the other regions of England and Wales.

GHRs for lawyers with more than 8 years of experience vary from £201 per hour (National Grade 3) to £409 per hour (London Grade 1). For lawyers with more than four years of experience the rates vary from £177 to £296. For more junior solicitors it is £146 to £226.

If you choose to pay your lawyers by the hour you should still ask for properly worked-out budgets for each stage of your case, including contingencies which may arise. This kind of cost budgeting is now a routine feature of civil court case management and is supervised by the courts. Judges expect to see it: you should too.

In order for both you and your lawyers to accurately estimate and agree on the likely hours of work and the costs of the various stages of a fraud case, you will need to provide accurate information about a number of things, such as the number of witnesses involved in a case and the quantity of documents that have to be reviewed and presented. And, as far as possible, you should provide this information as soon as possible, preferably right at the outset. Beyond those things, there are some aspects of a fraud case which are very difficult to predict.

Most difficult of all to predict will be the behaviour of your opponent. He may fight like a wounded rhino, run away or capitulate at the mere sight of a lawyer's letter; he may hire good lawyers or he may represent himself; he may play by the rules or try to bend or ignore them; he may comply with court orders or he may disobey them. Good lawyers have seen all of these things and refrain from making assumptions

---

19 You can see the full rate table at www.gov.uk/guidance/solicitors-guideline-hourly-rates. You will see that these guideline rates are getting quite old and so many lawyers have higher rates.

about what opponent parties will do. It is for that reason that is very important that you and your lawyers budget for various contingencies which may or may not occur.

We'll now try to be as practical as possible and look at what it may cost for you to bring a civil claim if paying by the hour.

3.14.1 The "Jackson Grid" in civil court claims

Lord Justice Jackson, a leading costs-reform judge, has conducted a major review into controlling costs in civil litigation[20] and has proposed a "grid" of typical *recoverable* costs for certain types of civil, monetary claims for between £25,000 and £100,000.[21] We shall call this grid the "Jackson Grid".

The Jackson Grid is designed for straightforward cases. This means that it is unsuitable for the scale and complexities of most fraud claims which typically involve at least one of the following factors:[22]

- claims for more than £100,000;
- proprietary claims (▷*Section 5.11, Proprietary claims*) and other claims which seek something other than monetary compensation are made;
- trials over three days;
- multiple defendants;
- obtaining and "policing" freezing injunctions;
- expert witnesses; and
- wider factors such as reputational issues at stake (i.e. the alleged wrongdoer's reputation).

The Grid's cost structure is too low for a typical fraud case. It is also probably too low for those claiming less than £100,000[23] because it does not allow for expenditure which is routine in even more modest fraud claims, such as fraud investigation costs and the cost of obtaining freezing injunctions. Lord Jackson does acknowledge the higher cost of lawyers based in London by allowing a 12.5% uplift for their fees, but excludes court fees (▷*Section 3.10, Civil court fees*). Finally, it is very important to note that the Jackson Grid focuses on recoverable costs (i.e. those you may expect to recover from a losing opponent) rather than the amounts you have to pay your own lawyers ("own lawyer costs"). Nevertheless, despite these caveats, the Jackson Grid is the only model available based on substantive research. It is therefore a useful start point for estimating both recoverable and own lawyer costs.

---

20 *Review of Civil Litigation Costs: Supplemental Report, Fixed Recoverable Costs*, the Right Honourable Lord Justice Jackson, July 2017.

21 Lord Jackson's proposal is that the grid of recoverable costs should apply to a new "intermediate" track of cases, which are too big to be dealt with in the existing "small" or "fast" tracks in the Courts and too small to be allocated to the "multi" track of cases in which the Courts deal with more complex, higher-value cases.

22 See Chapter 7, paragraph 3.2, of the *Review of Civil Ligation Costs … Fixed Recoverable Costs*. The Review does, however, envisage that there will be some cases which fall outside the usual parameters for inclusion in the new "intermediate track" but does not say what those cases ought to be.

23 Despite Lord Jackson's intention for it to be of universal application.

3.14.2 The "Jackson Grid" in a £100,000 fraud case

Let's think about a £100,000 fraud claim. The Jackson Grid's approach is to assume that the maximum sum recoverable for a case of this value should be £68,450 but makes no reference to additional costs of things such as freezing injunction applications which are routine in fraud claims. So, a more realistic fixed-recoverable costs figure might be £80,000. In this scenario, the victim would have to pay its own lawyer(s) approximately £115,000 (assuming the recoverable amount is 70% of the own lawyer costs paid).[24]

On these metrics, would you take the risk of bringing a £100,000 civil claim? Whilst is would be very painful to walk away from such a claim, you would have to think very carefully about the cost-benefit-risk calculus before committing your business to spending more than it lost to bring court proceedings.

It is (or should be) obvious that the English and Welsh justice system is not well suited to claims of modest value, particularly if those claims are also complex and uncertain. It is better suited to claims which are worth much more.

3.14.3 The "Jackson Grid" in a £1.5 million fraud case

Now let's adapt the Jackson Grid to a fraud case. We will set out figures for a civil fraud case in which £1,500,000 is claimed (*Figure 3.3*).

The values laid out in *Figure 3.3* are illustrative. If you were to ask a dozen lawyers what the typical costs are, you would get more than a dozen answers infused with yet more caveats. Nevertheless the matrix presents a reasonable overall view and provides a practical, constructive framework. We encourage readers to ask their lawyers to break down their budget proposals in the same manner. Doing so enables you to be more objective and more effective in evaluating the cost-benefit-risks of court proceedings.

There are innumerable variables which influence the matrix and could lead to lower or higher costs. As a general rule, the higher the value of a claim and/or the greater the significance the claim has for the wrongdoer-defendant, the more complex and hard fought the case will be, so increasing the total legal costs. In our adaptation, we:

- set higher figures in each stage than are in the Jackson Grid in order to reflect the fact that the claim is worth £1,500,000 rather than a maximum of £100,000;
- give figures for the recoverable costs of obtaining a freezing injunction and for "policing" that injunction (⊳*Section 4.8, Freezing injunctions*), which are routine stages of a fraud case but which do not feature in the Jackson Grid;
- give figures for the costs relating to the instruction of expert witnesses (for example forensic accountants and/or document examiners);
- show the figures both without and with a 12.5% London uplift; and
- ignore adverse costs in the event that the case is lost.

---

24 It may be possible to reduce these costs if you can instruct a barrister who is willing to run the case without a solicitor.

Figure 3.3: The "Jackson Grid" adapted to a £1,500,000 claim

Case Stages	**No uplift**	**Cumulative total**	**With 12.5% London uplift**	**Cumulative total**
Pre-action	20,000	20,000	22,500	22,500
Freezing injunction at commencement	30,000	50,000	33,750	56,250
Statements of case	10,000	60,000	11,250	67,500
Case Management Conference hearing	3,000	63,000	3,375	70,875
Disclosure	25,000	88,000	22,500	93,375
Witness statements (add 10% per witness if more than 3)	30,000	118,000	33,750	127,125
Experts reports (assuming light necessity)	30,000	148,000	33,750	160,875
Pre-trial review hearing	3,000	151,000	2,250	163,125
Trial preparation	50,000	201,000	56,250	219,375
Trial (two weeks)	50,000	251,000	56,250	275,625
Negotiations / Alternative Dispute Resolution	5,000	256,000	5,625	281,250
"Policing" the freezing injunction	10,000	266,000	11,250	292,500
TOTAL RECOVERABLE		266,000		292,500
TOTAL OWN LAWYER COSTS		380,000		417,857

(All figures are in £GBP and exclude VAT)

3.15 Fixed fee arrangements

Many lawyers are now prepared to work for clients with fixed fee arrangements. This means that they are prepared to pre-agree and stick to costs budgets either for the whole of a case or at least on a stage-by-stage basis. Certainly, this sort of arrangement will give you greater certainty than if you were simply paying by the hour. But is the overall result likely to be lower fees? And is it likely to produce good work that maximises the chances of winning your case?

Fixed fee arrangements work well if both sides to the agreement get approximately what they hoped for from the arrangement. In your case, the arrangement will work well if you feel that you received an amount of high quality work that matches your fixed cost outlay. Conversely, your lawyer will feel it worked well if he or she was adequately rewarded for the amount of work he or she has done. The ideal fixed fee is one in which the end result is one in which neither side feels that they have lost out but this is hard to achieve.

Where things go wrong with the fixed fee model is where either side feels that they got poor value for money: in the case of the client, that the lawyer did not work enough to justify the fixed fee; and in the case of the lawyer, that she did not get paid enough.

So how should you try to work out whether a fixed fee is a good deal, both for you and your lawyers? To judge the reasonableness of a proposed fixed fee, you will almost certainly have to look at the number of hours which the lawyers will work on the proposed budget. You should expect this information from your lawyers.

The number of hours to be worked will not only determine the fixed fee amount but is also important. That is because it must be a good estimate of the number of hours that lawyers need to spend on your case. After all, you will not want to pay more than is necessary and your lawyers will not give you an open-ended commitment.

Signpost

If and when you reach a deal with your opponent, it is essential that it is written into a binding settlement agreement and / or court order that you can readily enforce. Good lawyers will know the value of a tightly worded settlement agreement that does not allow your opponent to wriggle off the hook. ▷*Section 5*

If you want to have a fixed quote for all or part of your case, you probably need to expect to pay a premium for the benefit of this certainty, say 10% to 15%. Why? Think about what happens when you fix your loan interest rates with a lender such as with a mortgage. The bank charges you a small premium – built into its rate – in return for giving you the certainty of a fixed rate.

It follows then that if you are asking a lawyer to fix the cost of an item of work which exposes the lawyer to a risk of overruns, then perhaps it is reasonable to expect that this might cost you more. That is if the lawyer is doing his maths right.

On the other hand, many lawyers are not great at estimating the costs of a case, or even a stage of a case and optimistically underestimate how much work needs to be done. In this scenario the client ends up underpaying a lawyer who has agreed to do the case (or a stage of it) on a fixed fee.

If you are tempted to try and win at the expense of your lawyer, just remember that it will not be every lawyer who will be happy to work long hours for free on your case and an unhappy lawyer may not be the lawyer you want fighting your corner.

3.16 Alternative fee arrangements

These come in different forms. Conditional fee agreements (CFAs), which can be no-win-no-fee arrangements or no-win-low-fee arrangements; and damages-based agreements (DBAs).

No-win-no-fee arrangements have been around for many years for civil claims and you may have heard of them. Indeed, you may even have seen adverts on the television or on the back of buses telling you that you can make no-win-no-fee claims for personal injuries. We are not talking here about personal injury cases but about fraud. With that important distinction in mind, what follows is a summary of alternative fee arrangements, which come in two forms, the CFA and the DBA.

Not all lawyers will enter these arrangements. Those that do offer them will consider the risks, rewards and merits of each case. Law firms and barristers are commercial entities: they are not attracted to high-risk, low-reward cases. It is also for this reason that some lawyers may not enter into these agreements unless they properly understand the case.

In addition, lawyers may not enter into these arrangements unless and until they are confident that the defendant has sufficient assets to pay in the event that your case is successful. This would not be a problem if the defendant is a wealthy, stable UK corporation. However, if the defendant is an individual who may flee or dissipate his assets, the lawyers may insist on finding and freezing assets before agreeing to a CFA or DBA.

It may therefore mean that you first pay for the assessment of the merits and value of the case as well as the asset searches and freezing injunction (▷*Section 4, Tracing and securing assets in the civil courts*).

You may need separate agreements if you engage more than one lawyer. So if you instruct a solicitor and a barrister you may have two separate agreements. Alternatively you can make an agreement with a law firm which includes the cost of the barrister, effectively as a sub-contractor.

You must appreciate that an "alternative fee arrangement" comes at a price. So, whilst a lawyer may be prepared to take the risk of never being paid on a case he will only do so if you take the risk that you will have to pay him handsomely in the event of success.

Finally you need to consider "disbursements" carefully. Your lawyer needs to tell you at the outset about these costs, such as court fees, investigators and expert reports that would not be included in the alternative fee arrangement and that you must pay whether you win or lose and which will often have to be paid as and when they arise.

3.16.1 Conditional fee agreements

A Conditional Fee Agreement (CFA) is a litigation agreement where lawyer and client share the risk of litigation. They come in two forms:

- *No-win-no-fee agreements.* Instead of paying fees up front in the traditional way, such as an hourly rate, or a fixed fee, the lawyers only become entitled to payment of their fees in the event of a defined success. This sharing of risk does come at a price. If you enter such an agreement, you would have to negotiate and agree to pay the lawyers a percentage increase ("uplift") in their usual fees (known as their "basic fees") for working on your case. This uplift can be anything up to 100%. So imagine that you agree a success fee of 50%, you win the case and the lawyer's basic fees were £300,000, you would instead have to pay your lawyers £450,000. The uplift can't be applied to expenses such as court-issue fees.
- *No-win-low-fee agreements.* In these agreements, your lawyer works at a discounted base rate and in return you promise to pay the lawyer a corresponding success fee in the event of success. For example, you may agree a 30% discount on fees in the event of loss matched by a corresponding increase on fees in the event of a defined success. Imagine your lawyer's costs are estimated to come to £300,000. In the event of losing your case, you would pay £210,000. In the event of success, you would pay £390,000. The uplift cannot be applied to expenses such as court-issue fees. With no-win-low-fee agreements, lawyers usually require clients to pay the base fees that a are payable in any event as the case progresses. So if the lawyer is offering a 30% discount / uplift, then you will have to pay 70% of these "base" fees as they fall due.

You should be aware of two important features of CFAs. Firstly, they are usually made contingent on winning the case generally and not on winning a particular amount of compensation or being awarded a particular amount of costs. Secondly, the success-fee uplift *cannot* be recovered from your opponent; it has to be paid by you, in all probability from compensation you receive from the wrongdoer. Both of these features mean that you will pay a price for your CFA representation.

3.16.2 Damages-based agreements

The damages-based agreement (DBA) is a relatively new thing in England and Wales which has yet to gain real traction because of legal uncertainties in relation to their use and enforceability.

Like the CFA, a DBA is also an agreement in which the lawyers and client share the risk – and reward – of litigation. DBAs are different to CFAs in that they are contingent on the amount awarded by the court: the lawyers are paid a percentage of any damages recovered. This means that the lawyers receive nothing if the claim fails and nothing is recovered.

The law restricts the maximum that lawyers can receive under DBAs to 50% of the client damages. So, imagine that you agree to pay your lawyers 25% of any damages recovered from a wrongdoer and you are successful in claiming £500,000 from a wrongdoer, you would then have to pay your lawyers £125,000 out of the sum awarded to you *plus* any other disbursement costs.

3.17 Litigation funding

A fraud lawyer: "Two of the most important decisions for a victim of fraud are choosing the right legal team and getting the right sort of funding for a case. The right sort of funding will make seeking redress far easier."

Litigation funding is funding to help you bring a civil claim against wrongdoers. In reality it is only available for large cases running into many millions or tens of millions of pounds.

If you have a large case but either don't have the resources to mount the case or you would prefer passing the risk to a funder so as to avoid committing your own resources, then litigation funding may be attractive. Litigation funders are investors who are prepared for the high risks compared to other investment opportunities, but in return they demand high levels of profit on successful cases.

Like any investment, litigation funders assess cases on their value, merits, risks and returns if successful. They are only interested in cases with at least a 60–70% chance of success. These chances mean that they are only likely to generate a return in two out of three cases; they will lose their entire investment in a third of cases. Given these risks, lenders typically demand the higher of two calculations:

- 30% (or thereabouts) of the value of the financial recoveries you make in the case plus the loan amount; or
- four times (or thereabouts) the loan including the principal amount, to be paid from the financial recoveries.[25]

These high rates of return mean that only large cases are attractive to funders. Imagine you have a case in which you claim £250,000 from a wrongdoer which would cost £125,000 in your own lawyers' costs to bring to trial. It would be impossible to generate a £500,000 (4 × £125,000) return that a funder would want.

Signpost

The police or prosecutor may try to dissuade you from mounting a civil claim or ask you to wait until they have finished prosecuting the case. They may ask you to stay (suspend) live proceedings until the conclusion of the criminal case. This is usually not good advice. ⊳*Section 2*

25 You should not be expected to incur a potential liability beyond the level of financial recoveries. It would be very unwise to agree to such a possibility.

On the other hand, let us assume a completely successful £1,500,000 case with costs of £380,000 (a possibility within the range indicated in *Figure 3.3*), then:

Claim amount	£1,500,000
Recoverable costs, 70% of £380,000	£266,000
Total recovered	£1,766,000
Return to funder, 4 × £380,000	– £1,520,000
Net recovery	£246,000

This is not a good outcome for you, but it may be the only option if you simply do not have £380,000 and you cannot find lawyers to work on an alternative fee basis. Clearly litigation funding makes a lot more sense when the claims run into the tens of millions.

If you are interested in finding a litigation funder, a starting point is the website of the Association of Litigation Funders[26] were you can find further information, members and their code of conduct.

3.18 A comparison of funding methods

The various funding methods are set out side-by-side in *Figure 3.4* for a £1.5 million claim and £380,000 base costs.[27]

It is obvious from this comparison that pay by the hour and the fixed fees methods give you the highest recovery but at the greatest risk; litigation funding is likely to be the most expensive route; DBA and CFA methods are in between. The table also emphasises that you will not recover your full claim if your claim goes to trial because you will not recover all of your costs from the other side: courts always reduce your application for cost, typically to between 60% and 80% of your actual legal expenditure (▷*Section 3.11, Recoverability of costs in civil claims*). The only way to recover all your costs is by settling the case with the other side prior to going to court and including your costs in the settlement agreement (▷*Section 5.15, Compromising claims*).

26 www.associationoflitigationfunders.com.

27 The illustration ignores adverse costs (▷*Section 3.12, Adverse costs in civil cases*).

Figure 3.4: Comparison of funding methods in a £1,500,000 claim

	Funding method				
	Pay by the hour	**Fixed fee**	**DBA – 30% of recovery**	**CFA – 100% success[28] fee**	**Funder –4 × base costs**
Base costs	380,000	380,000	380,000	380,000	380,000
Unsuccessful claim:					
Your legal costs	380,000	430,000	0	0	0
Successful claim:					
Claim amount	1,500,000	1,500,000	1,500,000	1,500,000	1,500,000
Costs recoverable from defendant (70%)	266,000	266,000	266,000	266,000	266,000
Total recovery from fraudster	1,766,000	1,766,000	1,766,000	1,766,000	1,766,000
Your legal costs	–380,000	–430,000	–450,000	–760,000	–1,520,000
Net amount you recover	1,386,000	1,336,000	1,316,000	1,006,000	246,000

Warning: The figures in this table for a successful claim assume a total recovery of the claim amount and the recoverable costs from the wrongdoer. We've used that assumption to keep the comparison relatively straightforward. Unfortunately, most successful fraud cases are not that straight forward. Victims do not usually recover 100% of the amounts awarded to them by courts in judgments. They usually recover a lower percentage of the amount found due to them.

If we assume that the recovery from the wrongdoer in the event of success is £1 million, then the comparison of the different funding methods looks like this.

28 Typically, "success" will be defined as obtaining a favourable court award or settlement of a stipulated value.

Figure 3.5: Comparison of funding methods in a £1,500,000 claim with £1,000,000 recoverable from the wrongdoer

	Funding method				
	Pay by the hour	**Fixed fee**	**DBA – 30% of recovery**	**CFA – 100% success[29] fee**	**Funder – 4 × base costs[30]**
Base costs	380,000	380,000	380,000	380,000	380,000
Unsuccessful claim:					
Your legal costs	380,000	430,000	0	0	0
Successful claim:					
Claim amount	1,500,000	1,500,000	1,500,000	1,500,000	1,500,000
Costs recoverable from defendant (70%)	266,000	266,000	266,000	266,000	266,000
Total recovery from fraudster	1,000,000	1,000,000	1,000,000	1,000,000	1,000,000
Your legal costs	–380,000	–430,000	–300,000	–760,000	–1,520,000
Net amount you recover	620,000	570,000	700,000	240,000	0

3.19 Regulation of lawyers – making a complaint

If you are in any way dissatisfied with the service you receive from lawyers, you can complain. There are two principal regulatory routes. The Legal Ombudsman deals complaints relating to customer care and service. The professional regulators deal with matters of professional competency, e.g. failure to follow the Civil Procedure Rules, and misconduct such as dishonesty. The two main regulators are the Solicitors Regulation Authority (SRA)[31] for solicitors and the Bar Standards Board (BSB)[32] for barristers.

There are other professional regulators, but you are less likely to be dealing with their members in a fraud case: CILEx Regulation[33] for legal executives and Costs Lawyers Standards Board (CLSB)[34] for costs lawyers (those who specialise in dealing with disputes over lawyers' fees). All their contact details can be found on their websites.

29 Typically, "success" will be defined as obtaining a favourable court award or settlement of a stipulated value.
30 To come from and be capped by the total recoveries.
31 www.sra.org.uk/home/home.page.
32 www.barstandardsboard.org.uk.
33 www.cilexregulation.org.uk.
34 http://clsb.info.

If you complain to the Legal Ombudsman and it turns out to be a matter for one of the regulators, the Ombudsman will advise you and pass it to the relevant regulator. Similarly, if you call a regulator and the complaint is a service failure, you will be passed to the Legal Ombudsman.

3.20 Conclusions

In this section, we have discussed how to approach choosing, using and paying for lawyers. Some of the guidance we have given applies irrespective of the actions you take, whether complaining to the police, private prosecution or civil litigation. Other guidance has been more specific. Here are some concluding points and reminders of some key things.

- Do your research and select a skilled, experienced fraud lawyer.
- Although it is a reverse of the traditional route, it can make sense to first choose and engage a barrister who specialises in fraud. The barrister may then recommend bringing in a solicitor.
- Always pay close attention to your lawyer's advice; it should be a rare occasion that you do not follow that advice.
- Remember that it is your case and the lawyer is a contractor providing you with a service.
- Choose a lawyer you can work with.
- Do not underestimate your effort. The more you put in, the more efficient the lawyer will be, the better your case and the lower the cost.
- Insist on clear budgets and cost reports.
- Be aware that you will not recover all your costs if you win a civil trial case; and that if you lose your case you may end up with less than nothing.
- The same is true in private criminal prosecutions where you must expect to recover an even lower proportion of your costs and can still end up with no tangible results.
- There are alternative funding arrangements. Make sure you understand what is being offered and that they tend to bite hard into any compensation you receive.

Tracing and securing assets in the civil courts

4.1 In this section

- The importance of asset tracing
- The importance of speed
- Finding wrongdoers and assets
- Disclosure from banks and internet service providers
- Freezing assets
- Seizing property and evidence
- Warnings!

4.2 What's this section about?

This section introduces how you go about finding and freezing assets in the hands of fraudsters with the assistance of the civil courts.

The importance of asset recovery needs to be emphasised. There really is no point in a pyrrhic victory whereby you get a judgment for liability (win your case) but you cannot enforce it (actually get your money back).

Thinking about and planning asset recovery at the outset is crucial in fraud cases for different reasons. Firstly, fraudsters will often work very hard to make sure that you cannot find or enforce judgments against assets they hold or control. Secondly, if lawyers or litigation funders are not sure that judgments can be enforced, they will not consider alternative fee or funding arrangements (▷ *Section 3.17, Litigation funding*).

In this section, we set out the various possibilities for locating and preserving assets in the hands of the fraudsters and their associates so that if you win your claims you can be confident in recovering those assets. Some measures that you can take to identify where the money or other assets have gone are common sense, practical things that do not require the help of the courts (▷ *Section 1.14.4, Secure evidence*). Others require court intervention and, almost certainly, help from lawyers. These measures are the subject of this section.

4.3 Identifying wrongdoers and asset tracing

Essential to any recovery strategy is an effective way of determining the identity of the wrongdoers and a way of tracing money. These two things are usually linked.

"For whose benefit?"[1] Fraudsters almost always act out of greed or need. Follow the money trail to find out who benefited and you will usually find those responsible.

---

1 Shortened in the well-known Latin phrase "Cui Bono".

4.4 *Tracing and securing assets in the civil courts*

We will set out below the various legal steps you can take and court orders you can obtain to identify wrongdoers, track

> **Signpost**
>
> If you decide to do little or nothing, you would not be the first victim to decide to make that choice after learning of a fraud. But for many, if not most victims, doing nothing is unpalatable and unwise. ▷ *Section 2*

4.4 Time critical

> A fraud lawyer: "In asset recovery, the crux is to identify assets at the earliest opportunity that are capable of being frozen whether domestically or internationally without tipping off the fraudster. Such assets can then be frozen so that the fraudster cannot take further steps to make himself judgment proof."

Locating assets in the hands of fraudsters is usually time critical. This is true in all fraud cases but, perhaps, especially true in cyber fraud cases. Any investigation and court actions to locate and preserve assets must be taken as soon as possible. This is for three main reasons:

- Delays will mean that wrongdoers have more time to move and hide assets.
- Delays mean that they can and will spend assets.
- Delays may disqualify you from obtaining assistance from the court when trying to obtain court orders to help you locate and preserve assets.

Time and time again fraud lawyers are consulted by clients quite some time after a fraud has taken place. Here are a number of typical reasons:

- Very often, companies discover they are victims of long-running frauds months or years after they started.
- Some fraudsters adeptly cover their tracks making it difficult to detect and to identify the perpetrator.
- Many victims enter a period of denial before springing into action (▷ *Section 1.3, The slowly rotated dimmer switch…*).
- Victims sometimes turn first to the police, and only later realise that they need to do more of the running themselves (▷ *Section 1.8, Do you need specialist investigators?*).
- Victims approach non-specialist lawyers or other professionals and suffer unnecessary delay (▷ *Section 2.3, The victim merry-go-round*).
- Victims very often hesitate because of the costs and lack of awareness of alternative fee and funding arrangements (▷ *Section 3.16, Alternative fee arrangements*).

If you have experienced a delay, do not despair. With good advice and help, it may be possible to rescue the situation. It just may be harder, more complicated and more uncertain.

4.5 Applying secretly for court orders – words of caution

A fraud lawyer: "Full and frank disclosure is the sharp point between a solicitor's duties to his client and to the court. Instructing a lawyer you trust with that judgement call is vital."

Imagine that you have decided to ask the court to help to identify wrongdoers and to trace and freeze money and other assets. It would be useful, indeed essential perhaps, to be able to arrange that help from the court without tipping off the targets, the very persons who have defrauded you? After all, there is no point in telling such persons that you are lining up a court application to freeze their bank accounts. That would just alert them to the need to empty those accounts as fast as possible.

Luckily for victims, the courts are willing to listen to their applications in secret and not in the presence of suspects and their associates; and having done so the courts are then prepared to make orders which can then be unleashed on unsuspecting targets and / or on their banks and other asset holders. Such hearings are called "without notice" applications.

This facility for victims does come at a price. The price is candour. In exchange for being allowed to approach the court and obtain court orders in secret and without notice being given to those persons who the orders will affect, the court requires candour from the victims and their lawyers, what is usually called "full and frank" disclosure.

Full and frank disclosure must be given by every victim who applies for court orders without first warning the intended targets of those orders. In short, what this means is that the victim and its lawyers who apply for court orders in secret must:

- give a full account of the facts being presented to the court and include facts which may be *adverse* to the *victim-claimant* as well as those which are adverse to others;
- ensure that the court is not misled about any facts or features of the case; and
- ensure that the court is given a balanced analysis of the facts and the law on which the victim relies to show that it is a victim and entitled to the court orders being sought.

Perhaps the best way to think of this duty of candour is to think of the necessity of presenting the other side's case for them in the absence of that other party. Somewhat ironically, you are, in a sense, required to protect the interests of the wrongdoers because of their absence from the hearing. So, if you can think of a possible innocent explanation for the behaviour of the wrongdoers then you should raise that possibility, even if you then go on to say why it is unlikely.

Signpost

Ask a number of questions designed to test the knowledge and experience of the lawyers who will be working on your case. Although not easy to do, hopefully this guide will help you in that. ⊳ *Section 3*

If you fail to make full and frank disclosure, the targets of the secret orders will duly complain to the court about your lack of candour. The court will listen carefully to those complaints and, if the court find that the complaints are justified, the court can and may discharge the original orders made, leaving you without the protections of those orders, with heavy adverse legal-costs bills to pay to your opponents (⊳*Section 3.12, Adverse costs in civil cases*) and with your reputation heavily damaged.

Here are some examples of the sorts of things you should be candid about:

- Reasons for the delay between discovering the fraud and making your court application – most victim applicants have to explain a delay of some sort.
- If, since discovery of the fraud, you have had contact with the target fraudsters, you need to explain what has been said and done; you will need to produce copies of any communications between you and them and between your respective lawyers.
- In particular, you need to make the court aware of any "defences" which have been indicated by fraudsters or which are apparent from the evidence in the case.
- If you need to rely on evidence from individuals who may themselves have been involved in the fraud, this needs to be pointed out.
- If you are relying on evidence which you have obtained in questionable circumstances, you will need to alert the court to this.

If you take nothing else from this chapter, you should heed these warnings about candour. Get your approach right and your candour will act as a buffer dissuading and / or preventing the wrongdoer from challenging the secret court orders made against him. Get it wrong and you will embolden the wrongdoer to challenge the court orders and indeed you will face a discharge of those orders by the court with heavy costs consequences.

Happily, the duty of candour does lead to an upside for victims. If you diligently set out all the best arguments available to the alleged wrongdoer and still persuade the court to issue a freezing injunction or other kind of invasive order against the wrongdoer, then you will send a very clear signal to the wrongdoer that his position is weak and that resistance to the orders is likely to be futile. It may even persuade him or her that fighting the case generally will also be difficult.

4.6 Unleashing the nuclear weapons – further words of caution

> A fraud lawyer: "Whether you apply for a search order, Freezing order or Proprietary injunctions (or any combination) is one of the most critical decisions you can make in a fraud case. Very often the success of the entire action depends on that decision and the ones you make within the days that follow."

The powers introduced below are very strong and invasive powers to identify wrongdoers, and to trace and freeze money and other assets.

Used against a real fraudster and few have any sympathy at all but if used against innocent persons, real damage can be done to those innocents.

It is for this reason that the courts are very careful in authorising the use of these powers and will insist on various checks and balances to ensure that they are not abused.

Victims who wish the court to make invasive court orders have to pay a price. The price is not only court application fees (which are payable) but certain undertakings. We'll say more about the required undertakings in relation to each of the powers that we discuss below.

But having said all that, the courts' powers to assist victims of fraud are extensive and the courts are well set up to help. One victim was particularly impressed with the civil courts:

> "The experience of the company ... has been that the English courts and the legal system have been both efficient and responsive to its needs as a victim of a corporate fraud. The courts ... heard and dealt with applications in a prompt and practical manner, admirably balancing the company's entitlements with appropriate protections in place for third parties, such as banks and indeed the suspected perpetrator, in a fair and impressive manner. Judges and court offices personnel ... clearly understood the urgent nature of the applications and [were] very responsive as to time frames for hearings and issuing sealed orders. Remedies such as the Norwich Pharmacal Order are exactly what a victim of corporate crime requires to assist with effective asset recovery."

Signpost

In fraud cases the identity of the victim is not always clear cut, for example where there is a group of companies and a parent or holding company, and sometimes there are multiple victims. ⊳ *Section 5*

4.7 Norwich Pharmacal orders

Fortunately for victims, the civil courts have developed strong powers to help victims to identify wrongdoers and to help them trace assets. A key power is the ability of the court to make a so-called Norwich Pharmacal Order ("NPO" for short), a type of disclosure order.

A court can make an NPO against a person who holds information and / or documents which will help to:

- identify wrongdoers; and
- trace money or other assets which are considered to belong to a victim of fraud.

The essence of the NPO is that it can be granted against innocent persons who were used by wrongdoers to perpetrate the wrongs. It is not intended to implicate the holders of that information but merely to require their assistance.

Signpost

As more employees are drawn into the investigation as witnesses or to assist, you need to make it absolutely clear that it is a strictly confidential matter and any breach of confidentiality will be subject to disciplinary action. Managing confidentiality becomes increasingly difficult when third parties are brought into the enquiry. ▷ *Section 1*

It is possible to obtain NPOs against banks which require them to disclose to the victim:

- documents and information concerning the name, address and contact information they hold for bank account holders and signatories to accounts; and
- details of all transfers of funds and other transactions concerning funds in bank accounts, including the destinations to which funds have been paid from accounts.

And in both cyber fraud and commercial fraud cases, it is possible to obtain from telephone networks and internet service providers:

- identity and contact information for their account holders; and
- information and documents concerning the usage of accounts.

To get an NPO, you will need to be able to show to the court that:

- a legal wrong has been carried out, or arguably carried out, by an ultimate wrongdoer;
- the order is needed to enable action to be brought against the ultimate wrongdoer; and
- the respondent person against whom the order is sought must: (a) be mixed up in and have facilitated the wrongdoing; and (b) be able or likely to be able to provide the information necessary to enable the ultimate wrongdoer to be sued.

Specifically, in relation to the requirement that there is a need for an order, the victim must require the information sought in order to vindicate some right or take a step to protect himself arising out of the wrongdoing or potential wrongdoing.

It is not a requirement that the information is needed to commence civil-court proceedings or indeed that the victim intends to commence legal proceedings. It suffices that the victim wishes to identify a person, for example, to bring employment disciplinary proceedings or to make a complaint to the police.

When considering whether to make an NPO, the court will look at a number of relevant factors:

- the strength of the possible claim contemplated by the applicant for the order;
- the strong public interest in allowing an applicant to vindicate his legal rights;
- whether the information could be obtained from another source;
- whether the respondent to the application knew or ought to have known that he was facilitating arguable wrongdoing;
- whether the order might reveal the names of innocent persons as well as wrongdoers and if so whether such innocent persons will suffer any harm as a result;
- the degree of confidentiality of the information sought; and
- the privacy rights of the individuals whose identity is to be disclosed.

A fraud lawyer: "There are a number of legal routes a victim of fraud can take to improve their position before issuing a claim for recovery of assets. One really useful application which can be made is for disclosure of information from third parties (often banks). It's entirely possible that a victim might not know the name of the fraudster who targeted them, or whose account money was transferred into. An application can be made which compels the bank holding the account to provide certain pieces of information. This could include copies of bank statements, payment instructions, the account opening documents and so on. This can help a victim to determine whether there is any money left in the account and, if not, to see where it was transferred or what it was used to buy. You can also ask the court to 'gag' the bank so that they don't tip their customer off about your investigations.

Third party disclosure orders are a fundamental weapon in the victim's armoury as they enable victims to identify assets controlled by the fraudster or find out what has happened to the proceeds of the fraud from third parties such as banks. Because of their importance they are available in many countries and can be combined with gagging orders so as to prevent the third party ordered to provide the information from tipping off the fraudster as the existence of the order or the information provided to the victim."

When preparing your NPO application and drafting the terms your application will need to be very precise about these things:

- Precise about who it is that must provide the information. In the case of a corporate, this means being precise about which company is responsible for and holds the documents you want disclosed.
- Precise about the documents and information which must be disclosed. You must specify very clearly the particular documents or classes of documents which are held by the respondent to your application and say how and why it is that believe the respondent holds the information you seek. In the case of cyber fraud, this can involve some fairly technical explanations to the court about the relevant information and documents that the respondent will hold and you may need to use a digital forensic expert to provide you with the reasons for your requests.
- Precise about the time limits for provision of the information or disclosure that you wish to impose on the respondent to your application.
- Precise about the purposes for which you will use the information and documents you receive from the respondent to the NPO, which may include using the material for further investigating the fraud, for asset tracing investigations, for bringing civil proceedings, for making criminal complaints, and for internal disciplinary proceedings or employment cases.
- Precise about whether the respondent should be allowed to inform the alleged wrongdoer that you have made the application and obtained an NPO against that wrongdoer. If you do not want the respondent to be able to tell the wrongdoer, then you should ask the court to impose a non-disclosure order (commonly known as a "gagging order") on the respondent, barring it from revealing your application and its result to the wrongdoer for a limited period of time.

You will, almost invariably, need to offer to pay the respondent's costs of complying with the NPO which will be incurred by the respondent. For example, if you are asking for information and documents from a bank, you will have to be prepared to pay their reasonable costs of retrieving information and documents from storage and of making photocopies or electronic copies of these for you. These fees are typically quite small.

Lastly, when preparing an application for an NPO, you will have to decide whether the application should itself be made in secret to the court, that is, without notice to the respondent (for example, a bank). Your alternative is to alert the respondent that you will be making an application by giving notice. To determine which of these courses you take you need to consider the following:

- Is there a real risk that if you do alert the respondent to the NPO application that they might alert the alleged wrongdoer and so thwart the purpose of the NPO? In nearly all cases of fraud, the court will accept that it would be undesirable to alert a wrongdoer that you are seeking to establish his or her identity and to trace monies which have been fraudulently extracted from you. So the real question is whether the respondent can be trusted not to tip-off the wrongdoer deliberately or accidentally.
- Even if there is a risk that the respondent may tip off the potential wrongdoer, is it possible to eliminate or at least seriously reduce this risk whilst still giving notice to the respondent that an NPO will be sought against it? For example, many institutions will be sympathetic towards victims and have no real interest in alerting potential wrongdoers. In the case of banks, they are under a good deal of legal pressure not to tip-off fraudsters because of statute law. With these sorts of respondents, it is usually possible to negotiate a "gagging" agreement with them ahead of making your application for an NPO, which then allows you to make the application on notice to the respondent. Of course, any refusal to guarantee that they will not tip-off the wrongdoer would serve as a reason to make your application without notice.
- Would it in fact be helpful to give notice to the respondent, so that they can be part of the process of shaping an even more useful form of NPO than the one you have in mind, perhaps including details that you had not thought of? This can certainly be the case for NPO applications against internet service providers with whom it is particularly important to identify workable types of information that they actually hold and to identify other entities who may also hold information.

Typically, you will be faced with very little if any resistance from a respondent bank or telecommunications company. They have little to gain or lose from your application as the true target will not be them but will be the alleged wrongdoer. Most of the time these kinds of respondents are well-used to dealing with NPOs and will respond to them in stock fashion, that usual response being that they "neither object to nor consent to" the making of the order you are seeking from the court.

Given the lack of opposition from a typical respondent, making an NPO will often feel like an easy step. But beware. Judges are well disposed to making these orders but at the same time they do recognise that they are invasive. And even if you have informed a respondent that you are going to make an application before going to court, the court will carefully scrutinise what you are asking it to order. It will often have its own views as to the kinds of information or detail of information that you are entitled to receive from the respondent (and the same goes for the documents you are after). It will want to ensure that you get just enough for your purposes but not much more.

4.8 Freezing injunctions

4.8.1 Introduction to freezing injunctions

> A fraud lawyer: "One of the most powerful weapons available to a victim of fraud is the freezing injunction. It prevents the fraudster using or moving assets without a further Court Order. If a victim can act quickly enough the combined effect of having the proceeds of the fraud frozen (meaning no benefit was obtained) and access to funds to pay for a defence restricted can make all the difference."

Freezing injunctions (often called freezing orders) are the most commonly used of the court's "nuclear weapons". They are an essential power against fraudsters and others who launder or even just receive and hold the proceeds of fraud.

In short, they freeze all assets held by a wrongdoer up to the value of your claim (plus a reasonable amount for your expected legal costs). They are addressed to the wrongdoers (individual and / or corporate) but can also be served on the holders of assets. So, for example, they can be served on banks which hold funds for wrongdoers and require them to observe the terms of the freeze.

Once in place, a freezing injunction prohibits an alleged wrongdoer from dealing with his property, subject to some limited exceptions which we will come on to. Here's the standard wording for a worldwide freezing injunction:

> "Until the return date or further order of the court, [the alleged wrongdoer] must not without the prior consent of the Applicant's legal representatives:
>
> (1) remove from England and Wales any of his assets which are in England and Wales up to the value of GBP [amount]; or
>
> (2) in any way dispose of or deal with or diminish the value of any of his assets whether they are in or outside England and Wales up to the value of GBP [amount].
>
> Paragraph [the above paragraph] applies to all of [the alleged wrongdoer's] assets whether or not they are in his own name and whether they are solely or jointly owned. For the purpose of this order [the alleged wrongdoer's] assets include any asset which he has the power, directly or indirectly, to dispose of or deal with as if it were his own. [The alleged wrongdoer] is to be regarded as having such power if a third party holds or controls the asset in accordance with his direct or indirect instructions."

If you want to have a look at the entirety of a standard freezing injunction, you can find it on the Ministry of Justice's website along with some official (Practice Direction) guidance.[2] We'll say more about the "return date" below.

Freezing orders can exert a really powerful influence in a case. Fraudsters, by and large, hate them, as they strip back their ability to freely spend money and to dissipate their ill-gotten gains, damage their standing with banks and others who are notified of the freezing injunction and force them to reveal the whereabouts of assets, including those that are derived from the fraud.

For these reasons, freezing injunctions give victims the chance to get into the driving seat in the litigation against the fraudsters. After all, if you can discover the whereabouts of the stolen assets, find out how much the fraudster is worth and you know that the assets will remain frozen, you can proceed with some confidence in your claim and the fraudster may even feel compelled to give up the fight and negotiate an end to the case.

But take good note. Freezing injunctions can be expensive to obtain because of the care and detail that needs to go into an application to court for the injunction. We'll say more about the reasons requiring that care and detail below. And they can be expensive to "police". Once you have obtained a freezing injunction you will need to serve it on various institutions such as banks, all of whom will have the right to claim from you their expenses related to the work that they have to do in looking into whether they hold assets that are caught by the freezing injunction.

Your lawyers will also have to engage in costly long-running correspondence with the fraudster over things such as his or her right to take living expenses or legal expenses from the frozen assets. Yes, you do have to let the fraudster have a reasonable amount of money to eat, pay his mortgage and even pay for luxuries such as his or her children's school fees!

A fraud lawyer: "Fraudsters do not play by the rules. So suing a fraudster is very different from ordinary litigation. Freezing assets and seizing evidence before pursuing your claim is likely to be essential, and this can come as a shock to clients. The good news is that the courts are to here to help, even those in shadowy offshore jurisdictions (where fraudsters typically salt away the proceeds). A properly advised victim of fraud can unlock very powerful remedies. And whilst getting results has a cost associated, a trusted and specialist fraud litigator should always seek to ensure where money is to be spent a return on investment is likely to be made."

4.8.2 What kinds of assets can be frozen?

Any asset can be frozen, wherever it is located. Here are some examples:

- Cash.
- Money in banks and building society accounts (or to be legally precise, the wrongdoer's rights to be repaid money from banks and building societies).

2 www.justice.gov.uk/courts/procedure-rules/civil/rules/part25/pd_part25a#6.

- Shares, bonds and unit trusts.
- Real property (houses, offices etc).
- Personal property (cars, art work etc).
- Amounts owed to the wrongdoer by his or her debtors (or to be legally precise, the wrongdoer's rights to be repaid those amounts by his debtors).

4.8.3 Assets belonging to the defendant

The purpose of a freezing injunction is to freeze assets in which the wrongdoer has an interest. As you will have seen from the standard wording, a freezing injunction will explicitly state that it applies to:

- assets of the wrongdoer;
- including assets which he has the power, directly or indirectly to dispose of or deal with as if they were his own; and
- the wrongdoer is to be regarded as having such power if a third party holds or controls the asset in accordance with his direct or indirect instructions.

So, as you can see, the freezing injunction is very wide in its scope. It is designed to catch not only the assets physically possessed by a wrongdoer (cash, car and other personal items) but also his assets held by others, including banks and other financial institutions, friends and associates and so called "nominees".

A "nominee" is a person (or a legal person such as a company) who holds assets for another person. The key point here is that a nominee has no ownership-stake in the asset but instead merely holds the asset for the benefit of another.

It is also possible to ask the court to declare that assets held by a company should be treated as belonging to the wrongdoer, for the purpose of the freezing injunction, on the basis that the company structure is really a sham rather than genuine and real. But be aware, the law on this area is complex (so complex that it is hard for lawyers and even judges to understand and apply).

When asking the court to freeze assets which you think are owned by the wrongdoer but which are held by other persons for the wrongdoer, you need to be able to show the court that there is a "good reason for supposing" that this is so.

Lastly, as you will have seen from the standard freezing injunction wording that we set out above, a freezing injunction will freeze assets which the wrongdoer holds jointly with others. And so, it will act to freeze, for example:

- a house held jointly by a wrongdoer and his or her spouse;
- money and other investments in joint accounts at banks and other financial institutions; or
- personal possessions held jointly by a wrongdoer and his or her spouse.

4.8.4 Penal notice

This prohibition (freeze) is backed by a penal notice which is set out right at the start of the freezing injunction. It informs the alleged wrongdoer, as well as all those who have notice of it, such as banks and nominees, that to disobey the injunction would be a contempt of court and they could be imprisoned, fined or have their assets seized.

4.8.5 *Tracing and securing assets in the civil courts*

There are many cases of wrongdoers who have found themselves in breach of freezing injunctions. Some say they will comply but then move assets when they shouldn't. Some try to hide the extent of their assets when making disclosure of their assets and the whereabouts of any fraudulently extracted from the victim. Others are late with those disclosures. Some brazenly disregard court injunctions! Courts can and do hand out punishments to transgressors, but you and your lawyers will have to be vigilant to spot those transgressions, some of which will be concealed and prepared to enforce the terms of the freezing injunction, all of which will be time consuming and costly.

> **Signpost**
>
> Prosecutions require clear and cogent evidence of wrongdoing that is illegal, not just immoral or unscrupulous – evidence that builds a compelling picture of the fraud, its perpetrators and beneficiaries; evidence which the police, a judge or jury will believe. ▷ *Section 1*

4.8.5 Disclosure order

A freezing injunction will include, as standard, a requirement that the target must provide disclosure of all assets that he, she or it holds.

A disclosure order can be a powerful tool, enabling the victim to gather further information about the asset holdings of a wrongdoer. When that is then combined with the information the victim may already have concerning the wrongdoer's assets, a detailed picture can emerge of the assets which are now frozen under court order. This can enable a victim to evaluate whether a wrongdoer has sufficient assets to make with worthwhile continuing a claim against the wrongdoer.

The disclosure order will always inform the respondent that he may have the right to claim the so-called privilege against self-incrimination as a valid reason for declining to comply with the disclosure requirements of the order but also warn him that he should take advice about this. The warning is there because the right against self-incrimination is, to a large extent, limited by statutory provisions and so a target would need to be very careful about exercising the right.

4.8.6 Exceptions to the freeze

So far so good with the powers to freeze assets but there are the standard exceptions which you should assume would be written into any freezing injunction. The purpose of these exceptions is to allow the respondent to continue living and working whilst preventing him from spiriting assets away:

- the alleged wrongdoer will still be allowed to spend a reasonable amount of the money frozen to pay for his ordinary living expenses – the amount is limited and specified in the injunction;
- the alleged wrongdoer will also be allowed to use frozen money and other assets to fund his legal defence and to fight back against the imposition of the freezing injunction;

- the alleged wrongdoer will still be allowed to use his money and other assets to pay genuine creditors whom he needs to pay from time to time; and
- the alleged wrongdoer will still be allowed to use his money and other assets to continue his genuine business activities, trade or profession.

4.8.7 International reach of freezing injunctions

A freezing order issued in England and Wales may purport to have worldwide effect but if the wrongdoer holds assets in another country or territory you need to know that the English and Welsh courts' freezing injunctions may be of little effect unless and until you obtain a freezing injunction, or its equivalent in that other place.[3]

This is because the English and Welsh courts have no "jurisdiction" to make legally binding orders against third parties outside England and Wales except in two limited exceptions. The English and Welsh courts are able to make effective orders against a person who is:

- appointed to act under a "power of attorney" in relation to the wrongdoer's assets; or
- subject to the jurisdiction of the English / Welsh court and is given written notice of the freezing injunction at his residence or place of business within the jurisdiction of the English / Welsh court, and who is able to prevent acts or omissions outside England and Wales which would constitute or assist in a breach of the freezing injunction.

So, for example, you can expect that an English-resident "nominee" (a company or individual) that controls assets held abroad for the benefit of the wrongdoer must not deal with or dispose of those assets. The same would be true of an English bank which is able to prevent the wrongdoer from dealing with and disposing of monies and other assets held abroad.

Freezing orders in the international context are discussed further in *Section 7.*

> **Signpost**
>
> Frequently, in fraud cases, it is just as important and valuable to work out how much wrongdoers have gained by their actions, for example by investing the fraudulent proceeds, as you may be able to base your claim on this instead of or in addition to your own losses. ▷ *Section 5*

4.8.8 Effect on third parties

Wrongdoers can and do try to disobey freezing injunctions and continue to dissipate their assets, indeed in some cases they redouble their efforts to do so after being served with a freezing injunction.

---

3 England and Wales is one of the three distinct jurisdictions of the United Kingdom; Scotland and Northern Ireland are the other two. This guide is based on the authors' understanding of the law and practice in England and Wales.

This is why you will want to serve the freeze injunction on anybody who holds or controls assets which belong to the wrongdoer: not only does it freeze those assets, it also makes these third parties responsible for securing the assets.

Indeed, a key aspect of a freezing injunction is the fact that it requires persons other than the wrongdoer to ensure that its terms are not breached. So, for example:

- Banks and other financial institutions must observe the terms of a freezing injunction.
- HM Land Registry must not allow a transfer of real property and will, if you apply for it, register a caution against the register of land to warn potential buyers that the land in question is subject to a freezing injunction.

4.8.9 The process of obtaining a freezing injunction

What do you need to do and what would you need to show to obtain a freezing injunction from the civil court?

The first thing you will need to do to obtain a freezing injunction is to explain with the help of evidence, as far as is possible at this early stage, the:

- identity of the wrongdoer;
- wrongdoing perpetrated on you;
- assets you wish to freeze and their locations;
- persons who hold those assets and their relationship with the wrongdoer; and
- the risk that the assets will be dissipated if they are not frozen.

Your explanations will usually have to be given in a written statement called an "affidavit" and be accompanied by all key documentation ("exhibits") that needs to be shown to the court.

Let's look at those things in more detail.

> **Signpost**
>
> The credibility of evidence is not just based on what it is, but also on how and by who it was obtained. Maintaining the reliability and integrity of evidence is essential. ⊳ *Section 1*

4.8.10 Evidence of wrongdoing

Applications for a freezing injunction must be able to show to the court that there is a "good arguable case" that there has been a legal wrong which has caused you (the applicant) loss and for which the wrongdoer (the respondent) will be liable.

In order to obtain a freezing injunction against a person, you will need to show that you can bring what we call a money claim against that person. We deal with the various kinds of civil claim you may be able to bring in ⊳ *Section 5, Civil court claims.*

Showing a "good arguable" case involves setting out the various kinds of evidence that you have against the wrongdoer in a narrative backed up by documentary evidence, diagrams and so on. Your lawyer will be able to help you present your evidence in a manner which is clear, persuasive and accurate. The evidence does not need to be as strong as that required to prove your case at a trial. The courts recognise that the injunction is a preliminary step.

If you are applying for a freezing injunction without notice to the intended targets (i.e. secretly) then you must be candid with the court about your evidence and the strength of your case. You must give "full and frank disclosure" (⊳ *Section 4.5, Applying secretly for court orders – words of caution*). In practice this means explaining to the court the possible weaknesses in your case and identifying and showing to the court any documents which weaken your case. Here are a few examples of the kinds of evidence that could weaken your case and strengthen the position of a target:

- Evidence that suggests the wrongdoer was acting by mistake rather than deliberately and fraudulently.
- Evidence that the wrongdoer was himself duped by others.
- Evidence that you knew that you were being lied to but decided, for whatever reason, to carry on with the transaction in question.
- Evidence that you may not in fact have suffered any loss as a result of the fraud or such extensive losses as you claim.

> It is important that you have a constructive relationship with your lawyer, but do not be swayed solely by likeability and demonstrative sympathy with your plight. ⊳ *Section 3*

4.8.11 Risk of dissipation by the wrongdoer

To obtain a freezing injunction, a victim must be able to show to the court that if the court does not grant the injunction then there would be a "real risk that a judgment or award in favour of the claimant would remain unsatisfied" because of "unjustifiable disposal of assets".

You may be in possession of evidence that show's that the wrongdoer – knowing that he has done wrong – is intending to dissipate his assets. However, it is much more likely that you will not have such direct evidence and so will instead have to use circumstantial evidence to build your case that there is a real risk of dissipation.

Fortunately for victims, they often get off to a head start. That is because if the victim can show that the wrongdoer has committed a fraud it does not then take much to persuade the court that the wrongdoer would be prepared to dissipate his assets including those taken from the victim.

But it is not always the case that the wrongdoer whose assets you want to freeze is the main fraudster or even that he or she has acted dishonestly; he or she may just be a recipient of assets and subject to an "unjust enrichment" claim or an "unconscionable receipt" claim (⊳ *Section 5, Civil court claims*) and in these situations you would need to be careful to explain why that target's assets are nonetheless at risk of dissipation.

> **Signpost**
>
> What ought to be readily apparent from the Jackson Grid is that the cost efficiency of litigation increases with the value of the claim. In the biggest fraud cases (some are fighting over billions), it is commonplace for lawyers' fees to run into the millions of pounds, but it is a tiny fraction of the claim value. ▷ *Section 3*

But it is not always the case that the wrongdoer whose assets you want to freeze is the main fraudster or even that he or she has acted dishonestly; he or she may just be a recipient of assets and subject to an "unjust enrichment" claim or an "unconscionable receipt" claim (▷ *Section 5, Civil court claims*) and in these situations you would need to be careful to explain why that target's assets are nonetheless at risk of dissipation.

Here are the kinds of evidence you should look for and want to use if present in your case against the target whose assets you want to freeze:

- The circumstances of the fraud you claim has occurred mean that the target acted dishonestly.
- The target has already lied to try to disclaim liability for the fraud or conceal the whereabouts of its spoils and his assets or at least has been unco-operative.
- The target is unpredictable in his or her behaviour or beholden to somebody else who is dishonest.
- The target has a history of fraud, criminality, tax evasion, bad conduct and / or evading court orders.
- The target has already moved money or other assets in a way that is not just typical of normal business or personal expenditure.
- The target resident in another country in which it would be hard to enforce a judgment.
- The targets assets of a kind which would be easily moved and secreted away (e.g. cash or money in bank accounts).
- The target has few links or connections to the United Kingdom and so can easily "walk away" from this country.
- The target has a poor credit rating.

If you are applying for a without notice freezing injunction, you will have to be candid with the court not only about the evidence in your favour but also the evidence which favours the target whose assets you want to freeze. This means setting out and explaining evidence which would suggest that the target may not unjustifiably dissipate his or her assets, such as:

- Communications with the target in which s/he is candid and co-operative.
- Indications that the target has had the opportunity to move his assets but has not done so and does not intend to do so.
- The fact that the target has equity in real property in the United Kingdom which would not be quick or easy to dispose of.
- The fact that the target's assets are in a European country which would be relatively easy to enforce against.
- The target has a long-standing good clean record, credit score and reputation in business etc.

Ultimately, the court presented with all the evidence for and against making a freezing injunction will make a judgment call. Given good evidence that the target is a fraudster, it will usually make a freezing injunction, not least because it knows that once you bring a legal claim against a target this would have the effect of giving the target more reason to get on with dissipating his or her assets.

4.8.12 Without notice or on notice to wrongdoers?

A fraud lawyer: "The courts are littered with the corpses of cases where the parties have failed to be full and frank. Getting off on the wrong footing can sometimes mean never regaining true balance.

Freezing injunctions should not be considered lightly. Not only are they hard to obtain (the court will always put the case to the test) but they come at a high price: the evidence you submit will need to include not only your own arguments to support the request for an injunction, but also any arguments which might be made by your opponent. This is because the court usually hears an application for a freezing injunction without the fraudster being present to put their side of the story across. The court will expect a 'warts and all' account from an applicant. This is known as the duty of full and frank disclosure. Failures in this respect can result in your hard won injunction being released and you being penalised in costs."

When preparing an application for a freezing order, you will have to decide whether this application should be made (secretly) without notice to the wrongdoer or, alternatively, whether you should alert and give notice to the wrongdoer that you will be making an application against him, her or it. The relevant considerations are set out earlier in this section (⊳ *Section 4.5, Applying secretly for court orders – words of caution*).

4.8.13 The return date

If you have applied for and obtained a freezing injunction without notice, the respondent will be given the opportunity to come back to court to challenge the freezing injunction. The opportunity is the so-called "Return Date" which the court will have inserted in the without notice form of injunction that was granted.

The Return Date hearing is usually scheduled ("listed"), by the court, to take place some 7 to 14 days after the without notice hearing. It is the first opportunity for the person whose assets have been frozen (as well as anybody else affected by the freezing injunction) to come back at you and dispute what you have been saying to the court.

The person whose assets are restrained is entitled to:

- criticise your evidence and arguments on which you relied to obtain the without notice freezing injunction;
- show that you failed to properly present all the available evidence and arguments that you were aware of; and
- provide evidence which that person holds and which presents the case, or the risk of asset dissipation, in a different light.

In many cases, persons whose assets have been frozen do not fight back; they prefer to live with the freezing injunction than to try and fight against it. But others do. You may be able to predict the likely response in your case but rarely can you discount the possibility of a fight-back. One thing which above all else will most likely lead to a fight-back is if you fail to be candid when explaining your case to the court at the without notice hearing.

4.8.14 Cross-undertaking in damages

The so-called "cross-undertaking in damages" is the price paid by an applicant for a freezing injunction. Here's what it looks like:

> "If the court later finds that this order has caused loss to the Respondent, and decides that the Respondent should be compensated for that loss, the Applicant will comply with any order the court may make."[4]

The applicant is the victim (you) and the respondent is the person whose assets are frozen by the freezing injunction. The purpose of the cross-undertaking is to give the person whose assets are frozen some measure of protection against a loss because their assets have been frozen.

A liability to pay compensation to the person whose assets are frozen can arise in two circumstances. Firstly, if the freezing injunction is discharged by the court because it turns out that you obtained the freezing injunction in an unlawful manner. Secondly, if the freezing injunction is discharged because you lose your underlying claim against the person whose assets are frozen.

Save in some exceptional circumstances, the undertaking you would have to give would be unlimited in its amount of potential liability. That is because the court does not try to foresee or limit the amount of loss which a person may suffer as a result of having assets frozen. You must therefore heed the advice of an experienced lawyer before committing yourself to cross-undertakings.

When applying for a freezing injunction, you will have to provide evidence of your ability to meet a liability to the respondent if that were to become due. This means providing evidence of your company's net asset position.

You may also be required to "fortify" your cross-undertaking in damages. It means lodging some form of security in a solicitor's account or even with the court itself.

4.8.15 Cross-undertaking to pay third party costs

To obtain a freezing injunction, you also have to be prepared to pay the reasonable costs of compliance with the order of the third parties on whom you serve a copy of the freezing injunction. The court will require you to "undertake" to be responsible for those costs.

So, for example, if you serve a copy of the freezing injunction on a bank who you know or suspect holds money for the wrongdoer then you must expect to have to pay the bank's administrative costs of determining whether it holds bank accounts for the wrongdoer and of freezing those accounts.

---

4 www.justice.gov.uk/courts/procedure-rules/civil/rules/part25/pd_part25a#6.

4.9 Proprietary injunctions

4.9.1 Introduction to proprietary injunctions

Another way to "freeze" assets is to obtain a so-called "proprietary injunction". A proprietary injunction can be made on its own or in conjunction with a freezing injunction. So, what's the difference?

The purpose of a proprietary injunction is to preserve the status quo of assets in a proprietary claim (▷ *Section 5.11, Proprietary claims*) and prohibit the fraudster from doing anything with specific assets that you are trying to recover. Proprietary claims can have significant advantages over monetary claims (▷ *Section 5.11.4, The advantages of proprietary claims*).

Here is typical wording for a proprietary injunction:

> "Until after the return date or further order of the Court, the Respondent must not remove from England and Wales or in any way dispose of or deal with or diminish the value of the Proprietary Injunction Assets whether or not they are in the Respondent's own name and whether they are solely or jointly owned. For the purpose of this order the Proprietary Injunction Assets include any asset which the Respondent has the power, directly or indirectly, to dispose of or deal with as if it were his / her own. The Respondent is to be regarded as having such power if a third party holds or controls the asset in accordance with his / her direct or indirect instructions."

Signpost

Using a proprietary claim, you can "trace" your property into the hands of others. If, for example, a fraudster extracts money from your company and then passes that money to a company or to a spouse or family member then you may be able to recover the money from that other person. ▷ *Section 5*

4.9.2 Conditions for grant of a proprietary injunction

When deciding whether to make a proprietary injunction a court has to exercise a judgment based on a number of things. In short, you will need to be able to show to the court that:

- *There is a serious issue to be tried.* You must have at least an arguable case that you will succeed. This is obviously not the same as saying that it is probable will win your case or even that you have a good case.
- *Damages would be inadequate*. You must be able to show that without the proprietary injunction you would not otherwise be adequately compensated by damages payable by the wrongdoer. The point is that there is no need to freeze assets if you can simply collect damages from the wrongdoer at the end of the case which equal the value of the assets you want to freeze. The counter argument, usually available to a victim, is that if the wrongdoer dissipates the asset in question and indeed has no other assets or would also dissipate his other assets then the wrongdoer will not be good for any damages he is ordered to pay.

- *The applicant is in a financial position to compensate the person whose assets will be frozen.* That means being able to show that you would be able to compensate the person whose assets are frozen in the event that you lose your case and that person has suffered losses as a result of the asset freeze. If you cannot show this because you have little assets, or perhaps because most of your assets were taken by the fraudster then the court may still grant you a proprietary injunction but would have to consider the next factor, the balance of risk.
- *The balance of risk of doing an injustice to either party (otherwise known as the "balance of convenience" test).* If both you and your opponent stand to lose from a proprietary injunction because neither would be guaranteed damages to cover losses arising from the grant or not of the injunction, then the court can still grant the injunction if it considers, on balance, that you face a greater risk if the injunction is not granted than the risk faced by your opponent if the injunction is granted.

4.9.3 Disclosure order in support of a proprietary injunction

If you have identified a target against whom you want to obtain a proprietary injunction you may also want to force him to give you disclosure to help you identify, locate and freeze the assets which are the subject of the proprietary injunction; and in appropriate cases the court will make such an order at the time of granting a proprietary injunction.

In particular, you will want to know and the court will typically order a target to reveal:

- the nature and location of assets which were acquired by the target and which are the subject of your proprietary claim;
- what has become of those assets and if they have been transferred or paid away in exchange for other assets then what is the nature and location of those other assets; and
- the identity of all persons who exercise any control over those assets.

As set out above, in the relation to freezing injunctions, a proprietary injunction disclosure order would have to contain standard wording to protect the rights against self-incrimination of the target of the order.

Signpost

In preparing your claim and throughout your case, you must remain clear-sighted about your financial objectives and possible compromised outcomes. ▷*Section 5*

4.9.4 Can the wrongdoer use or spend proprietary injunction assets?

A great advantage of a proprietary injunction (over a freezing order) is that the terms of the injunction will, typically, bar a wrongdoer from using the assets to pay:

- legal costs or living costs; and
- creditors.

The rationale for this is that you are claiming a proprietary interest in the assets, essentially claiming that you own the assets or will, as a result of winning your case, be declared to become the owner of the assets which are frozen.

Only if the person holding the frozen asset has no other assets which are not subject to the non-proprietary claim would he, she or it be allowed to use / spend from the proprietary assets which are frozen by the injunction.

4.9.5 Evidence and other issues

If you decided to apply to the court for a proprietary injunction, you will need to observe the kind of court procedures set out above in relation to freezing injunctions. Indeed, in most fraud cases, an applicant for a proprietary injunction will simultaneously apply for a freezing injunction against wrongdoers.

4.10 Other injunctions

It will, in appropriate cases, also be possible for you to obtain other forms of interim injunctions against wrongdoers pending the resolution of your claims against the wrongdoer. These can be, for example, in support of claims concerning trade secrets and breaches of confidence (⊳ *Section 5.12, Protecting and reclaiming information, associated property and intellectual property*). The courts have the power to grant injunctions, for example, to:

- prohibit misuse of your trade secrets or confidential information; or
- require products that have been manufactured with the use of your trade secrets to be recalled and to be delivered up to you for safekeeping.

4.11 Search orders

A fraud lawyer: "Search orders are expensive, can be tricky to obtain and carry a high burden for the victim and the legal team. Obtaining them is only the beginning: forensic computer experts and teams of lawyers are needed to execute the order and later analyse the results of the search. Speed and surprise are of the essence in execution – technologically savvy defendants may have set up 'kill' systems that try to wipe their computers or devices and which take only seconds to activate. That said, search orders offer an invaluable opportunity to recover property or obtain evidence that would otherwise never see the light of day."

The most invasive and dramatic of all of the court's "nuclear weapons" is the search order, sometimes still known by its old name, the Anton Piller order.

You can see what the standard search order looks like on the Ministry of Justice's website.[5]

5 www.justice.gov.uk/courts/procedure-rules/civil/rules/part25/pd_part25a#7.1.

> **Signpost**
>
> Persons entrusted with responsibilities such as directors and agents will often have duties to report information. Directors have the duty to report suspicions of fraud committed by persons within a company and a failure to do so would be a failure of that legal duty. ▷ *Section 6*

A search order is an order against a named person, requiring him, her or it, to provide your legal team (and a supervising solicitor) with access to a property (home, office, or even a car) to search for and seize specified items which you claim belong to you as well as evidence. In the case of documents that are relevant to your case, you would be entitled to take copies and if necessary to remove them from the premises in order to copy and return them two days later. Here's what you can get access to search for:

- *Stolen, fraudulently extracted or unlawfully taken property.* This can obviously include items of personal property such as computers and manufacturing or office equipment but can also include cheques, lists of customers and other items which belong to you.
- *Documents which would assist a claim against the wrongdoer.* This would be any kind of electronically stored or paper documents which are likely to help you build a case against a wrongdoer. Typical examples, include emails and text messages between wrongdoers.
- *Documents which would assist in the tracing and freezing of assets.* Typical examples include evidence in relation to the movement and location of assets (both those subject to a proprietary claim and others), such as bank account documents and statements, emails and texts between wrongdoers and associates to whom assets have been transferred.

A search order does not allow your searching party to breakdown doors or otherwise force access to a property. Instead, it demands that the person controlling access to a property must give your "supervising solicitor" (more about this person below) and your searching team access to all searchable areas such as locked cabinets, safes and computers. In the case of computers, the search order will require the person who has the computer to provide details of all passwords for access to the computers and any encrypted documents. Your search team can include IT experts.

Given that a search order is the most invasive of all of the court's orders, the court will only grant a search order based on a number of important conditions and safeguards. Those conditions and safeguards are:

- *Extremely strong evidence of the underlying claim.* As that suggests, you must be able to show sufficiently clear and cogent evidence that you have been defrauded.
- *Very serious actual or potential harm if not granted.* You must be able to show that without the search order being made you could suffer very serious harm. An example would be that the wrongdoer would destroy important or crucial evidence of his wrongdoing or destroy evidence of what has become of stolen assets.

- *Clear evidence that the target has the relevant items or documents in his possession.* These are the kinds of items or documents discussed above.
- *Real possibility that the relevant items or documents may be destroyed.* You must be able to show that without the search order, the wrongdoer would set about destroying the relevant things. Essentially, you must be able to show that nothing short of a search order would do. So for example, if the court made an order requiring the wrongdoer to disclose and hand over all relevant items there is a real possibility that he would not only disobey the order but destroy the documents in question. This can be inferred from the nature of the underlying fraud of which the target is accused by the victim but such an inference would not be inferred in every case.
- *Cross-undertaking in damages.* The court will require you to give an undertaking to be responsible for any losses suffered by the target of the search order and which would become payable as a result of the order being discharged due to your fault or discharged as a result of your losing the underlying case against the target.
- *Full and frank disclosure.* You must be candid and open about all aspects of your application and the evidence presented in support of it, alerting the court to potential weaknesses in your underlying case and in your application for the search order. It extends to the information you give to the court in support of your cross-undertaking in damages. This is the quid pro quo for asking for such an invasive order at a without notice (secret) hearing.
- *Supervising solicitor.* To obtain a search order, you would need to agree to a protective procedure involving an impartial independent solicitor, called a supervising solicitor. This solicitor, paid for by you, would have to be present during the search of the relevant premises and be responsible for compiling an accurate report of what was searched, taken and / or copied and for ensuring that the person who is the target of the order understands his basic legal rights and that those rights are respected. Those rights[6] include the right to receive legal advice, the right to challenge the order requiring entry to the premises (the target can delay entry of the supervising solicitor for a maximum of two hours in order to make an urgent challenge), the right to claim legal professional privilege, and the right to claim the so-called privilege against self-incrimination. In respect of the latter, see above in relation to freezing injunctions.

4.12 Conclusions

This section has set out the range of legal powers available to victims in tracing and securing assets in the civil courts. Thinking about tracing and securing the assets of the wrongdoer at the outset is crucial, otherwise a successful judgment in your favour may turn out to be a pyrrhic victory. The courts are there to help victims but obtaining the various orders is a complex business which requires the assistance of skilful, experienced lawyers.

6 These privileges are complex and beyond the scope of this guide.

Civil court claims

5.1 In this section

- Who can bring claims
- Valuing claims
- Alleging and proving claims
- Proprietary claims
- Monetary claims
- Claims concerning trade secrets and confidential information
- The claim process
- Trials

5.2 About this section

In this section, we set out to guide you through the most important features of bringing a civil claim before the courts. We will tell you about starting a claim, about the stages of a claim and what to expect at a trial of your case. You will also learn about valuing your claims and negotiating a settlement.

We will also discuss the key ingredients of the main kinds of claims which are made in fraud cases before the civil courts. Some of these will come across as rather dry and technical. We include these descriptions because if you bring a claim you will need to know what it is that you have to prove to succeed.

We will use plain English, but at the same time prepare you for discussions with lawyers by introducing some key legal terms.

5.3 The right to bring civil court claims

Any company or individual who has been the victim of wrongdoing has the right to bring claims before a civil court, whether the High Court in London or another court in England or Wales. Your lawyer will give you advice on the choice of courts available to you. There are two basic conditions:

- The claim must be based on a recognised legal wrongdoing, as opposed to a question of immorality.
- It must be brought by the correct victim(s) against the correct wrongdoer(s).

The second condition may seem obvious, but in fraud cases the identity of the victim is not always clear cut, for example where there is a group of companies and a parent or holding company, and sometimes there are multiple victims. Your lawyer will help you work out which is the correct claimant company or companies.

> **Signpost**
>
> You will not know at the outset what might become vital to the investigation in your case. Something disregarded early on may become relevant later. Record everything which may become relevant from the moment you begin to have concerns and keep going with that until the conclusion of the case. ⊳ *Section 1*

5.4 Valuing your claims

If you are thinking of bringing a civil claim against wrongdoers, you will, rightly, want to know how much you stand to gain by doing so. We start here with an introduction to some of the things you will need to think about.

When lawyers and courts talk about the value of a claim, they essentially mean the financial value to be gained by the person bringing the claim or to be lost by the person defending it depending on who wins or loses the case (or wins or loses part of it). This is not the same as talking about the emotional or reputational issues surrounding the bringing or defending of a case.

When we talk about the financial value to be gained by the person bringing the claim, we are being very precise: if the claim is brought by your company, then you will be valuing your company's claim. This is for good reason. Having identified which person should be the claimant, it is that person that can and must articulate its claims. Other persons are not entitled to make claims unless they too have valid claims and become claimants.

How should you go about assessing the financial value of your case?

If you want to maximise the amount of your claims whilst avoiding inconsistencies, double-counting your losses and other conceptual errors, you are likely to need the help of lawyers. But you can do a great deal of thinking and preparation to set yourself and your lawyers on the right road to optimising your claims.

> **Signpost**
>
> Solicitors, as a general rule, spend less time in court and more time preparing client cases, interviewing the client, witnesses, corresponding with opponent lawyers and so on. They tend to specialise quite early in their careers so it is unlikely that you will find a solicitor who is equally expert in the civil and criminal courts. ⊳ *Section 3*

We suggest that you start by thinking about the financial value according to two different principles both of which may be features of your claims:

- work out how much you think that you have lost; and
- work out how much you think that the wrongdoers have gained.

These can be different if the fraudster has made additional profits by using the money or assets taken from you, for example by investing the money or buying and selling an asset for a profit.

5.4.1 How much have you lost?

You will need to think about as many aspects of your losses as you can, starting with your direct losses. Here are some examples of direct losses:

- How much money was fraudulently extracted from your bank account?
- How much money did you pay out against fraudulent invoices?
- How much money did you pay out against inflated invoices?
- What was the value of cash stolen?
- What was the value of other property or information stolen?

Next, you should think about any indirect losses that you have suffered. Here are some examples of those:

- What interest have you had to pay as a result of being deprived of money?
- What interest could you have earned if you had not been deprived of money?
- What business opportunities have you lost as a result of being deprived of your money or other property?

> **Signpost**
>
> Be careful not to be seduced by grand predictions (even well-meaning ones) of likely victory when you are meeting a lawyer for the first time. It would be unwise for you to feel comforted by imprudent advice at such an early stage. ⊳ *Section 3*

5.4.2 How much have the wrongdoers gained?

Frequently, in fraud cases, it is just as important and valuable to work out how much wrongdoers have gained by their actions as you may be able to base your claim on this instead of, or in addition to, your own losses. For example:

- What was the value of the bribe received by your errant director / employee?
- What is the current value of the property fraudulently taken, bearing in mind that assets can go up in value?
- What is the current value of any other property which has derived from that which was originally taken?
- What was the value of the business opportunity that should have come to your business but which was secretly exploited by your errant director / employee?

5.4.3 Valuing your claims – reality check

Whilst you will want and need to maximise and fully articulate the values of all of your claims that you bring, there is also a reality check that you need to make at the outset of your case and need to keep coming back to throughout your case.

This is because the true expected value of your case is not just the amount being claimed; you also need to be well aware that the value is affected by a number of other factors:

- all the legal costs;
- all the time you and people working for you spend on the case;

- whether the time spent on the case causes you to miss business opportunities;
- any costs that might result from publicity;
- any consequences resulting from your customers, suppliers or competitors knowing you are engaged in litigation;
- whether your time and money could be better invested in business opportunities which are more profitable than recovering your losses;
- the chances of succeeding in getting a judgment;
- the chances of recovering all your losses; and
- the chances that you will lose and have to pay the defendant's costs.

It is important to be very commercially-minded about litigation and to view it in the same way as you would any other investment. It would be bad enough if you were to invest in a case and it failed to deliver. It would be doubly bad if you also failed to exploit real business opportunities because of the distraction, time and money spent on the case.

To put you in the right frame of mind in considering whether it is worth pursuing a case you should regard the fraud loss as a sunk cost. You then regard it as a possible *gain* from the litigation. Even if you desperately need to recover the stolen property or money, it helps to think of litigation in this hard-headed way.[1]

Then you can draw up a cost benefit schedule. Forecasting the cost of management time, adverse publicity and missed opportunities may be difficult, but including these more intangible costs can be important, as the table below illustrates. The cost benefit scenario in *Figure 5.1* is based on a £1,500,000 loss and claim (▷ *Section 3.18, A comparison of funding methods*).

Figure 5.1: Cost benefit schedule

	Cost if lose, £	**Court order if win, £**	**Gain if win, £**
Fraud loss recovery	–	1,500,000	1,500,000
Own legal costs	–380,000	266,000	–114,000
Intangible costs	–50,000	0	–50,000
Opponent's costs	–266,000	–	–
Total	–696,000	1,766,000	1,336,000
Chances of success / failure	30%	70%	

In this example you will have to consider and compare the:

- 70% chance that you will win the case and make a net recovery of £1,336,000, versus
- 30% chance that you will lose the case and lose a further £696,000 by bringing the unsuccessful proceedings.

---

1 It is worth noting that people are more exercised and motivated by the loss of money or assets than by gaining what they do not have. You will want to be conscious of the fact that you may have this feeling. That is a perfectly understandable emotion but it needs to be disregarded when figuring out the expected value of a claim and whether or not you can and should bring court proceedings.

Even if the intangible costs were zero, the potential gain from the case would be a maximum of £1,386,000. It is £114,000 less than your original loss because claimants do not recover all their costs from defendants (▷*Section 3.11, Recoverability of costs in civil claims*).

The figures above assume a total recovery of the fraud loss from the wrongdoer. Unfortunately, that is not a typical outcome. It is much more usual that a victim recovers less, sometimes a lot less, because the fraudster has already illegally spent much of the money, or most frustratingly, is lawfully using it to pay his lawyers. Let's re-work those figures, to reflect this reality. Let's assume that you are only able/likely to recover £1 million from the wrongdoer. Here's what the cost benefit schedule now looks like.

Figure 5.2: Cost benefit schedule – claimant's perspective based on partial recovery from the defendant

	Cost if lose, £	**Court order if win, £**	**Actual recovery, £**	**Gain if win, £**
Fraud loss recovery	–	1,500,000	1,000,000	1,000,000
Own legal costs	–380,000	266,000	0	–380,000
Intangible costs	–50,000	0	0	–50,000
Opponent's costs	–266,000	–	–	–
Total	–696,000	1,766,000	1,000,000	570,000
Chances of success / failure	30%		70%	

In the above scenarios, would it make more commercial sense to take the loss on the chin, learn from the experience and invest the £380,000 that you would otherwise have to spend on your own legal fees in, for example, new equipment or revenue streams which yield an annual £100,000 profit contribution with a 90% chance of success?

Some companies have coherent anti-fraud policies which aim to send out a zero-tolerance message by pursuing fraudsters. For these businesses, the risk and cost calculations are less relevant. You should also bear in mind that the mere prospect of litigation is enough to encourage some fraudsters to settle quickly.

You should continue to review the cost benefit analysis as the case progresses. This will either confirm that you are doing the right thing in continuing the case or, if things turn bad then the cost benefit analysis may encourage you to drop the case. If you do end up in that difficult position, you should bear in mind that, if you abandon the case, the defendant will expect you to pay his costs to date and that will almost inevitably be the result at court.[2] Your lawyer will need to advise you carefully in order to avoid or minimise these costs.

---

2 If you want to abandon a claim, you may be able to negotiate what lawyers call a "walk away" or "drop hands" deal, in which the case is abandoned and each side bears their own costs. But don't count on being able to do that.

> **Signpost**
>
> You will not recover all your costs, it is more likely to be between 60% and 80%. ▻ *Section 3*

We'll return to the issue of case valuation when we deal with the settlement of claims (▻ *Section 5.15, Compromising claims*). We will look at the value of a claim from the perspective of both the victim-claimants *and* the wrongdoer-defendants. We'll also discuss the assumptions and variables that need to be carefully considered and worked into your cost benefit calculations. We will even show you some mathematical equations that might help you arrive at an expected value to you of your case.

5.5 Commencing proceedings

A court case will begin with a 'Claim Form' in which you have to set out all the kinds of claim you are bringing. In order to get a case up and running, you – or most probably your lawyers – will have to prepare the Claim Form, obtain a court-approved copy of it from the court (for which you will have to pay a fee – ▻ *Section 3.10, Civil court fees*) and then formally serve the court-approved claim form on your opponent.

The court approval for the issue of your Claim Form comes in the form of a court stamp (officially, a "seal"). It does not mean that the court has agreed that there is merit in your claims, it simply means that you have paid the court fee, the claim is registered and has a reference number so that it can track the progress of your case. Oh, and your company has now officially become the "Claimant" and your opponent is now a "Defendant".

> **Signpost**
>
> The sooner you bring a claim the better and commencement of a case should, if at all possible, be coupled with seeking court freezing orders or other protective measures against the wrongdoers right at the start of your case. ▻ *Section 2*

5.6 It's your case and you must prove it

As a claimant, you have the responsibility to progress your claims. This means that you must do most of the running when it comes to making sure that a timetable is adhered to. It is unfair, but the defendant will be in no hurry and is likely to obstruct your progress whenever he can.

As the claimant, the *burden of proof* is on you to prove your case to the *standard of proof* required for civil claims. The civil standard is the balance of probabilities, which essentially means that, to be successful, it is your company which must satisfy the court (a judge) that your case is more likely to be correct than the defendant's case.

If your case goes to trial – and you should always assume that it will – then you and your lawyers will have to work hard to prove your case to the satisfaction of the court. One alternative to trial is a settlement of your case, which should always be on your mind (▷ *Section 5.15, Compromising claims*). The other alternative is abandonment of your case, which would be costly and highly unattractive.

We say more about trial and settlement below. For now, we will just emphasise this: it is critical that you behave and conduct your case in a manner that will both enhance your credibility and maximise your chances of success if and when you arrive at trial.

> **Signpost**
>
> Investigating fraud is not about 100% certainties. It is only in rare cases that all the damning documentation has been preserved and the wrongdoers confess their guilt. Fortunately, that level of certainty is not necessary in order for you to protect your business and to bring action against wrongdoers. ▷ *Section 1*

5.7 Don't litigate by correspondence

What do we mean by this? Lawyers like talking. They also like writing. And when they think the client wants action, they swing into action. Sometimes this means writing long letters delivering ultimatums in a hectoring tone to vent their client's grievances; and sometimes all of this before even bringing any claims or organising freezing injunctions and the like against wrongdoers.

Are these long letters effective as against a fraudster? Well, it doesn't take a genius to work out that a fraudster's response to long letters from lawyers is either to ignore them altogether or to find a way of engaging in long drawn-out correspondence to render the victim-lawyer's ultimatums meaningless all the while quietly getting on with dissipating assets to make themselves judgment proof.

So what should you do instead? Well, first and foremost, an expert fraud lawyer will judge whether any correspondence with a target defendant is even appropriate before beginning proceedings. This is because in most cases the victim's lawyer ought to be thinking about whether the victim can and should go to court to obtain a freezing injunction, and perhaps other protective measures, to secure assets before alerting the wrongdoer to the fact that his or her fraud has been discovered (▷ *Section 4.8, Freezing injunctions*).

As and when it is necessary to correspond with the wrongdoer, a minimalist approach to correspondence usually works well. Polite, crisp deadlines which are then adhered to are far more effective than protracted and confusing correspondence that can be ignored or exploited by the fraudster.

5.8 Legal jargon

You probably will not be surprised to hear a lot of legal jargon is still used by lawyers (and judges) in and out of court. This is especially so when it comes to explaining the kinds of claims brought by victims of fraud. Here is what could be a typical conversation between a lawyer and a (confused) client (only slightly exaggerated for effect):

> *Lawyer:* You have a number of causes of action you can pursue.
>
> *Client*: Yes, I know that he caused my company a lot of damage.
>
> *Lawyer*: I'm not talking about damages at the moment, we'll come on to those later. I'm referring to the fact that you have both tortious claims and equitable wrong claims to bring.
>
> *Client*: There was nothing equitable about how my former director behaved and its the company that's had a tortuous time since he ran off with its money.
>
> *Lawyer*: Yes, and because he owed fiduciary duties, you can bring tracing claims to get restitution of your property.
>
> *Client*: I just want my money back.
>
> *Lawyer*: Of course, and that's what I'm talking about but first we need to claim that title in your money is revested in your company and then we can make the errant director a constructive trustee of all the substitute property he now holds.
>
> *Client*: I'm not quite following you; my former director was clearly more destructive than constructive.
>
> *Lawyer*: Yes, and you bear the burden of proof of showing that – of course, he will invent an exculpatory defence which you will then have to rebut.

You should learn some of the most important legal words from this guide but we cannot and do not try to teach you them all. As you receive advice and watch your court case unfold you will learn the most important legal terms but you should not wait until the end of your case to understand them: ask your lawyer for clear explanations in plain English and if legal terms have to be used, ask for clear explanations of these as well.

> **Signpost**
>
> The importance of asset recovery has to be emphasised. There really is no point in a pyrrhic victory. ▷ *Section 4*

5.9 Overview of the different kinds of claims in fraud cases

It is highly probable that the kinds of allegations (lawyers call them claims) you will need to consider are those that have been developed by the courts over hundreds of years. These kinds of claims are usually referred to as "common law" claims, although even that is not quite the right jargon in some cases. Nevertheless, we shall refer to all court-created claims as common law claims.

What will perhaps surprise the reader is that the word "fraud" does not feature in most of the titles of the claims which are available to victims of fraud.[3] Instead, the common law uses terms such as: "deceit", "conspiracy" and "knowing receipt". In addition to the common law is legislation, which provides useful additional kinds of claims. We'll say more about those below.

The common law caters for most cases and where it does not, statute law fills the gaps. There are, however some uncertainties and complexities in the law relating to fraud. Lawyers (including judges) who do not regularly deal with civil fraud cases can find themselves as confused as the client.

We think the most useful way to explain the types of possible claims is by reference to their objectives and effect. Broadly speaking there are two categories of claims.

The first kind are claims which enable you to directly recover property which is yours or which will be declared to be yours; and we shall call them *proprietary claims* (sometimes called "*in rem*" claims).

The second kind are claims the aim of which is to enable you to claim monetary compensation or some other amount of money from the wrongdoer. We shall refer to these as *monetary claims*.

Lawyerly alerts:

- This guide provides an overview.
- We explain the most common types of claim relating to fraud, but others may apply in particular situations.
- We do not set out the various legal defences which wrongdoers may rely on.
- We do not set out the various time bars which prevent claims after certain periods of time.

5.10 Some cautionary words about alleging fraud and dishonesty

It may be utterly obvious to you that you are a victim of fraud and also who did it. But, and it is a significant but, the person you think of as a fraudster is also entitled to his day in court and is innocent until found liable by the court. He or she is entitled to protection from being wrongly denigrated, defamed and so on.

It should be remembered that the bulk of cases before the civil courts are about unpaid bills, boundary disputes, negligence, unintentional personal injuries and so on. Whatever their value and impact on the claimants, these cases do not include allegations which seriously impugn the reputation of the alleged wrongdoer.

3 The only kind of claim which explicitly refers to fraud is that under Section 423 of the Insolvency Act 1986, headed "Transactions defrauding creditors". Although this can be a useful claim, it is not as common as the other claims we have discussed and so we have not included it in this guide.

Civil courts expect claimants to be very cautious in making serious allegations such as fraud. Therefore, fraud claims must be based on credible material which establishes a "prima facie" case. Improperly made fraud allegations can and do backfire spectacularly. The court will expect you and your lawyer to show clear and cogent evidence to support fraud allegations.

However, despite these cautions, there are advantages to proving fraud: they include longer time periods for claims, greater levels of damages and more rights to track down and recover your money.

A key advantage of using an experienced fraud lawyer is that he or she will have a well-trained nose for spotting fraud and will be able to rule out innocent explanations. He or she will also fully understand the concerns of courts in relation to the fraud allegation, when it should be made and when claims should be framed *without* alleging fraud.

Signpost

When gathering documents, you will need to preserve their integrity as well as get them well ordered for presentation to your lawyer. This usually means keeping the original documents in the same state and order as you found them in your files and business records but then making copies and putting those copies into chronological order for your lawyer. ⊳ *Section 3*

Claimants have to set out (in lawyers' speak: "particularise") the nature and facts of their claims to justify the type of claim they are bringing to the court. Below, we introduce a number of kinds of claims. Some of them contain allegations of fraud or dishonesty; others do not.

Although it feels good to allege fraud and dishonesty when bringing a claim against wrongdoers, it is sensible to first consider whether the same or similar result can be achieved without having the additional responsibilities that come with alleging and having to prove the fraud or dishonesty.

5.11 Proprietary claims

The essence of a proprietary claim is that it seeks to vindicate your right to the return of property which belongs to you or which the court declares ought to belong to you. If successful the court would order the wrongdoer (and others, holding your property) to return it to you.

The law concerning proprietary claims is about as confusing as the law can get. If you delve into the law books and case reports, you will find all kinds of difficult jargon and conceptual difficulties which even judges and lawyers find very difficult to understand and apply.

We will explain your legal rights by separating out different kinds of property and rights.

Signpost

If you have identified a target against whom you want to obtain a proprietary injunction you may also want to force him to give you disclosure to help you identify, locate and freeze the assets which are the subject of the proprietary injunction; and in appropriate cases the court will make such an order at the time of granting a proprietary injunction. ▷ *Section 4*

5.11.1 Proprietary claims to tangible personal property and cash

You may have lost goods because of theft or fraud. Similarly, you may have lost hard cash. We think that your proprietary rights to recover tangible personal property[4] and cash are best summarised as follows:

- You will generally always have the right to ownership and possession of tangible personal property that was stolen from you[5] if that property still exists. Neither the thief nor the recipient of the stolen property acquires title to the property.[6] It remains yours. This is even the case where the recipient is entirely innocent and has paid money for your property.
- The same is true in respect of stolen *cash* if it still exists in cash form in the hands of the thief or is gifted by the thief to another person. But if the thief passes the cash to an innocent recipient in a commercial transaction, then you would lose the right to the return of the cash from the recipient of it.
- The same rights apply to tangible personal property or cash which has been disposed of by a director or other agent of your business who made the disposition without having actual authority to do so.
- The same rights apply to tangible personal property or cash which has been fraudulently extracted from you (i.e. by a deceitful representation).
- You *may* have the right to ownership and possession of money paid out by you by mistake (the law is uncertain on this).

5.11.2 Proprietary claims to money paid out from your bank account through the banking system

We'll now look at the more common situation, where the victim loses money through the banking system.

- You will have the right to ownership and possession of money which has been fraudulently paid away by a signatory to your company's bank account without your company's informed consent.

---

4 Not land or intangible property.

5 For example, received as cash from your bank account, or taken from your petty cash.

6 This position can change if, for example, a person buys the property in another country and that country's laws would grant that buyer a right to ownership of the property.

- The same rights apply to money disposed of by a director or other agent of your business who made the disposition without having actual authority to do so.
- You will have the right to ownership and possession of money which has been fraudulently extracted from you by false representations which induce you to pay the money away.
- You will have the right to ownership and possession of money which has been fraudulently extracted from you by means of hi-jack of your bank account – at least if you are not able to obtain a re-credit of the amount taken from your bank (⊳ *Section 2.5, Getting your money back from your bank or the receiving bank*).
- You *may* have the right to ownership and possession of money paid out by you by mistake (the law is uncertain on this).

5.11.3 Wider proprietary claims to property and money

There are situations in which the courts will grant you the right to become the owner of property – any kind of property – as if that property had become yours as a result of the wrongdoing against you:

- You will have the right to ownership and possession of the profits secretly made by a fiduciary (⊳ *Section 5.13.4*). So if, for example, one of your directors exploited his knowledge of your business and its opportunities to pursue his own opportunities as a side-line rather than passing those on to your business, then the court can order that the secret profits made by the wrongdoer-director have become your secret profits.
- You will also have the right to ownership and possession of the money received by a person by way of a bribe in the course of their business on your behalf (⊳ *Section 5.13.9*).

5.11.4 The advantages of proprietary claims

What is really significant and advantageous about proprietary claims is that:

- They can apply to property which is derived from the original property which was stolen or fraudulently extracted from you. So if a fraudster extracts money from you but then buys a car with that money, you would be able to claim the right to take ownership and possession of the car. Similarly, if for example a fraudster used your money to repay a mortgage on her house, you would have the right to a "charge" over the house for the value of your money which would then enable you to force a sale of the house to obtain the value of your money.[7] Lawyers and courts often refer these kinds of claims to derivative assets as "equitable tracing claims", or simply "tracing" claims. In technical legal terms, "tracing" is not actually a kind of claim. It is instead a route to a "remedy" that the court can allow. It is a set of rules by which the courts allow victims to show that assets now in the

---

7 In technical legal terms, this would be called a remedy of equitable subrogation. You would be entitled to be subrogated to (meaning "stand in the lender's shoes in respect of") the rights that the mortgage lender had before the mortgage was repaid.

hands of a wrongdoer were derived from assets that came from or which the victim was entitled to.

- They can lead to greater recovery than your loss at the time of the fraud. So, for example, if a fraudster steals money from you which he then uses to buy a house you will be able to claim ownership and possession of the house. If the house has gone up in value then you will benefit from that gain. (Obviously, if the house has depreciated in value, this kind of claim will be less valuable.)
- They take priority over other unsecured debts of those who hold the property which is due for restoration to you (whether it is your original property or is something derived from your original property). They also take priority over asset-freezing and realisation of assets by criminal-court actions by government agencies against persons holding your property.
- They can reach beyond the first recipient of stolen or fraudulently extracted property or money. Using a proprietary claim, you can "trace" your property into the hands of others. So if, for example, a fraudster extracts money from your company and then passes that money to a company or to a spouse or family member (a frequent occurrence) then you *may* be able to recover the money from that other person (subject to what we say below in relation to third person defences to such claims).

But beware. A tracing exercise gets much complex and uncertain – both evidentially and legally – when assets have been converted and mixed with other assets by a wrongdoer.

A useful way to think about proprietary claims is to remember that that they were originally designed to allow victims to recover specific, identifiable items of property, for example a stolen work of art, a house, a vehicle or a bag of gold coins. Tracing claims as we know them today are a much more modern invention.

The law has had to keep pace with the development of money transaction and banking systems. And it here when things become most challenging. For example, distinguishing your stolen money in a bank account from that belonging to others or claimed by other victims or owed to legitimate creditors is difficult. So too is dealing with transactions where there is no straight conversion from one asset to another.

These kinds of cases present multiple challenges both evidentially and legally. The courts have developed certain "rules" or "presumptions" that can guide the tracing exercise and these help. But at the same time the courts do still require victim-claimants to be able to establish their tracing claims within defined parameters. There must be a sufficient "nexus" between the assets that were taken from the victim (or to which the victim was entitled to) and the assets in the hands of the wrongdoer which are the target of the tracing claim.

Signpost

Given that a search order is the most invasive of all of the court's orders, the court will only grant a search order based on a number of important conditions and safeguards. ▷ *Section 4*

5.11.5 Defences by third party recipients of property in proprietary claims

It is important for you to know that a third person who receives property which is derived from your property (i.e. not the original property itself),[8] such as a spouse or family member may be able to assert a defence to your tracing claim called the "bona fide purchaser for value defence".

The defence works like this. If the third person can prove that he purchased the property in question with an adequate payment in good faith and without knowing about your interest in the property then he or she would be able to succeed in defending against your claim and you would have lost the right to the return of your property.

In practice, the two most important elements of this defence are:

- Whether the third person gave adequate value for the property he or she received. If you can show that it was a gift to her then you defeat the defence.
- Whether the third person had notice of your rights over the property. To determine this question, the court will consider what facts the third party knew at the time he or she acquired your property. It will want to know whether the third person had suspicions but ignored those suspicions. It will look at whether the price paid for your property ought to have alerted the person to the existence of a problem. And it will look at these things according to what should have been reasonable behaviour by the third person. In one case, a court described the issue for it to determine as being whether a reasonable person with the recipient's attributes should either have appreciated that a proprietary claim probably existed or should have made enquiries or sought advice, which would have revealed the probable existence of such a claim.

5.12 Protecting and reclaiming information, associated property and intellectual property

The protection of confidential information, indeed trade secrets, is very important to businesses. Important information comes in a huge variety of forms; examples include, business plans, scientific formulae, customer lists, financial information, price lists and bid information. The same is true of intellectual property.

Industrial espionage has always been around. As has misappropriation and use of confidential information by errant directors and employees. In the early days, data thieves would misappropriate paperwork or simply photograph it. Then came the photocopier. Next, floppy discs. Then email, memory sticks and hacking. Cyber fraud in all its guises has made corporations more vulnerable to attack, not just from within but also from without.

---

8 This is because, under English law, stolen property will always remain the property of its original owner, the victim, who is able to obtain its restoration from either the thief or any other third person who has acquired that original property, whether or not the third person paid for the property. As set out in the main text, this absolute right does not exist in relation to restoration of property which has been derived from the original property. It may not also apply where the original property has been taken out of the UK and sold in a foreign country whose law is different from that of the UK.

5.12.1 Trade Secret Regulations

The Trade Secrets (Enforcement, etc) Regulations 2018[9] (we'll call them the "Trade Secret Regulations") stipulate in very clear terms what is to be protected and how. It is trade secrets that are to be protected. A "trade secret" is defined as being information which:

- is secret because it is not generally known among or readily accessible to persons within the circles that normally deal with the kind of information in question;[10]
- has commercial value because it is secret; and
- has been subject to reasonable steps under the circumstances, by the person lawfully in control of the information, to keep it secret.

The (victim) "holder" of a trade secret is entitled to sue the person who unlawfully acquired information from the holder, as well as any other persons who acquire the holder's information, to protect that information.[11]

The Trade Secret Regulations empower the courts to grant both interim injunctions (▷ *Section 4.10, Other injunctions*) and final injunctions prohibiting the use of the confidential information itself and also prohibiting the exploitation of that information through production, sale and distribution of "infringing goods". Finally the regulations empower courts to order that the confidential information and infringing goods be delivered up and forfeited to the person from which the confidential information was unlawfully taken.

The Trade Secret Regulations define "infringing goods" as being "*goods, the design, functioning, production process, marketing or a characteristic of which significantly benefits from a trade secret unlawfully acquired, used or disclosed*".

These are potent legal powers. If somebody steals information from you – whether in paper form or electronically stored form – you are entitled to have that information back. And if it has been used to make some gadgets or other commercial product, you may be entitled to have those handed over to you, so that you become the legal owner of those goods.

As we say above, all of this protection hinges on the holder being able to show that the acquisition, use or disclosure of its trade secret was "unlawful". The Trade Secret Regulations say that to be unlawful, the acquisition, use or disclosure must constitute a "breach of confidence". This is statutory language and the courts will have to interpret the meaning of this phrase. When doing so, they are highly likely to look at the case law that the courts have developed to define what is a breach of confidence.

---

9 Introduced into UK law to give effect to Directive (EU) 2016/943 on the protection of undisclosed know-how and business information (trade secrets) against their unlawful acquisition, use and disclosure.

10 The exact wording in the Regulations is a bit more detailed: "secret in the sense that it is not, as a body or in the precise configuration and assembly of its components, generally known among, or readily accessible to, persons within the circles that normally deal with the kind of information in question".

11 The victim is also entitled to recover compensation for what has been suffered as a result of the "unlawful" acquisition, use and/or disclosure of the confidential information.

5.12.2 *Civil court claims*

The Trade Secret Regulations also make clear that they do not replace or limit the protections developed by the courts but combine with and complement those other protections. The regulations also make clear that they do not prevent the courts from developing and providing wider protections to holders of trade secrets. Let's now look at breach of confidence claims.

5.12.2 Breach of confidence claims

Breach of confidence is a type of claim which has been developed by the courts over a period of nearly 200 years. A victim will be able to succeed in a breach of confidence claim if it is able to prove all of the following ingredients:

- the claim must concern information which is clear and identifiable and capable of being confidential or private;
- a reasonable expectation that the information is confidential or private;
- the infringer, whether the person who misappropriates the information or a secondary user of the information, must know that the information is confidential; and
- the infringer misuses the information (but note that a holder of confidential information is also able to obtain an injunction to prevent its misuse).

What does it take to prove that the infringer knows that the information is confidential? In the case of a director or employee, this will be straightforward if the information in question is highlighted as confidential in his contract with the victim company. In other cases, there is more scope for arguments. It is certainly clear (from a legal perspective) that a person will have sufficient knowledge to become a wrongdoer if he has actual knowledge of the circumstances giving rise to the reasonable expectation of confidentiality. It is also clear that a person will have sufficient knowledge for liability, if he would have had such knowledge but for his wilful blindness. Beyond that, the law becomes much less clear.

The courts can protect your confidential information by ordering those who might misuse it (or continue to misuse it) to cease that activity and to hand over to you your confidential information.

5.12.3 Copyright and other intellectual property claims

Laws exist to protect intellectual property rights, namely your rights to copyrights and designs and patents and your rights to protect any trademarks you hold. It is important that you know that these other rights exist, although they are beyond the scope of this guide.

5.13 Monetary claims

We describe here a number of types of claim that entitle the victim to be paid a sum of money by the wrongdoer. We shall refer to these as "monetary claims" as we think that this is the best generic description for them, although it is right to say that legally they are called by a variety of more specific names.[12] The following monetary claims may be available to you as a victim of fraud:[13]

- breach of contract;
- unjust enrichment;
- breach of fiduciary duties (including those owed by directors);
- breach of trade secrets and breach of confidence;
- conversion;
- deceit;
- causing loss by unlawful means;
- bribery;
- conspiracy;
- dishonest assistance; and
- knowing or unconscionable receipt.

Monetary claims seek a payment of money from the wrongdoer to your company. Their main purpose is to put you back into the position you would have been in but for the actions of the wrongdoer. The court orders the defendant to pay the compensation within a short period of time. If he fails to pay, the courts will assist in enforcing the payment and we say more about enforcement at the end of this section of this guide.

Which claim or claims are most suited to your case depends on the features of the case including: whether the defendant had a duty of trust towards your company; whether there is a contractual relationship with the wrongdoer; and the nature of the conduct of the wrongdoers.

5.13.1 The advantages and disadvantages of monetary claims

The advantages in bringing monetary claims are:

- They are easy to understand in the UK and overseas.
- There are routine enforcement mechanisms and, if necessary, bankruptcy (of individuals) and winding-up (of corporates) to give effect to money judgments.
- They entitle victims to be compensated for the full value of their losses even where the wrongdoers no longer hold any benefits from the relevant wrongdoing. So even if the wrongdoers have spent the money stolen from you, you are entitled to enforce your money judgment against their other assets (e.g. houses).
- They entitle victims to be compensated for their lost opportunities. For example, if you were fraudulently induced to buy a certain business which turns out to be no good, you will be entitled to claim for the fact that you missed out on the opportunity to purchase a different business that would have proved to be successful and yield profit and value to you. This can mean you end up with compensation which exceeds the amount of money you actually lost.

---

12 There are common law damages claims, equitable compensation claims, claims for accounts and claims for restitution.

13 There are others, such as a claim under section 2(1) of the Misrepresentation Act 1967, which are not included in this guide.

5.13.2 *Civil court claims*

- Monetary claims (and their results in terms of orders or settlements)[14] in respect of fraud claims continue to be enforceable against wrongdoers even if and after wrongdoers are bankrupted and discharged from bankruptcy.

> **Signpost**
>
> Often persons prefer to live with a freezing injunction than to fight against it. But others do. One thing which above all else will most likely lead to a fight-back is lack of candour when explaining your case to the court at the without notice hearing. ▷ *Section 4*

The most important disadvantages are:

- They give you no priority as a creditor. If the offender's debts including your compensation order exceeds his assets and he is bankrupted, you can only recover a proportionate amount. Without a freezing injunction controlling the amount the offender can spend, he can spend as much as he likes up to the point the order is paid or enforced (▷ *Section 4.8, Freezing injunctions*).
- If the offender has transferred money or property to others you may be able to pursue those recipients under insolvency laws but it can be very expensive.
- Criminal prosecutors are increasingly seeking "confiscation orders" to deprive criminals of their gains. Offenders may have to pay these orders before satisfying any other creditor (▷ *Section 6.7.3, Seeking compensation and restitution*). Sometimes foreign courts ask courts in England Wales to secure "external orders" (▷ *Section 7.4.4, Restraining assets in E & W in support of foreign criminal cases*) and these too can be a threat.
- Other victims may secure civil-court orders. If any of these claims are "proprietary" claims, they will have priority over the wrongdoer's assets.

We'll now review the make-up of various kinds of monetary claims. This will allow you to understand what you have to prove to succeed with these claims.

> **Signpost**
>
> The applicant for a freezing injunction must be able to show to the court that there is a "good arguable case" that has been a legal wrong in respect of which the victim has suffered loss and for which the wrongdoer whose assets are to be frozen will be liable. ▷ *Section 6*

5.13.2 Breach of contract

If you are or were in a contractual relationship with any company or individual involved in the fraud, then you should take a good long look at that contract and take advice on its interpretation.

14 Although this would depend on the characterisation of liability and terms of the settlement.

A claim based on a contract is *not a fraud claim* but will often be an important kind of claim for a business because the victim will not normally have to prove any actual dishonesty by the wrongdoers, only that they failed to honour a contractual obligation. This is especially so if the contract includes explicit terms proscribing behaviours such as over-charging, conflicts of interest, paying inducements.

If you succeed in bringing a contract claim, you will be entitled to compensation in an amount that puts you into the position that you would have been had the wrongdoer not breached the agreement. So, for example, if the wrongdoer stole money from you, the court will make orders that compensate you for the losses that you suffered and which you would not have suffered had there been no theft.

Employee contracts (including those of Directors) are interpreted in accordance with employment law as well as more general contract law. Employees have so-called duties of "fidelity" towards their employers; essentially meaning that they are contractually bound to act honestly in their work for and within the employer's business.

Downsides to contract claims compared with fraud claims are that:

- they may be barred or limited in scope or amount by the contract;
- the compensation you are awarded by the court may be more limited than in fraud claims; and
- they are more likely to become time-barred more quickly.

> **Signpost**
>
> Fraud cases are often far more complicated than other kinds of cases. You may also find yourself up against a wrongdoer who knows his way around the law and who may have lawyers who are expert in defending him against your allegations. To go it alone should be your last resort. ▷ *Section 3*

5.13.3 Unjust enrichment

Unjust enrichment claims (historically referred to as "restitution claims") provide claims in situations in which no contracts or no effective contracts govern the relationship between the parties.

The basic ingredient is that a person has been enriched at the expense of another. In a fraud case, this means enrichment – in money or property – by the wrongdoer at the expense of a victim.

Victims can only sue the first person to have received money or property and be unjustly enriched, not people to whom the assets were subsequently transferred.

In addition, for a victim to be able to successfully sue a wrongdoer for unjust enrichment, it must be able to show that the wrongdoer was "unjustly" enriched.

What is "unjust" is not judged by some vague notion of fairness or by an exercise of discretion by a judge dealing with a case. In order to succeed, a victim must be able to show that the wrongdoer's receipt was of a kind recognised by the courts as being unjust.

5.13.4 *Civil court claims*

The courts only recognise certain kinds of enrichment as unjust including:

- receipt following mistake, including a mistake induced by fraud, for example, a mistaken payment or an overpayment; and
- receipt for which consideration is due but not given, for example, a payment is made for goods or services which are not then supplied.

A victim is entitled to compensation equal to the amount of enrichment. Victims cannot claim for losses above that amount. So, for example, a company which mistakenly pays a sum of money to a supplier after the supplier deliberately submitted two invoices for the same work is entitled to the amount of overpayment. But the company cannot claim – in an unjust enrichment claim – for additional losses based on what it would have done with the money had it not lost that money.

A valuable feature of an unjust enrichment claim is that a victim may not have to prove dishonesty; it may be enough simply to show that a contract was entered into by mistake or has failed for another reason.

5.13.4 Breach of fiduciary duties

A victim will be able to claim compensation from a wrongdoer who was at the time of the wrongdoing a "fiduciary" to the victim owing fiduciary duties which he breached.

A useful and much-quoted legal (case-law) definition of a "fiduciary" is the following:

> "A fiduciary is someone who has undertaken to act for or on behalf of another in a particular matter in circumstances which give rise to a relationship of trust and confidence. The distinguishing obligation of a fiduciary is the obligation of loyalty. The principle is entitled to the single-minded loyalty of his fiduciary."[15]

The following are examples of fiduciary relationships which are legally well established:

- solicitor (the fiduciary) and client;
- agent (the fiduciary) and principal;
- business partners (each are fiduciaries);
- directors (the fiduciaries) and company;
- directors (the fiduciaries) and creditors of their company if the company is insolvent;
- employee (the fiduciary) and employer, in certain circumstances; and
- joint venture parties (each are fiduciaries), in certain circumstances.

Signpost

Although it is vital that you negotiate the best deal, be aware that it is very difficult for lawyers to make predictions about costs at an initial discussion. ▻ *Section 3*

15 *Mothew v Bristol & West Building Society* [1996] EWCA Civ 533.

What are the fiduciaries' duties? The following are well established (and for ease of reference we refer to the beneficiary of the fiduciary duties as the "other"):

- A duty to act loyally in the interests of the other.
- A duty to act in good faith in the interests of the other.
- A duty to avoid conflicts of duties between their own interests and those of the other.
- A duty not to misuse or misappropriate the other's property.
- A duty not to make a secret profit (or to allow a third party – such as a family member – to make a secret profit) from his position without the informed consent of the other.

An important feature of breach of fiduciary duties is that they do not always necessitate explicit claims of dishonest conduct by the wrongdoer: it is enough that the wrongdoer has breached the relevant duty.

A victim who is successful in showing that a fiduciary has breached his duties to the victim is entitled to claim:

- compensation for his losses suffered as a result of the breach; and / or
- a sum of money – known as an "account" – equivalent to the profit made by the fiduciary.

5.13.5 Breach of trade secrets and breach of confidence

We have already set out the ingredients for these claims (▷ *Section 5.12.1, Trade Secret Regulations* and ▷ *Section 5.12.2, Breach of confidence claims*). In both cases, the court may award compensation to the victim whose information has been misused by a wrongdoer. The court can award compensation to the victim for its losses and can also disgorge profits made by the wrongdoer as a result of his misuse of the trade secrets or other confidential information, ordering the wrongdoer to pay the total of those profits made to the victim.

5.13.6 Conversion

Another strange-sounding claim. You could think of this – in general terms – as your right to claim compensation when personal property[16] has been taken from you without your authority. Personal property means real objects and can include, for example, computer hardware and paper files. It can also include cash.

To succeed with a conversion claim, you need to be able to show that:

- you had possession of the property in question or had the immediate right to possession of that property; and
- the wrongdoer deliberately deprived you of your rights to possess and use your property.

If you succeed in a conversion claim, the court's order will be made on the basis that you should be restored to the position you were in before and the wrongdoing. You

16 A conversion claim applies only to tangible personal property. It cannot be used to claim for land, or indeed for intangible property, such as intellectual property and electronic data.

will be entitled to monetary compensation for all of the harm that you suffered as a result of the actions of the wrongdoer.

5.13.7 Deceit

Deceit is explicitly a fraud claim. A victim will show that he was the victim of deceit if he can prove all of the following ingredients:

- the wrongdoer made a representation of fact to the victim;
- the representation was false;
- the wrongdoer knew that it was false, or did not believe it to be true, or was reckless about whether it was true or not;
- the wrongdoer intended the victim to rely on the representation;
- the victim did rely on the representation; and
- the victim suffers loss because of relying on the representation.

You will have noticed that the test of dishonesty is quite widely drawn and includes recklessness. It is enough that a person *suspected* that his or her statement was inaccurate or that he or she neglected to inquire into its accuracy or that he or she was ignorant as to whether the statement was true.

Here are some well-worn examples of behaviour that the courts will find deceitful if they involve dishonesty; some also amount to a breach of contract and unjust enrichment by the wrongdoer:

- mis-selling a product or service based on false statements;
- agreeing to pay for something with no intention to make payment;
- selling company shares to subscribers on a false prospectus;
- selling company shares to buyers, making false statements about the profitability of the company;
- presenting a false invoice for payment;
- declaring that goods have been dispatched or delivered when they have not;
- making false promises to creditors to persuade them to extend their credit or dissuade them from calling in or enforcing loans and trade credit and so on;
- persuading an accounts department to release company funds based on false information;
- giving a cheque as payment knowing that it will be dishonoured; and
- giving a forged cheque as payment.

If you succeed in a deceit claim, the court's order will be made on the basis that you should be restored to the position you were in before the wrongdoing. You will be entitled to claim monetary compensation for all the harm you have suffered as a result of the wrongdoing.

Signpost

When deciding whether to bring a case you need to factor in the potential costs you would have to pay to your opponent in the event of losing your case or part of your case. It is difficult to predict those costs at the outset of a case but you should probably assume that they would be at least as high as your own legal costs expenditure. ▻ *Section 3*

5.13.8 Causing loss by unlawful means

Causing loss by unlawful means (also known as "unlawful interference") consists of:

- interfering with the freedom of a third party in respect of that party's economic relationship with the victim;
- which is unlawful as against that third party (and which is actionable by the third party, or which would have been actionable by the third party if it had suffered loss);
- which is intended to cause loss to the victim[17] – it is enough if the perpetrators acted deliberately with knowledge of its consequences for the victim;[18] and
- which does in fact cause loss to the victim.

Rather confusing, even to lawyers. So, let's try and make it more understandable…

The essence of the unlawful interference claim is that it allows a claim by a victim who was only an indirect victim of the unlawful conduct of the wrongdoer. Here are some examples:

- The wrongdoer is a sub-contractor on a construction project. He provides fraudulently inflated invoices to the contractor who in turn submits bills also based on those inflated figures to the client-victim. The initial deception by the sub-contractor was focused on the contractor but if the sub-contractor is aware that a knock-on consequence is that the contractor would charge higher amounts to the client-victim, then the client-victim can bring a claim against the sub-contractor.
- The wrongdoer defrauds a third party, which in turn means that the third party is unable to honour its contractual obligations to the victim or to enter into business with the victim as it would have done but for the harm it suffered.
- The wrongdoer is a director who asset-strips the company she controls leaving that company unable to pay a creditor (victim).
- The wrongdoer has a letter of credit in his favour under which he must prove dispatch of goods to entitle him to call for payment under the letter of credit. The wrongdoer forges shipping documents to fraudulently claim under the letter of credit. He calls for payment from his own bank who in turn collects payment from the victim's bank. The victim was not the direct recipient of the dishonest presentation of the forged documents but has suffered as a result and may bring a claim against the wrongdoer.

If you succeed in a claim of causing loss by unlawful means, the court's order will be made on the basis that you should be restored to the position you were in before and the wrongdoing. You will be entitled to monetary compensation for harm that you suffered as a result of the actions of the wrongdoer.

17 Harm to the victim can be the dominant end result sought by the wrongdoer's interference with the third party.

18 It could be that the harm to the victim is the means by which the wrongdoer intends to obtain some other result, such as a benefit for herself. And, therefore, it is no defence that the perpetrator only intends to enrich himself. But on the other hand, it is not enough that harm to the victim is only a foreseeable consequence of the interference with the third party. If that is the case, the person who carries out the interference would not be liable.

5.13.9 Bribery

A payment to a director, employee or agent of a company is presumed to be made with a corrupt motive or intention to persuade or influence the agent if the victim company is not informed of that payment. The same is true in relation to secret payments to a partner in a partnership which are not known to the other partners.

The motive of the director, partner, employee or agent is irrelevant: receipt of the secret payment is enough to give rise to an irrebuttable presumption that the director, partner, employee or agent was improperly induced in the carrying out of his role.

The principal is not required to prove that the secret payment was given specifically in favour of a particular contract, since the payment may have been given in order to win favour generally. But if the payment does relate to a particular contract, then the amount of the secret payment is *always* deemed to have inflated the price paid by the victim company by at least the amount of the secret payment. If the victim alleges loss or damage beyond this he must prove it.

A victim is entitled to claim:

- A sum of money equivalent to the amount of the secret payment (from both of or either of the payer and the recipient).
- That the secret payment received by the director, employee or agent is held for the victim who is entitled to these monies – a form of proprietary claim (see ⊳ *Section 5.11, Proprietary claims*).
- That the person who received the secret payment must pay to the victim a sum of money equivalent to the profit made by the recipient. If the value of property obtained has declined in value since the date it was received by the director, employee or agent, he is obliged to pay for the difference between the present value of the asset and the value of the asset when it was received. When assessing what profit or advantage has been obtained it is necessary to look at the whole situation in the round before deciding what is practically just.
- Where a director, employee or agent places his benefit from his breach of fiduciary duties into a partnership or company, the whole profit received by the partnership or company and not just the benefits he personally received.

5.13.10 Conspiracy

Your lawyers may tell you that you can bring an "unlawful means conspiracy" claim. And you'll be thinking that this is another strange-sounding and rather antiquated description for a legal claim. Don't be put off, an unlawful means conspiracy claim can be a very effective kind of claim.

An unlawful means conspiracy is:

- an agreement (in legal language, a "combination") between two or more persons;
- to use unlawful means;
- pursuant to which unlawful action is taken;
- aimed at the victim;
- resulting in damage to the victim.

For the unlawful means conspiracy to be aimed at its victim it is enough if the perpetrators acted deliberately with knowledge of its consequences for the victim and it is no defence that the perpetrator only intended to enrich himself.

> **Signpost**
>
> The purpose of a proprietary injunction is to preserve the status quo in relation to a proprietary claim so as to prohibit the wrongdoer from doing anything with specific assets that are the subject of the proprietary claim. ▷ *Section 4*

The unlawful means conspiracy claim can be very useful. This is because it can be based on a wide variety of unlawful behaviours, including criminal conduct by the conspirators as well as civil law wrongs. Here are a couple of examples of behaviour that would amount to unlawful means:

- The conspirators agree to present you with false information in order to induce you to enter into an agreement. For example, they are sellers of shares in a business which you are acquiring and in the due diligence stage of your purchase of the shares, the sellers agree to deliberately misrepresent information to you, or agree to put forward information to you being reckless as to whether or not the information is correct.
- The conspirators agree to hack into your computer system to steal your customer lists and pricing information (see ▷ *Section 6.6, Cyber crimes*).

You may also be told that you can bring a "lawful means conspiracy" claim. A lawful means conspiracy is:

- an agreement (in legal speak here, a "combination") between two or more persons;
- a predominant purpose of which is to harm the victim-claimant;
- pursuant to which action is taken;
- resulting in damage to the victim.

The distinguishing feature of the lawful means conspiracy claim is that you have a legitimate claim even if the actions of the wrongdoers were inherently lawful: the claim arises from the fact that the predominant purpose of the conspiracy was to cause you harm. To show that the predominant purpose was to harm you, you would have to undermine any suggestion that the conspirators were just pursuing their own business interests, such as legitimately competing against you. You would need to show that their overriding intention was to cause you harm. They really would have had to be out to get you.

If you succeed in a conspiracy claim, the court's order will be made on the basis that you should be restored to the position you were in before and the wrongdoing. You will be entitled to monetary compensation for all of the harm that you suffered as a result of the actions of the wrongdoers.

5.13.11 Dishonest assistance

A dishonest assistance claim is a claim against a person who has helped another person, who is a fiduciary, deprive a victim of money or property. The main ingredients of the claim are:

- First, there needs to have been a trust or fiduciary relationship but the trustee or fiduciary need not have been dishonest.
- Secondly, the assister-wrongdoer must have dishonestly induced the breach or assisted in the breach.

Examples include laundering the proceeds of a theft by an employee or inducing a director with a bribe.

The victim is entitled to claim that the assister-wrongdoer has a personal liability to pay to the victim not just for losses caused by his assistance but for all losses which resulted from the breach of trust or breach of fiduciary duties.

5.13.12 Knowing or unconscionable receipt

To succeed in a claim of knowing or unconscionable receipt, a victim must be able to show that:

- it had assets held for it under trust or which were the subject of a fiduciary relationship;
- those assets were transferred in breach of that trust or fiduciary relationship duties;
- they were transferred to a person who received those assets for his or its own use; and
- that recipient's knowledge was such that it would be unconscionable to allow the recipient to retain the value of the assets.

A classic example of knowing / unconscionable receipt liability is that of a spouse or associate who receives a gift of misappropriated monies, knowing that they had been misappropriated.

What is much less easy to explain, and indeed much less easy for the courts to grapple with, is what is meant by the term "unconscionable". Although susceptible to further argument before the courts, it is highly likely to include:

- wilfully shutting one's eyes to the obvious possibility of the wrongdoing;
- wilfully and recklessly failing to make such inquiries as an honest and reasonable person would make;
- knowledge of circumstances which would indicate a probability of wrongdoing to an honest and reasonable person; and
- knowledge of circumstances which would lead to an honest and reasonable person taking advice which would reveal a probability of wrongdoing to an honest and reasonable person.

5.13.13 Intimidation and economic duress

If a victim has been threatened with an illegal act and as a result has been coerced into action (or indeed inaction) which has caused the business to suffer harm, then the victim is entitled to claim compensation from the wrongdoer who made the threats. A victim is also entitled to claim compensation if the illegal threat is made against another person which then directly leads to the result that the victim suffers harm.

This kind of claim will be of most use to victims of cyber blackmail and other similar threats. For example, the victim may have his computer systems disabled by a virus and the perpetrator then demands a ransom as payment for restoring the victim's computer system to normality. There are two different kinds of claim, one called intimidation and other called economic duress.

> **Signpost**
>
> If you choose to pay your lawyers by the hour you should still ask for properly worked-out budgets for each stage of your case, including contingencies which may arise. This kind of cost budgeting is now a routine feature of civil court case management and is supervised by the courts. Judges expect to see it: you should too. ▷ *Section 3*

5.14 Overlapping and alternative claims

The facts of fraud cases often mean they fit into different types of claim. It is common therefore that fraud claims are pursued under multiple heads of claim and quite normal that claims overlap or are alternatives to each other. There are good reasons for doing this:

- If you fail with one kind of claim you may succeed with another.
- Different claims offer different remedies and you may want a combination of remedies.
- You may not be sure which kind of remedy you want and so you may want to keep your options open.
- If you start off with one type of claim and later find you want to introduce another, the courts may bar you from doing so.
- You can't lose a case against a defendant and then start another case against that same person using a different kind of claim.

If you do bring multiple claims, particularly those which overlap, you and your lawyers will have to take care to make sure that they are carefully presented and that one does not damage another. This isn't a serious risk, it is just a matter of properly presenting your claims.

For example, your primary case may be that a contract was and is void either at the time of its purported formation or as from some later date. Your secondary case may be that, if it was or is not now void, you are entitled to enforce the contract against the wrongdoer. You can't get judgment for both. So, faced with these alternative cases, the judge in your case would have to determine whether you succeed in your primary case, or in your secondary case (or indeed in neither case).

If you do bring multiple claims, do not get carried away with thinking that you can make multiple recoveries from a wrongdoer or group of wrongdoers. You can only recover the total amount of compensation that you are entitled to.

At the point of court judgment, you may be required to elect which remedies you wish to have reflected in the court order to be made against the wrongdoer;

if the alternatives would be inconsistent with each other in respect of a particular wrongdoer, then you must choose which one you want.

The classic and much-cited example of the need to exercise a choice is a bribery case. In a bribery case, the victim, when suing a person who has been bribed (for example, an employee) ultimately must choose between either recovering the bribe (or property derived from it) *or* being compensated by the bribee for the damage caused to the victim as a result of the bribe. The victim cannot have a combination of both. So, the victim has to consider which is worth more and then "elect" which one to have enshrined in a final court order against the wrongdoer. Which one is better may depend not just on the amount each is worth at face value but which one is more valuable in the circumstances. What do we mean by this? Let's test it with some hypothetical facts.

Imagine that an employee of your company was given a £1 million bribe as a sweetener to pave the way for your company to contract with the bribing supplier. Imagine also that the corrupt relationship with the supplier led to £2 million of false and exaggerated charges for contract variations which funded the bribe. You sue the employee. Your claim is in two categories. You have a proprietary claim against the employee to recover the £1 million bribe money that he has received (and to trace it into any other property he has acquired with the bribe money). And you have a claim for damages in the sum of £2 million, the amount that you lost. The court finds in your favour on both counts. You then have a critical choice between two remedies: the £1 million proprietary claim or the £2 million monetary claim. Which of the two alternative remedies on offer should you take?

Taking these alternatives at face value, you would be keen to elect for the remedy of damages. Easy!? But what if the ex-employee is going bankrupt and has a stack of debts owed to a number of others. The cost-benefit-risk calculation surfaces again. The proprietary claim becomes the more valuable of the two because the £1 million worth of money and assets that are derived from the bribe belong to you and do not have to be shared with the ex-employee's other creditors (⊳ *Section 5.11.4, The advantages of proprietary claims*). The £2 million monetary judgment may be apparently worth more but is less valuable because you have to share the recovery of assets proportionately with numerous creditors. Even if the ex-employee is not facing bankruptcy, there is one other scenario that may cause you to choose to prioritise the proprietary claim over the monetary claim. That is if the ex-employee has invested the bribe money so well that it is now worth more than the £2 million plus interest that you would be entitled to recover in the monetary claim.

The only serious downside to bringing multiple claims is time and costs; it will cost you both to make out and then prove different claims. You should also bear in mind that multiple claims will also increase the defence costs. But, in many cases, the additional time will be minimal since the core elements of your work will have to be done and apply to whatever kind of claim is articulated. And the same is true for the work to be done by your opponent.

5.15 Compromising claims

5.15.1 Be prepared to compromise

A fraud lawyer: "Whilst the idea of reaching a settlement with a fraudster might stick in the craw, the benefits of drawing a line under a fraud and moving on can be enormous: the legal spend comes to an end, the staff who are dealing with the case are freed up, the pressure of running litigation stops and the anxiety associated with being a witness and potentially being cross examined is instantly alleviated. Some of these can be easily quantified and set off against a settlement sum, others are harder to convert to pounds and pence, but their value should not be underestimated. Your legal team will help you to understand what a reasonable settlement sum might be, taking into account all these aspects, the strength of your case and the likely cost of going all the way to trial."

You would be forgiven for thinking: "I want my day in court", "I want him cross-examined by my barrister to show what a liar he is", or "How can I reach a deal with him?" (or all of these things!). So why then are we going to talk about compromise?

Signpost

Sometimes, witnesses are reluctant to speak up because they are afraid of the suspect or are unnecessarily worried that they will be somehow blamed. They must be protected and assured. ▻ *Section 1*

Most civil-court claims never make it all the way to trial because they are settled by the parties on terms which each is content with. Very often, content in this sense does not mean happy, indeed parties may be unhappy about the settlement agreement. It means that the parties are content to compromise their objectives and settle matters in preference to the costs, anxieties, uncertainties and risks of continuing the litigation.

Compromise should certainly be on your mind. Civil-court fraud cases are not about revenge. Nor should they be brought for the purpose of ruining an opponent's reputation. They are about money and other financial objectives.

Signpost

Most difficult of all to predict will be the behaviour of your opponent. He may fight like a wounded rhino, run away or capitulate at the mere sight of a lawyer's letter; he may hire good lawyers or represent himself; he may play by the rules or try to bend or ignore them; he may comply with court orders or disobey them. ▻ *Section 3*

If you bring a claim in the civil courts, it is essential that you are prepared to compromise it at the right value. This is not only because your opponent may be keen to settle your case in an acceptable way but because the court will expect you to compromise if a fair deal is offered and may even punish you financially if you do not.

And perhaps most importantly, there are very few if any cases which can be said to be a sure bet one way or the other. Deciding, for whatever reason, that you are simply not interested in any form of compromise would be a very risky and unwise strategy.

Parties to a civil-court case are free to compromise the dispute between them at any time. They may do so at any stage of the case. Some cases settle soon after the wrongdoer feels the pressure of a freezing injunction (▷ *Section 4.8, Freezing injunctions*) and others settle much later in the proceedings. It is even very common for parties to reach a compromise on day one of a trial or even at some other point during the trial.

Finally, in this introductory piece, remember the truism: you don't just get what you deserve, you get what you negotiate.

5.15.2 Calculating the right compromise outcome for you

A fraud lawyer: "There used to be a theory that you couldn't mediate on fraud cases. It wasn't true. There are very few cases which couldn't be settled if the parties want to try to reach a compromise. Where a case involves fraud there may be an unwillingness to make any compromises in terms of what might be accepted from the perpetrator, but that's why careful cost/benefit analysis and the consideration of the costs involved in taking a case to a defended trial are necessary. There is usually a benefit to both parties in accepting an early settlement, even if that means accepting a slightly lower sum."

In your preparation before bringing a claim and indeed throughout your court case, you must remain clear-sighted about the financial outcome you desire as well as the kind of outcome you would accept as a compromise with the wrongdoer.

You'll remember we have already looked at the valuation of claims (▷ *Section 5.4.3, Valuing your claims – reality check*). The example we set out was based on a £1,500,000 claim. We presented the case through the eyes of the victim, which gave you the following cost benefit schedule based on a full recovery of the £1,336,000 judgment value after a trial (*Figure 5.3*).

Figure 5.3: Cost benefit schedule – claimant's perspective based on full recovery from the defendant

	Cost if lose, £	Court order if win, £	Gain if win, £
Fraud loss recovery	–	1,500,000	1,500,000
Own legal costs	–380,000	266,000	–114,000
Intangible costs[19]	–50,000	0	–50,000
Opponent's costs	–266,000	–	–
Total	–696,000	1,766,000	1,336,000
Chances of success / failure	30%	70%	

19 Management time etc.

You'll remember that, in this example, you (the victim) will have to consider and compare the:

- 70% chance that you will win the case and make a net recovery of £1,336,000, versus
- 30% chance that you will lose the case and so lose a further £696,000 by bringing the unsuccessful proceedings.

Now let us look at it from the defendant's perspective (*Figure 5.4*). Whether win or lose the case, the defendant loses money: the only question is, how much? The defendant will be considering and comparing:

- 70% chance that he will lose the case and have to pay out £2,196,000, versus
- 30% chance that he will win the case and still make a loss of £164,000.

Figure 5.4: Cost benefit schedule – defendant's perspective based on full recovery from the defendant

	Cost if lose, £	**Court order if win, £**	**Gain if win, £**
Judgment debt	–1,500,000	–	–
Own legal costs	–380,000	266,000	–114,000
Intangible costs	–50,000	0	–50,000
Opponent's costs	–266,000	–	–
Total	–2,196,000	266,000	–164,000
Chances of success / failure	70%	30%	

By combining the two positions (*Figure 5.5*), it immediately becomes apparent that the defendant is in a far worse position both in terms of risk and cost.

Figure 5.5: Comparison of outcomes for claimant and defendant

	Claimant wins case	**Claimant loses case**
Claimant	70% : +£1,336,000	30% : –£696,000
Defendant	70% : –£2,196,000	30% : –£164,000

Very often the reality of their poor prospects only dawns on defendants when they are properly advised and confronted with these positions. This leads us to a vital point. Many defendants will not even entertain engaging in negotiations until claims are issued *and* they become convinced that the claimant is willing to go all the way to trial.

The claimant is also faced with a dilemma. Trying to persuade a defendant to settle a case before bringing a claim also gives the defendant the opportunity to delay things and dissipate his assets and/or the assets that have been stolen from the victim. Most fraud lawyers would advise a victim to bring the claim against the wrongdoer and at the same time obtain a freezing injunction against him which can then be served on the wrongdoer without warning so as to freeze his assets.

5.15.2 *Civil court claims*

The combination of intransigence and defiance from defendants together with the strategic imperative to freeze the wrongdoer's asset without prior warning to him means that it is, typically, all but inevitable that a victim will have to spend money to issue a claim in order to freeze the assets held by the wrongdoer and force him into seeking proper advice and confronting the realities of their position.

Now let's focus in on the comparison of the outcomes for the claimant and the defendant if their dispute goes all the way to trial (*Figure 5.5*). None of these outcomes are especially attractive – the *only* net winners in all four scenarios are likely to be the lawyers. The question then arises whether a negotiated settlement would be more appealing, and what it might look like.

If both parties to the dispute are of equal bargaining power and are rational, and that can be a big if, then the *bargaining range* for a negotiated settlement prior to accruing any costs sits between the worst outcome for the defendant and the best outcome for the claimant. The bargaining range represents the limiting parameters for a rational negotiation that avoids the anxieties, risks, costs and distractions of going to a full trial. In its simplest form, the bargaining range is defined purely by the value of the claim:

Bargaining range [claim basis]:

–£1,500,000 (defendant) to +£1,500,000 (claimant)

At the outset of disputes, inexperienced litigants naturally base their views of the bargaining range on the rights and wrongs of a claim and its value. If both parties are strongly minded to settle immediately, then the bargaining range based solely on the claim value holds true. Critically however, this "claim basis" bargaining range ignores the alternative: the mounting costs of continuing with the litigation and ultimately having the case decided at an expensive trial. You, the claimant, must understand that the rights and wrongs of disputes are less salient to settlement negotiations than the economics of the alternative. Negotiations are about the avoidance of costs and risks, they are not about delivering perfect justice. The art and purpose of the negotiation is to achieve a settlement wherein both parties fare better than the average economic value outcome of going to trial. Both parties ought to be advised of the bargaining range should the case be decided at a trial. From *Figure 5.5*, it would be as follows.

Bargaining range [defendant's worse case to claimant's best case trial basis]:

–£2,196,000 (defendant) to +£1,366,000 (claimant)

You, as the claimant, may think it entirely sensible for the defendant to pay over £1.5 million than face the significant risks of losing £2.2 million. Your opening position would undoubtedly be £1.5 million plus your own legal costs that you have already incurred. Nevertheless what would you be willing and what would you need to concede to avoid the uncertainties of a trial? A rational offer from a defendant using the 'trial basis' bargaining range would be no more than £1,366,000 because he will have been advised that this is likely to be the maximum that you could gain by going all the way to trial because you would not be awarded 100% of your costs (⊳*Section 3.11, Recoverability of costs in civil claims*). The reality of litigation and negotiations is that in most cases the settlement figure will be lower than you want and deserve. So, should you get an agreement for anything approaching £1.3 million and receive the money in full, you will be doing very well indeed.

The problem with the bargaining positions above is that they do not adequately accommodate the chances of success. What does it really mean when a lawyer says to you that your probability of winning is 70%?

Some lawyers, especially in America, address this problem by using economic concepts to estimate the so-called economic value (EV)[20] of cases. The approach is based on probabilities and calculates what an average outcome would be for a given projected chance of success. As some cases will yield more than the average and some will return less, the method is not accurate in forecasting the financial outcomes of an individual case. However, assuming that your case is average, then these calculations do provide you with an estimate of the typical return that you could expect. Again, this approach does require that lawyers are very realistic with their assessments, that both parties to the dispute are rational and that parties' bargaining power is equal.

The method is simple – you multiple value by probability for each outcome and then add them.

For our example (▷ *Figure 5.5*), the expected value (EV) for the claimant is:

$$EVc = (£1{,}336{,}000 \times 0.7) + (-£696{,}000 \times 0.3) = +£726{,}400$$

The expected value (EV) for the defendant is:

$$EVd = (-£2{,}196{,}000 \times 0.7) + (-£164{,}000 \times 0.3) = -£1{,}586{,}400$$

Introducing the risk element and average outcomes, the 70% chance of succeeding at trial, has reduced the gap between the claimant's and defendant's positions. In this case the bargaining range has narrowed, and is defined by the expected value calculations.

Bargaining range [expected values trial basis]:

–£1,586,400 (defendant) to +£726,400 (claimant)

Looking at this bargaining range, you the claimant may think that the defendant should be prepared to pay £1,586,400 now in order to avoid the 70% risk of losing at trial and so losing a total of £2,196,000. But as that would mean that the defendant has to pay you more than you lost (i.e. the claim value of £1.5 million), he will be resistant to that and may consider the combination of risk and average outcome as acceptable and elect to go to trial.

The defendant may also consider that an offer of £726,400 would be entirely rational for both himself and you the claimant given that this is your expected value of the case going to trial. You, the claimant would probably regard this as miserly minimum, deciding that you would rather take your chances at trial.

We need then to look for a settlement figure that is acceptable to each of the parties. Luckily, if they are prepared to settle the dispute and avoid the costs of trial, the parties do have the opportunity to find such a figure which is better for both parties than the expected values of taking the case to trial.

If both parties are prepared to negotiate a settlement in which the defendant pays out less then £1,586,400 and the claimant recovers more than £726,400, then they will both fare better than the average trial outcome for the given parameters.

---

20 Some call it the "net expected value" (NEV), but we prefer to use the term "expected value".

5.15.2 *Civil court claims*

The mid-point between the two expected value (EV) positions is a rational outcome for both sides that avoids the uncertainties and costs of a trial. The calculation for the mid-point, namely the amount to be paid by the defendant to the claimant, is:

Settlement mid-point = 0.5 × (EVc – EVd)

For our example:

Settlement mid-point = 0.5 × (£726,400 – –£1,586,400) = £1,156,400

For the defendant, this mid-point means that the defendant pays out £430,000 less than its economic valuation (–£1,586,400) and £1,039,600 less than his worst outcome at trial (–£2,196,000).

For the claimant, the mid-point means the claimant receives £1,156,400, which is £430,000 more than its economic valuation (£726,400) and avoids the uncertainties of full litigation that may lead to a loss of £696,000.

What you will see from this example is that each side gains by £430,000. The total gain to both parties is, therefore, £860,000. This is the total amount of legal expenditure and management costs which, on our example, could be avoided if the parties were to settle the case rather than take the case to trial. You could think of this as the "cake" to be split by the parties. As we have said, our view is that the most rational settlement is likely to be the mid-point, namely splitting the cake in half, if the parties have equal bargaining power.

It is very tempting to think that the splitting of the "cake" should reflect the probabilities of success of winning and making the expected recovery. So in our example, where the claimant has a 70% chance of success, it is tempting to think that she should receive £602,000 (£70%) of the £860,000 cake, meaning that it would be fair that the defendant pays a sum of £1,328,400 to the claimant to compromise the case. But we think that approach is not the right approach. This is for two reasons. Firstly, the probabilities (in this example, 70/30) are already built into the parties' expected values of their cases. Secondly, if one runs the figures in our examples through a full range of different probability scenarios, starting with a 0% chance of success to a 100% chance of success to the claimant and splits the "cake" according to those probabilities then one sees that at 0% chance of success the claimant would have to pay £696,000 to the defendant, and at 100% chance of success, the defendant would have to pay £2,196,000 to the claimant to settle the case. Neither of these alternatives are real alternatives to trial. They are, simply, the expected trial results when one thinks about either 0% or 100% chances of success for the claimant.

For the sake of simplicity, our example does presuppose that neither side has yet incurred recoverable costs that need to be factored into the expected values equations, and if you were doing these calculations for real, you would want to build those into the equation. But the point of setting out the example as we have is to enable you to understand that there is likely to be a windfall that is available for you and your opponent to split between you if you avoid further expenditure on lawyers and if you avoid spending further management time on the case: the "cake" to be split by the parties.

So far in this discussion, we have been looking at the expected values of a case where the victim claimant is able to make a full recovery from the wrongdoer-defendant. Unfortunately, many if not most fraud claims are not that straightforward. It is frequently the case that a victim-claimant will not be able to make a full recovery because the wrongdoer no longer has sufficient assets to satisfy the claim in full. Introducing the problem that the defendant no longer has the assets to satisfy a claim further worsens the claimant's outcome. We looked at this problem earlier (▷ *Figure 5.2*). To demonstrate how the expected values change, let's look again at *Figure 5.2*, which shows the cost benefit figures from the claimant's perspective where the maximum that the claimant can recover is £1,000,000.

We then need to compile the cost benefit schedule from the defendant's perspective.

Figure 5.6: Cost benefit schedule – defendant's perspective based on partial recovery from the defendant

	Cost if lose, £	**Court order if win, £**	**Gain if win, £**
Judgment debt recoverable	–1,000,000	–	–
Own legal costs	–380,000	266,000	–114,000
Intangible costs	–50,000	0	–50,000
Opponent's costs	–	–	–
Total	–1,430,000	266,000	–164,000
Chances of success / failure	70%	30%	

For this example, the expected value (EV) for the claimant is:

EVc = (£570,000 × 0.7) + (–£696,000 × 0.3) = +£190,200

The expected value (EV) for the defendant is:

EVd = (–£1,430,000 × 0.7) + (–£164,000 × 0.3) = –£1,050,200

You will see from these figures that the bargaining range collapses.

Bargaining range [limited assets, expected values trial basis]:

–£1,050,200 (defendant) to +£190,200 (claimant)

This means that, on average, a typical asset-poor trial defendant would face total wipe out and a typical claimant would recover a fraction of her claim. In these circumstances, a reasonable settlement enables the defendant to keep some meaningful assets and ensures that the claimant fares better than average at trial. In this example, the trial-avoidance "cake" to be split between the parties remains £860,000 and the settlement mid-point is:

Settlement mid-point = 0.5 × (£190,200 – –£1,050,200) = £620,200

With a sweep of the probabilities, the above examples show that the expected values modelling drastically reduces the value of a claim. Striking a deal at the mid-point may also appear unfair to an aggrieved victim. But the expected values modelling is logical, it is the rational point of settlement. Very often, legal disputes are about mitigating the losses caused by wrongdoers rather than full recovery. This is the reality of litigation and it is therefore right that it becomes the reality of a negotiation.

5.15.2 *Civil court claims*

The methods and examples introduced here are illustrative but also realistic. Their purpose is to encourage you to assess your case with a hard business head, both objectively and economically. Too often victims and defendants are far too optimistic, and too often lawyers fail to properly consider or properly explain risks and outcomes. The methods set out here give you some tools to engage your lawyers (and yourselves) in meaningful discussions about risks and recovery. Hopefully these tools will help you make informed decisions so that you avoid becoming one of the many litigants who only say, "I didn't realise", when it is too late.

There are too many other assumptions and variables that crop up in the variety of fraud cases to try and list them all in this guide. But here are some that you may have to consider in your case.

The likely recoveries from the defendant

We have already spent some time looking at this issue and shown you the difference between a case in which the claimant is likely to make a full recovery and one where she is likely to make just a partial recovery from the defendant of the sums which the court orders the defendant to pay. You may be faced with a range of possibilities when it comes to recovery. So long as you can arrive at sensible assumptions about these and the probabilities associated with each different level of recovery, it is possible to factor a number of probabilities into the expected value calculations.

Your probability assessments

You will be dependent on your lawyers for their advice on the probabilities of winning or losing the case (or achieving a best outcome versus a worst outcome). You can and should expect your lawyers to give you there assessments of the probabilities. Lawyers call this giving advice on the "merits" of a case. They are well used to giving such advice to clients but it is not an easy thing to do. Lawyers may tell you to expect a range of possible outcomes. For example, they may say that the chances of achieving a particular best outcome are between 50% and 70%. You'll then have to figure out your calculations from there. You also need to appreciate that lawyers can and do change their minds about the probabilities of winning and losing a case as a case progresses.

The wrongdoer's probability assessments

What you will not know is how your opponent thinks of his probability of success. You will not anything about the advice he or she may have received on chances of successfully defending against your case versus losing the case. That advice will be confidential to the wrongdoer, in the same way that the advice you receive is confidential to you. In a negotiation, the wrongdoer or its lawyers is likely to tell you that they do not accept your assessment of the probabilities and they may give you theirs. Of course, if you are right about the probabilities then you can proceed with confidence to use those probabilities to calculate values. But, right or wrong, you need to remember that the other side may be working to a different set of probabilities and you will have to figure that into compromise negotiations and any equations you formulate to calculate the expected value of the case to your opponent.

Appetites for risk

Although your opponent may have been advised that he has only a 30% chance of successfully defending against your claim, he may actually think those are really good odds! After all, if he is a career fraudster, he probably has a much bigger appetite for risk than an average person. The upshot of this is that even if it ought to be apparent to your opponent that the odds are stacked against him, he may not feel that way. Alternatively, the defendant may be terrified of being publicly exposed as a fraudster and so think that a 30% chance of being exposed is horrendous. Factored into this is the fear that the defendant may have that being publicly exposed would increase the risk that the police would take interest in the case and bring a prosecution.[21]

Multiple defendants

If you are suing more than one wrongdoer, you will need to factor that into your cost benefit analysis as well. Claiming against more than one fraudster typically *increases* your chances of winning and recovering assets because you have two or more targets. If you succeed against all wrongdoers, you would usually be entitled to judgment against them all on a joint and several liability basis, meaning that you can enforce against just one or all of them and choose which one you enforce against first (assuming that you do not want to bring simultaneous enforcement actions). And although you cannot make double recovery, the potential unfairness of it all as between the multiple fraudsters will not be your problem.

5.15.3 Methods and tips to reach compromise

> A fraud lawyer: "There are two important forces at play with settlement – commercial and emotional. The latter should not be underestimated. Fraud often involves betrayal of trust and dishonesty, causing anger and distress in victims which can make thoughts of settlement unpalatable. Here time is an important factor. Strong emotions can mellow after a while, and time tends to wear away the resolve of defendants to fight when the expensive and stressful reality of litigation becomes felt. With time, settlement can become a realistic option despite initial resistance from both sides. Also, where personal relationship existed before the fraud, mediation can be a cathartic experience for the victim, offering the opportunity for to make an informal statement telling their story, and have it heard by the perpetrator."

There are different ways in which you try to reach a compromise with your opponent. The main ones used are these:

- *Direct communication between you and your opponent.* There is no bar on your speaking with the person you consider to be the wrongdoer but beware of the fact that if he is a fraudster, he could be slippery and even just playing for time when speaking with you.
- *Direct communication between your lawyer and your opponent's lawyer.* This can be on the telephone, in a meeting or by emails or letters.

---

21 You will need to be advised on how best you can legitimately benefit from these fears that the wrongdoer is likely to have. But do not go thinking that you can effectively blackmail the wrongdoer into a compromise. You can't. And do not think that you can guarantee to the wrongdoer that you will not, for example, give evidence in any police investigation that is underway. You can't guarantee that.

- *Mediation.* The courts and the law generally encourage parties to consider mediation as a means of trying to reach a compromise of court disputes. In a mediation, the parties share the cost of appointing a neutral mediator (often but not always another lawyer) who then tries to mediate a compromise between the parties.

In each of these settings, when trying to compromise civil claims, the communications between the parties and between their advisers are what are called "without prejudice" communications.[22] This is a special status, meaning that the exchanges of information, offers and counter offers remain confidential to the parties and, as a general rule, neither party would be entitled to reveal those communications either to the outside world or to the court.

Exactly how and when you try to negotiate a conclusion to your case will be a matter for you to decide on based on the advice that you receive from your lawyers. Being in business, you may have strong ideas about how the negotiation should run and what proposals you should make to your opponent. That is a good thing as this is your case and you must have the final say in its outcome.

There are a number of things that you can and should think about and do to enhance your chance of getting a good deal. Most of these things are well known to experienced business people who are often expert negotiators. But we think that it is important to remind ourselves of them, given the complexities of a fraud case negotiation in which your emotions will run high and in which the wrongdoer may be prone to further bad behaviour:

- *Prepare.* Always prepare heavily for any negotiation. The truism that proper preparation prevents poor performance is true! The fact that you have been defrauded and think that you have the upper hand in the case does not mean that the negotiation will be easy. It is likely to be difficult. Have at your fingertips all the important information that you will need.
- *Create variables.* Be creative to create as many variables as you can think of that may be put into the deal. And think of which ones are most attractive to you and which ones are most attractive to the other side.
- *Value the variables.* Put values on all the possible variables. These will include the value of court judgments, your legal costs, the other side's legal costs, lost business opportunities if you spend more money and time on the case and anything else that will need to be factored into calculations.
- *The "cake".* Work out what the "cake" is that is up for a split between the parties. By creating variables (▷ *Section 5.15.2*), you may be able to enlarge the cake. But whether you can or can't, you must be clear and realistic about the composition and value of the "cake" that is up for division between the parties. The cake is your opportunity to find a win-win situation for both you and your opponent. (By win-win, we mean an outcome that is a good alternative to the uncertainty, cost and risk of going to trial.)
- *Red lines.* Decide on your red lines. You have to know what your walk-away point is going to be.

---

22 To be more precise, the full term used is "without prejudice save as to costs" because, if the case does not settle, the negotiations may be opened up to the court at the conclusion of a case for the court to judge the reasonableness of the parties' positions when the court is deciding what cost orders should be made.

- *Choose the negotiation setting*. Make sure that you will be comfortable at the negotiating table. If you want the wrongdoer-defendant to feel as comfortable as you then choose a neutral venue (neither your lawyers' nor his lawyers' offices).
- *Avoid grandstanding and attacking*. The start of a negotiation can be tricky. Emotions are running high and even the lawyers are primed to attack and defend. You must avoid making attacks. You must also avoid grandstanding or making sweeping generalisations or statements aimed at trying to show how powerful you are feeling in the negotiations. Attacking or grandstanding is more likely to lead to anger, resentment and intransigence on both sides, all of which will make it harder to remain at the bargaining table and harder to reach a compromise.
- *Build rapport*. Whatever you think of your opponent (the wrongdoer) and whatever you think of his lawyers, it is vital that you understand that you and your lawyers will need to build a rapport with the other side. You can start with small talk and go on to find whatever common ground you can, even if the only common ground is simply the desire to reach a rational settlement.
- *Listen*. There's a reason that you have two ears and only one mouth! Really listen to what the other side has to say. You may discover that they are interested in things that you had not thought about and which can increase the size of the "cake" or give you the opportunity to trade different things than you had planned to trade to reach an acceptable outcome.
- *Avoid being salami sliced*. This means, do not end up agreeing some things at the outset of the negotiation – such as the value of some, but not all, of the variables at play. The best rule of thumb is to be clear that nothing will be agreed until everything is agreed.
- *Discuss "interests"*. Initially, try to keep the negotiation focused on the interests of the parties and how both parties can make gains through the negotiations. Avoid making proposals and getting locked into negotiating positions until you have built a rapport, listened to your opponents and expressed your interests. You can agree with the other side that neither side will make any proposals until you are both happy that you have finished discussing your interests.
- *First proposal*. After you have finished discussing the parties' interests, aim to be the first to make a proposal. By doing that, you will create a benchmark that will be harder for the other side to deviate from too widely.
- *Ambitious but credible proposals*. Unless you are up against really foolish opponents (and that is not likely and you should never assume that) then the reality is that you are going to have to be credible with your proposals. This does not mean abandoning ambition and caving in. It just means being reasonable. A reasonable position should have the effect of drawing in your opponent and keeping him at the bargaining table. An unreasonable position is likely to have the opposite effect.
- *Smaller and smaller movements*. Both you and your opponent are likely to have to keep moving towards a settlement point. You need, however, to signal that you will not keep on moving indefinitely. The best way to do this is to make any movements you make smaller and smaller so that it becomes clear that you are unwilling to make any further significant movements.
- *"If you, then I"*. This is both a linguistic point and a strategic one. Experienced negotiators always use this formula of words. You should say, for example, "If you accept this, then I will accept that" rather than "I will accept this if you accept that". It's widely recognised that the "If you, then I" formula is more

assertive. It also serves to remind you that you should never make a movement without getting something in return.

- *Careful with ultimatums.* You can make ultimatums and your last and final offer may well be presented as an ultimatum. But be careful. They have the potential to blow up the negotiation if deployed too early.
- *Tough on the issues, not on the negotiators.* Whatever you think of your opponent and his lawyers, you need to hold back from letting rip with your feelings about them. Telling your opponent that he is an undeserving crook may be exactly what you want to do and may be 100% accurate. But it will not encourage compromise. If you are getting annoyed, suggest a break and go compose yourself.
- *Cool in the face of provocations.* Keep your cool if the other side misbehaves or launches into tirades against you. Keep calm and politely tell your opponent that you recognise he is being provocative and that it will not work. If you are feeling riled as a result, suggest a short break to compose yourself.
- *Final offers.* Final offers should be decisive, requiring just one last small movement from either side to reach a deal. You can present alternative choices but each of the choices must be clear and unambiguous and capable of resolving the whole dispute between the parties.

5.15.4 Getting a binding and effective compromise agreement

If and when you reach a deal with your opponent, it is essential that the lawyers who are involved in the negotiation are then able to express that deal in a written and binding form of agreement and / or court order that you can readily enforce. This is referred to as a "settlement agreement". Experienced lawyers know the value of a carefully and tightly worded settlement agreement that does not allow your opponent to wriggle off the hook after doing a deal.

It is obviously crucial that you actually get the settlement monies or other assets from the wrongdoer under the settlement agreement. One key tactic is to make sure that the freezing and proprietary injunctions remain in place until the fraudster complies with all the terms of the settlement agreement. It is also important to ensure the conclusion of your case against the defendant is dependent on his full compliance with the settlement agreement, entitling you (but not the defendant) to set aside the settlement agreement and revert to suing him if he does not comply with the settlement terms.

Warning: in cases involving more than one wrongdoer, if you reach a compromise with one or more but not all of the wrongdoers, it is very important that you do not damage your continuing claims against other wrongdoers. You will need legal advice on the settlement agreement's impact on any claims you may have against other wrongdoers, making sure that you preserve your rights against these other parties.

5.16 The steps leading to trial

To progress your case to trial, a number of basic stages will have to be dealt with and the court has a duty to actively manage your case to make sure that it progresses in good order. You and your lawyers have a duty to adhere to all the relevant procedural rules of the court (of which there are many) and the procedural orders made by the court in your case. Any failure by you to adhere to the rules and orders can have very serious effects as, if in breach, you may be barred from pursuing lines of claim or barred from recovering certain legal costs. Here are the most basic stages:[23]

- *Statements of case*: each party must explain in brief terms (or "plead") their case in written statements of case. The victim-claimant must prepare Particulars of Claim and each Defendant must prepare a Defence. The purpose of these statements is to provide each side with a good understanding of how the other side's case is presented. These documents include "statements of truth" which must be signed by parties or their lawyers confirming that the documents contain truthful assertions.
- *Case management conference hearing*: after the statements of case have been exchanged, all parties will be required to attend court for a so-called case management conference hearing (CMC). Prior to the hearing the parties' lawyers have to agree on a neutral but accurate short statement of the case as well as the issues that are in dispute and which will in due course have to be determined at the trial. Before the hearing, the parties also have to produce detailed cost budgets showing their estimated legal spends throughout the lifetime of the case.
- *Standard disclosure*: each party in the case is obliged to disclose all documents which may assist it to win its case and which may harm its prospects. This can be a very time-consuming and expensive stage in a case. It is open to parties to agree to dispense with this stage but you would need to be carefully advised about whether a dispensation is likely to work to your advantage. A fraud case will often throw up some really interesting and challenging issues. Your opponent may be refusing to hand over documents that he should disclose. He may attempt to destroy the incriminating evidence he holds. He may even present forged documents, leading to authenticity challenges on your part. Because you are alleging fraud, it is even possible that you may be able to force your opponent to hand over documents that passed between your opponent and his former lawyers to impugned transactions. All of which can lead to arguments and applications to the court seeking determination of issues surrounding the disclosure of documents.
- *Factual witness statements*: each party must put together and provide written statements of the witnesses that they intend to call to give evidence at the trial. These statements need to be comprehensive and to cross-refer to important documents (called "exhibits") which each party wishes to rely on to prove its case. The statements need to be comprehensive and very carefully worded because they will stand as so-called evidence-in-chief of the witnesses who have made those statements. Witness statements must be signed by the makers of the statements, with a declaration which confirms the accuracy of the information given in the witness statements.

23 There are other stages which may occur but to describe all contingencies is beyond the scope of this guide. One stage worth mentioning is the possibility of summary judgment. If the claimant believes the evidence shows that the alleged fraudster has *no realistic prospect* of success in defending all or part of the case, then the claimant can apply for what is known as summary judgment, which, if successful, would shorten proceedings. However, if unsuccessful, the effect is usually to lengthen proceedings.

- *Experts' reports*: each party will also divulge reports of experts they rely on (and in respect of which the court has given permission to deploy). There is a good deal of procedural law and practice concerning expert evidence which is beyond the scope of this guide.

> **Signpost**
>
> It is important to note that your lawyers can only offer limited assistance in preparing you for court. Lawyers may familiarise their witnesses with the process of giving evidence but, unlike TV courtroom dramas, they cannot coach them on its content. ▷ *Section 1*

5.17 Civil trial

> A fraud lawyer: "A well known QC announced to me and my client on the way to court that a fraud trial is like acting with animals and children, you don't know what the hell will happen. That wasn't particularly reassuring, but after the trial extended from one week to four as the other side called an additional eight witnesses, I took his point. (We won.)"

Before getting into a breakdown of the structure of a trial, we need to give you some health warnings about fraud trials generally.

When you arrive at trial, the posturing is over. The fight really begins. And despite the fact there are rules of trial, it will feel like a bare-knuckled, no-holds-barred fight! Each side will be pumped-up and ready to "have his day in court".

Your lawyers will have been working intensively for days, weeks or months ahead of the trial, preparing their opening statements and their cross-examination for your opponent and her witnesses. In fact, both sides' lawyers will have burned the midnight candle and will be expecting to live on a fair amount of adrenaline and fast food in the coming days, weeks (or even months!). It's a stressful business. As one lawyer described it: "A trial is a life shortening event!". That isn't to say that this stress is all negative. Good trial lawyers manage it well and can even thrive on it. What then about you?

It is really important that you prepare yourself for the stress of the trial. You too will be in the cauldron. You and others from your business may be giving evidence. In the final lead-up to the trial, your lawyers will be firing last-minute questions at you, and that is just a taste of what is to come when you give evidence. Your opponent is very likely to come up with some new or late-served evidence. She may make a late application to ask the judge to admit further lines of evidence, or to bar you from making certain arguments or relying on certain evidence.

It is important that you (and your lawyers) are conscious of the heated fraud trial atmosphere, as it is quite likely to affect both your lawyers' and your decision-making. You may hear a bluntness in your lawyers' views that you had not heard before. They may seem more interested in what the judge has to say than what you are thinking. A pumped-up lawyer may be less amenable to settlement just at a moment when you may be stressed out and keen on seeking a compromise.

> A fraud lawyer: "The trial is the pinnacle of the court proceedings. It involves hazards, possible surprises and potential reversals of fortunes. It is therefore very important to prepare the client for what to expect at trial. And for lawyers to prepare themselves as well!"

What then about the structure of the trial? Here, we also need to give you some health warnings.

Yes, trials are structured, and are the culmination of a fairly ordered timetable that leads up to trial. You will know the issues to be determined at trial that are set down in statements of case. You will be familiar with the evidence in witness statements supported by documents. Your lawyers will have told you what you can expect to be questioned about at trial. You will know how many days or weeks the trial is scheduled for. From all this, you will have pictured what the trial may look like and feel prepared for all eventualities. But then … the trial starts and much of that orderly nature flies out of the window. It is highly likely that the trial will deliver a number of surprises. To be prepared, you must expect the unexpected.

The trial of your civil case will be presided over by just one judge. He or she would listen to all the evidence in the case, the arguments and speeches of the advocates. In a trial there are set times when witnesses are called into court for questioning and there are set times when the advocates argue the cases of their respective clients.

> **Signpost**
>
> You should also be aware that whilst giving your evidence orally to the court (which may last a few days) you are in "purdah" which means you cannot speak to anyone about the case, including your own lawyers during court adjournments, whether lunch breaks or overnight. ⊳ *Section 1*

Subject to the many warnings that we have given about the unpredictability of trials, here is a simple view of what a trial will typically look like:

- Claimant's advocate makes a speech telling the judge what the case is about, goes through the key documents in the case and tells the judge which witnesses are coming to court to give oral evidence.
- Defendant's advocate may then do the same, explaining the case from the defendant's perspective (but in many cases the defendant does not take this opportunity at the start of the case).
- Claimant's advocate introduces ("calls") in turn each of the claimant's witnesses who have come to court, asking them to confirm the truth of their written statements.
- Defendant's advocate questions ("cross-examines") each of the claimant's witnesses after each is introduced.
- Claimant's advocate may question ("re-examine") each of the claimant's witnesses just in relation to anything new which has arisen from the defence advocate's questioning.

- Defendant's advocate introduces ("calls") in turn each of the defendant's witnesses who have come to court, asking them to confirm the truth of their written statements.
- Claimant's advocate questions ("cross-examines") each of the defendant's witnesses after each is introduced.
- Defendant's advocate may question ("re-examine") each of the defendant's witnesses just in relation to anything new which has arisen from the claimant's advocate's questioning.
- Claimant's advocate makes a closing speech, explaining the evidence that has been heard and considered and putting that together with the relevant legal principles to say why it is that the claimant's case has been successful in showing that the defendant engaged in the wrongdoing and should pay compensation etc.
- Defendant's advocate makes a closing speech, explaining the evidence and legal principles and saying why it is that the claimant has failed to show that the defendant is liable to pay compensation etc.
- Claimant's advocate makes a final speech just responding to the defendant's advocate's closing speech.

After the conclusion of the evidence and the arguments, the judge would then have to arrive at a judgment about who did what and when and whether the wrongdoer(s) are liable for their wrongdoing as alleged by you. And if so, how much compensation the wrongdoer(s) must pay or what other remedy you are entitled to (for example, a proprietary claim remedy).

It is possible that the judge would give an immediate judgment in favour of one party but in most cases the judge will adjourn your case and then spend a few days, weeks or months preparing a written judgment which explains his or her decisions. When the judgment is ready you would be called back to court for the judgment to be "handed down".

Finally, as a last step, after the judge has given judgment, the liabilities of the wrongdoer(s) would then have to be spelled out in an order of the court, ordering the wrongdoer(s) to make payment of compensation to you, or take such action as necessary to return property to you and so on. At the same time the court would make an award in relation to your entitlement to recover your legal costs from the losing party, but remember that would not recover all of those costs (⊳ *Section 3.11, Recoverability of costs in civil claims*).

If you have come this far and have an order of the court against the wrongdoer, you would then need to enforce that order.

5.18 Enforcing court orders

> A fraud lawyer: "Enforcement isn't the end of a case, it's the beginning, because if there's no recoverable asset, the rest is pointless."

If you win your case and have a court order in your favour, you will be entitled to enforce that order by various legal means. But before getting to enforcement, the wrongdoer will be given an opportunity to pay or observe the order of the court voluntarily.

In the case of monetary claims (▷ *Section 5.13, Monetary claims*), the person who is ordered to pay becomes a judgment debtor and is usually given two weeks to voluntarily pay the amount due. Where a defendant is ordered to do something, such as to return property to you, the defendant will be given a reasonable amount of time to do that.

If the person who has been made the subject of a court order refuses to comply with it voluntarily, then you would have to resort to legal enforcement methods.

For money judgments, you will be entitled to use one of these direct enforcement methods to enforce the court order. In each case you would need to seek and obtain the relevant enforcement order from the court:

- *Third party debt order*: having money held in the name of the wrongdoer in, for example, banks transferred to you.
- *Charging and possession and sale orders over land*: you will be entitled to "charge" and then take "possession" of land belonging to the wrongdoer in order to sell that land and realise the amount that you are owed under the court order.
- *Attachment of earnings*: amounts owed to you would be deducted and paid to you from an individual-wrongdoer's employment wages.
- *Bailiff*: a court-appointed bailiff would attend the wrongdoer's premises to seize personal property to sell in order to realise the amount owed to you.

If a person refuses to pay a money judgment within the allotted time, you are also entitled to bring insolvency proceedings against that person if his/her/its so-called centre of main interests (COMI) is in the UK.[24] If your opponent is an individual, you would be entitled to petition for his or her bankruptcy. If the judgment debtor is a company, you would be entitled to petition for its winding up. The absence of payment in either case means that you would almost certainly be successful and as a result the individual would be made bankrupt or the company would be wound up.

Signpost

You must appreciate that an "alternative fee arrangement" comes at a price. So, whilst a lawyer may be prepared to take the risk of never being paid on a case, he will only do so if you take the risk that you will have to pay him handsomely in the event of success. ▷ *Section 3*

An insolvency practitioner would then be appointed to collect in the debtor's assets to pay you as well as any other creditors of the insolvent person. This means that you have to share all available returns on asset realisations with all other unsecured creditors pro rata the amounts owed to you and the other creditors.

24 Insolvency law and practice is another specialist subject and what follows is just a very brief introduction.

This can be a serious disadvantage. Furthermore, even before making any returns to you and other creditors the insolvency practitioner(s) would be entitled to be paid for their professional services out of the liquidated assets. Their fees can really mount up and they are the first in the queue. Secured creditors, typically banks and mortgage lenders, are second in line. You and other unsecured creditors are all at the tail end and any residual is shared out pro rata with the amount owed to each creditor.

Proprietary claims have a distinct advantage over monetary claims in insolvency and bankruptcy. Proprietary court orders instruct the relevant person(s) to return to you the specific property which is yours. This is important. It is your property and is not regarded as part of the assets of the bankrupt person or insolvent company. Therefore no other creditor has claim over it and it cannot be shared out amongst the creditors, whether they are secured or not.[25] Under these circumstances the court orders the fraudster to return the real property to you. When a fraudster has transferred the property to another person, typically a spouse, the court can order that person to return your property to you. Any refusal to obey such a court order would be contempt of court.[26]

The hardest enforcement cases are, generally, those in which the wrongdoers have transferred assets to many recipients and / or to recipients and locations overseas.

In large cases, it is common for victims to engage lawyers in other countries (or "jurisdictions") to find assets and then bring enforcement cases in those overseas locations. We briefly deal with this type of international enforcement in *Section 7.5, UK-based victims seeking help from overseas jurisdictions*.

Even in smaller cases involving a stubborn or evasive judgment debtor, you may have to go back to court for assistance in forcing the defendant to reveal the whereabouts of property, to answer questions about assets and so on.[27]

Until a defendant has paid money due from him or has returned or made available property which is the subject of a proprietary order, the defendant would remain subject to an appropriate form of freezing injunction or proprietary injunction (▷ *Section 4.8, Freezing injunctions* and ▷ *Section 4.9, Proprietary injunctions*).

5.19 Conclusions

Given the complexity of the law, it is important that you do not have too many fixed ideas about what kind of case you can or cannot bring before you take and receive expert help in identifying and formulating claims that are likely to succeed and best meet your objectives in winning a case against wrongdoers.

Although well short of an in-depth look at the law of civil-court fraud claims, this guide should at least help you to understand the advice you receive from your lawyers and to follow what is said and decided in court hearings.

---

25 The only exception to this is when a creditor has a secured interest over the same asset, such as a mortgage over a house in which the claimant has a proprietary right.

26 Contempt of court is punishable by up to two years in prison and/or a fine or so-called "sequestration" of assets of the person in contempt. The subject of contempt involves some fairly complex substantive and procedural law and is beyond the scope of this guide.

27 The relevant procedures for this are beyond the scope of this guide.

Having some knowledge should help you to make better choices and decisions. It will help you to query and probe the advice you receive and fully engage with the legal claims you choose to bring. This last point is really important.

If and when you choose to bring civil-court claims against wrongdoers, you must remain fully engaged at all times. If not, then your case will begin to drift, and guess who will notice that? Your opponent, the wrongdoer, will be the first to notice, and after that, so too will the court.

Remaining fully engaged means remaining in the driving seat at all times and keeping the wrongdoers on the back foot. This not only requires full engagement with the court process but it also means proper preparation of your claims and proper preparation of your evidence that you deploy in your claims.

Proper preparation also means careful cost budgeting at the start and throughout your case, so that you have enough money to pay your lawyers at each stage of the case and do not end up stalling and causing delays and do not get outgunned by the wrongdoer who may also be using and paying for lawyers.

Lastly, do think about the eventuality of a trial and how you will prove to the court that you are right and your opponent did wrong. Think carefully about how you will prove to the court the level of your losses as a result of the wrongdoing. And be prepared to compromise your claims if and when the right opportunity comes.

Criminal investigations and criminal court prosecutions

6.1 In this section

- Criminal fraud
- Bribery
- Cyber crimes
- Compensation order
- Restitution orders
- Reporting fraud
- Police and prosecutors
- Police priorities
- Private prosecutions
- Prosecution process
- Trial

6.2 Introduction

If you're reading this section, you've either decided that a police-led investigation and state-sponsored prosecution is for you or perhaps you are just still trying to work out what you want to do and so are reading this section for more information.

Our aim in this section, is to explain, briefly, what amounts to a crime of fraud and what amounts to a crime of bribery, describe the way in which these cases are dealt with by the public agencies and the criminal justice system in general and set out what, if any, financial reparations you can expect to secure through the criminal courts.

Financial reparations are very important to most victims of fraud. One study has shown that 97% of victims want financial reparations.[1] Given their importance to victims we will spend a good deal of this section dealing with the criminal courts' powers to award compensation and restitution to victims of fraud.

Complaining to the police or the Serious Fraud Office (SFO) and asking them to investigate your case is free. Free in the sense that you will not have to pay the public authorities or the criminal courts a penny.

The reality is, however, that if you do wish to have your case investigated and prosecuted, your chances of getting this to happen are likely to be improved if you have a lawyer helping you in preparing your evidence and in liaising with the police and prosecutors.

---

1 Button, M., Tapley, J. and Lewis, C. (2013), "The 'fraud justice network' and the infra-structure of support for individual fraud victims in England and Wales" *Criminology and Criminal Justice, 13*(1), 37–61.

6.3 Private prosecutions

If you are thinking of bringing your own private prosecution of a wrongdoer, then you should find much of this section useful as a start to understanding how things work in criminal justice. It can only be a start as it would be essential that you engage a lawyer to advise you on the correct allegations to make and to present your case in court.

If you want to bring a private prosecution you would have to know a lot more than is in this guide because of the heavy responsibilities which are placed on private prosecutors.

You also need to know that the powers of investigation which are available to public investigators (police and SFO) are largely unavailable to you. For example, you cannot carry out dawn raids and arrests. Nor are you able to obtain restraint orders in support of the private prosecution unless and until you actually launch a court case and given that the investigation and preparation for the prosecution may take a considerable amount of time, you may miss out on freezing assets held by the wrongdoer.

> **Signpost**
>
> Private prosecutions require a good deal of expertise and resources. To win, you must comply with the same procedural and evidential laws and rules that govern the conduct of the police and public prosecutors. You must also prove your case to the criminal standard of proof. You may not have the same resources which the state can muster to investigate and prosecute a fraud; nor will you have all of its powers. ⊳ *Section 2*

You also need to know that bringing a private prosecution will cost you money, even if you are entitled to be reimbursed some of your expenses (⊳ *Section 3.13, Recoverability of costs in private prosecutions*).

6.4 What is criminal fraud?

We set out here the ingredients that go to make up a criminal offence of fraud under the Fraud Act 2006.[2] There are three main kinds of fraud criminalised by this Act. In all cases, a person would only be guilty of the conduct, if he or she also had a dishonest state of mind.[3]

> **Signpost**
>
> It is not legitimate to use criminal investigation and prosecution for the purpose of putting pressure on the wrongdoer to reach a financial settlement with you. If you threaten or ring a prosecution you must be prepared to see that through to the end. ⊳ *Section 2*

2 There are other kinds of criminal offences which could come under the fraud umbrella but those are beyond the scope of this guide.

3 A discussion of the meaning of dishonesty for the purposes of the Fraud Act 2006 is beyond the scope of this guide.

6.4.1 Fraud by false representation

Here are the statutory ingredients for this offence:[4]

"(1) A person is in breach of this section if he–
(a) dishonestly makes a false representation, and
(b) intends, by making the representation–
(i) to make a gain for himself or another, or
(ii) to cause loss to another or to expose another to a risk of loss.

(2) A representation is false if–
(a) it is untrue or misleading, and
(b) the person making it knows that it is, or might be, untrue or misleading.

(3) 'Representation' means any representation as to fact or law, including a representation as to the state of mind of–
(a) the person making the representation, or
(b) any other person.

(4) A representation may be express or implied.

(5) For the purposes of this section a representation may be regarded as made if it (or anything implying it) is submitted in any form to any system or device designed to receive, convey or respond to communications (with or without human intervention).

What sorts of representations can form the basis of this offence? Clearly, expressly spoken or written false representations are included, such as:

- a verbal or written demand for a payment which the wrongdoer knows he is not legally entitled to;
- a statement that 1,000 pallets of goods were delivered when the maker of the statement knows that only 900 were shipped; or
- a promise to repay a loan if granted, when in fact the borrower has no intention of repaying it.

The provision states that they need not be expressly spoken or written by the wrongdoer but can also be implied by his conduct. Here are some examples of implied representations:

- Tendering payment with a cheque knowing that it will be dishonoured.
- Tendering payment with a stolen or forged cheque or payment card.
- Showing a forged pass to gain entry to a building site with the intention of then stealing goods from the site.

---

4 Section 2 of the Fraud Act 2006.

> **Signpost**
>
> The very fact that you have brought criminal proceedings may make the wrongdoer and his associates fight harder than they would had you just brought a civil claim. Threatened with prison for himself and others (for example, a spouse) he has strong incentives to think creatively to come up with a defence and little incentive to capitulate or reach a compromise with you. ⊳ *Section 2*

6.4.2 Fraud by failing to disclose information

Here are the statutory ingredients for this offence:[5]

> "A person is in breach of this section if he–
> (a) dishonestly fails to disclose to another person information which he is under a legal duty to disclose, and
> (b) intends, by failing to disclose the information–
> (i) to make a gain for himself or another, or
> (ii) to cause loss to another or to expose another to a risk of loss."

The key to this offence is that there must be a "legal duty to disclose" information which a person fails to honour. Legal duties of disclosure can occur in a number of ways:

- It may be a requirement of a contract that a person must provide certain information at relevant times. For example, an agent-distributor of your goods may be under a duty to keep you informed of the quantity of goods which have been sold so as to entitle you to payment of the sums arising from those sales.
- Persons entrusted with responsibilities such as directors and agents will often have duties to report information. For example, a director will have duties to report suspicions of fraud committed by other persons within a company and a failure to do so would be a failure of that legal duty.
- A director of a company will also be under a legal duty to report to the company any personal interest he has in a transaction entered into by the company.

6.4.3 Fraud by abuse of position

Here are the statutory ingredients for this offence:[6]

> "(1) A person is in breach of this section if he–
> (a) occupies a position in which he is expected to safeguard, or not to act against, the financial interests of another person,
> (b) dishonestly abuses that position, and
> (c) intends, by means of the abuse of that position–
> (i) to make a gain for himself or another, or
> (ii) to cause loss to another or to expose another to a risk of loss.
>
> (2) A person may be regarded as having abused his position even though his conduct consisted of an omission rather than an act."

---

5 Section 3 of the Fraud Act 2006.
6 Section 4 of the Fraud Act 2006.

The essence of this offence is that a person has a position of trust which he then abuses. Here are some examples of conduct, if coupled with dishonesty, which would amount to an offence by a director, partner, agent or employee:

- Secretly becoming financially interested in a supplier-business to the principal company or partnership.
- Misappropriation of company or partnership assets, such as money in bank accounts or company stock.
- Theft or cloning of confidential information.
- Leaking confidential information to a rival business.
- Accepting a bribe (there is also a separate offence of bribery – ⊳ *Section 6.5, Bribery*).
- Failing to pursue a business opportunity so as to enable himself to pursue it as a personal opportunity.

Signpost

The police and prosecutors focus on the offenders with the aim of obtaining the minimum evidence required to first secure guilty verdicts and then proportionate sentences, all at the lowest cost. Their main interest in the damage caused to the victim is limited to these ends; it is not to fully quantify victims' losses. ⊳ *Section 1*

6.4.4 Gain or loss

What amounts to a gain or loss for the purpose of the three main Fraud Act offences? Here is what the statutory provision says:[7]

> "(2) 'Gain' and 'loss'–
> (a) extend only to gain or loss in money or other property;
> (b) include any such gain or loss whether temporary or permanent;
>
> and 'property' means any property whether real or personal (including things in action and other intangible property).
>
> (3) 'Gain' includes a gain by keeping what one has, as well as a gain by getting what one does not have.
>
> (4) 'Loss' includes a loss by not getting what one might get, as well as a loss by parting with what one has."

6.5 Bribery

Bribery (often referred to as "corruption") is a key feature of many cases affecting business. That is because in many cases fraud on a business is an "inside job". In the case of bribery, an outsider will have corrupted the insider (or perhaps the other way around) to carry out the fraud on the business.

---

7 Section 5 of the Fraud Act 2006.

The Bribery Act 2010 makes very clear what will amount to an offence of bribery. The offences are, broadly-speaking, split into two main categories. Firstly, offences of giving bribes; and, secondly, offences of receiving bribes. We concentrate here on the kinds of bribery which are mostly likely to cause loss to a company.[8]

6.5.1 Bribing another person

Under the Bribery Act 2010:[9]

> "A person ('P') is guilty of an offence … where–
> (a) P offers, promises or gives a financial or other advantage to another person, and
> (b) P intends the advantage–
> (i) to induce a person to perform improperly a relevant function or activity, or
> (ii) to reward a person for the improper performance of such a function or activity."

As can be seen from the words in the statute, the essence of the offence is the inducement or rewarding of another for the improper performance of that person's "relevant function or activity". The definition of "function or activity" includes "any activity connected with a business" which would certainly encompass the functions and activities of directors, employees and agents.

A giver of an advantage is guilty if he "intends" that it will have the unlawful effect. There is no need to prove "dishonesty" on the part of the wrongdoer, although this of course may be an appropriate description of his or her conduct. This intention is usually inferred from the secrecy of the payment and the effect that it has.

Here are some examples of bribery:

- Paying a procurement director in money or in kind so as to sell more or sell at higher prices to his company.
- Providing excessive hospitality (e.g. shopping trips, use of a holiday home) to a sales person in order to obtain his company's products or services at cheaper rates.
- Giving gifts to an HR director so as to obtain a better employment package or payoff.
- Promising the recipient a new job; for example, secretly promising a director a renewed role if he facilitates a takeover bid of his company.

6.5.2 Receiving a bribe

Under the Bribery Act 2010:[10]

> "(1) A person ('R') is guilty of an offence if any of the following cases applies.

---

8 We do not deal with the offences of bribery of public officials.

9 Only part of section 1 of the Bribery Act 2010 is reproduced here. Omitted is the case 2 "facilitation" offence which is of less relevance to victims of fraud in the UK.

10 Only part of section 2 of the Bribery Act 2010 is reproduced here. Omitted is the case 4 "facilitation" offence which is of less relevance to victims of fraud in the UK.

(2) Case 3 is where R requests, agrees to receive or accepts a financial or other advantage intending that, in consequence, a relevant function or activity should be performed improperly (whether by R or another person).

...

(4) Case 5 is where R requests, agrees to receive or accepts a financial or other advantage as a reward for the improper performance (whether by R or another person) of a relevant function or activity.

(5) Case 6 is where, in anticipation of or in consequence of R requesting, agreeing to receive or accepting a financial or other advantage, a relevant function or activity is performed improperly–

(a) by R, or

(b) by another person at R's request or with R's assent or acquiescence.

(6) In cases 3 to 6 it does not matter–

(a) whether R requests, agrees to receive or accepts (or is to request, agree to receive or accept) the advantage directly or through a third party,

(b) whether the advantage is (or is to be) for the benefit of R or another person.

(7) In cases 4 to 6 it does not matter whether R knows or believes that the performance of the function or activity is improper.

(8) In case 6, where a person other than R is performing the function or activity, it also does not matter whether that person knows or believes that the performance of the function or activity is improper."

In summary, the law criminalises receipts (or anticipated receipts) of advantages which are conferred on a person (or which are anticipated to be received by a person) in return for the improper performance of that person's function or activity (or those of another person).

6.6 Cyber crimes

Cyber crimes are prosecuted using three key sections of the Computer Misuse Act 1990. All three sections are concerned with hacking type crimes. Sections 1 and 3 address cyber-dependent hacking crimes, and section 2 deals with cyber-enabling hacking. However, these hacking laws are very rarely used. Prosecutions are most often brought for the underlying offences, such as fraud or theft, and not for the use of computers in those offences (⊳ *Section 1.4, What is fraud?*).

6.6.1 Theft of money in bank accounts and other intangible property

One of the most important criminal offences for victims of acquisitive cyber crime became law long before the advent of modern computing. It is plain simple theft under the Theft Act 1968. The offence of theft[11] applies to all forms of property, both tangible and intangible. "Property" (for the purpose of the theft offence) "includes

11 Set out in section 1 of the Theft Act 1968.

money and all other property, real or personal, including things in action and other intangible property". A "thing in action" includes money in a bank account. Intangible property includes intellectual property, such as copyright materials.

6.6.2 Unauthorised access to computer material

Under section 1 of the Computer Misuse Act 1990, a person is guilty of the "unauthorised access offence" if:

- he causes a computer to perform any function with intent to secure access to any program or data held in any computer, or to enable any such access to be secured;
- the access he intends to secure, or to enable to be secured, is unauthorised; and
- he knows at the time when he causes the computer to perform the function that that is the case.

The courts have dealt with the question as to the authority an employee has and decided that an employee can be guilty of this offence if the employer has clearly defined the limits of the employee's access to programs and data held by the employer.

The courts have dealt with the question as to the authority an employee has and decided that an unauthorised access prosecution can only be sustained if the employer has clearly defined limits on the employee's access to programs and data. This is important because an employee can only be guilty of the unauthorised access offence if he breaches these clearly defined authorisation rules to gain access to programs or data.

6.6.3 Unauthorised access with intent to commit or facilitate commission of further offences

Under section 2 of the Act, a person is guilty of the unauthorised access with intent offence if he commits the unauthorised access offence with intent:

- to commit an offence to which this section applies; or
- to facilitate the commission of such an offence (whether by himself or by any other person).

An offence under this section is defined very widely and would certainly include offences such as fraud, theft of a credit balance in a bank account, and blackmail.

6.6.4 Unauthorised acts with intent to impair, or with recklessness as to impairing, operation of computer, etc

The purpose of section 3 of the Act is to criminalise conduct such as distributed denial of service attacks which disable a victim's computer system, as well as other attacks. The legal provision reads:

A person is guilty of an offence if:

- he does any unauthorised act in relation to a computer;
- at the time when he does the act he knows that it is unauthorised; and

- either the person intends by doing the act to:
  - impair the operation of any computer;
  - prevent or hinder access to any program or data held in any computer;
  - impair the operation of any such program or the reliability of any such data; or
  - enable any of the above to be done;
- or the person is reckless as to whether the act will do any of those things.

6.7 Compensation orders and restitution orders

Victims of fraud frequently are unaware that the criminal courts can order the convicted wrongdoers to award them compensation or restitution. Even police officers and prosecutors can be unfamiliar with these court powers.

We introduced these concepts earlier (▷ *Section 2.7, Complain to the police*). In this section, we will expand on both compensation and restitution. But before we get into too much detail, it is worth reminding ourselves of the basics.

A compensation order is a court order which requires the convicted wrongdoer to pay a sum of money to the victim of his offending whether or not the assets available to the wrongdoer derive from his offence against the victim. Although criminal courts are obliged to consider making compensation orders, on current interpretation of the law, victims have no right to address a court (either themselves or through a lawyer) and no right to seek a judicial review a court's refusal to make a compensation order. We think that this is a bad state of affairs and overdue for challenge and change.

A restitution order is also a financial order but is focused on restoration of victim's property to the victim. This can be the property which was "stolen" (which includes property extracted by fraud) from the victim but can also be personal property[12] which "represents" the original property which was fraudulently extracted from the victim. So, if a fraudster uses fraudulently obtained money to buy shares he can be ordered to hand over those investments to the victim.

The really interesting thing for victims who have a restitution claim is that they do have the right to address the criminal court (themselves or through a lawyer) when seeking a restitution order. Very few victims are aware of their rights to claim restitution through the criminal courts. In fact, very few lawyers are aware of this.

Crown Prosecution Service (CPS) guidance states that "… compensation orders should only be made in simple straightforward cases", and the courts should only make restitution orders in "the plainest of cases".[13] We do not think that these approaches are helpful or right for victims. But the CPS are correct to say that they are current principles that guide courts in their decision-making; albeit that the courts do appear poised to modify their traditional approach – as we set out below.

As a result, you must beware that that the criminal court may not declare itself competent to deal with compensation or restitution in your case unless you have a really "straightforward" case for compensation which does not lead to argument over

12 This cannot include land which is outside the scope of restitution orders.
13 www.cps.gov.uk/legal/s_to_u/sentencing_and_ancillary_orders_applications/#a01.

the amount of your losses etc; or the "plainest" case for restitution which does not involve complicated arguments concerning your entitlement to restitution.

Signpost

Civil proceedings are usually faster and cheaper than criminal proceedings and, given the lower standard of proof required for success, are easier to win. ⊳ *Section 2*

We need to stress – and will continue to stress – that if you are pinning your hopes on obtaining compensation or restitution from the criminal courts, you need to be very cautious in doing so: the criminal justice system does not have a great record when it comes to delivering adequate compensation to victims of fraud.

Now, with those warnings in place, let's take a closer look at compensation orders and restitution orders.

6.7.1 Compensation orders

The power of the criminal courts to make compensation awards is contained in a statute, the Powers of Criminal Courts (Sentencing) Act 2000. Section 130 of that Act states that:

> "A court [when dealing with a person convicted of a criminal offence] may make an order … requiring him … to pay compensation for any … loss or damage resulting from that offence or any other offence which is taken into consideration by the court in determining sentence.
>
> A court must consider making a compensation order in any case where this section empowers it to do so.
>
> A court shall give reasons, on passing sentence, if it does not make a compensation order in a case where this section empowers it to do so.
>
> Compensation … shall be of such amount as the court considers appropriate, having regard to any evidence and to any representations that are made by or on behalf of the accused or the prosecutor."

Theoretically there is no limit to the amount of compensation the criminal courts can award but case law has limited the amount which can be awarded to the maximums which would be available through the civil courts (⊳ *Section 5.4, Valuing your claims*).

If you are pinning your hopes on a criminal court compensation order, you will need to strike a balance between being ambitious about the amount you can and should claim for your losses and being realistic and trying to keep the explanation and calculation of your losses as simple as possible.

As we have set out in an earlier section of this guide (⊳ *Section 2.7.1, Criminal compensation orders*), the traditional approach of the courts has been to avoid dealing with complexity when it comes to deciding on entitlement to compensation or the appropriate amount to order.

In essence, the criminal courts have, historically, been encouraged to deal only with "simple, straightforward" cases. This is particularly disadvantageous for victims of fraud, given that establishing a loss and its amount will often not be simple and straightforward.

The justification for this approach is that the criminal courts lack sufficient competency and resources to deal with complex questions of compensation which are best left to the civil courts.

In recent years there have been signs that the criminal courts will start to take a different attitude to more complex cases of compensation. Particularly helpful are two Court of Appeal cases in which the Court decided that it is right for criminal courts to compensate victims even in complex cases, particularly if the civil-court route would be unrealistic, impractical or unaffordable.

There are some other limitations with compensation order powers:

- Victims have no right to be heard by the criminal courts in respect of requests for compensation. This means that they have no right to address courts or to ask lawyers to do so. Which means that they have no direct voice in relation to compensation.
- Victims are reliant on compensation being pursued for them by the police and prosecutors involved in their case. Victims will often have to push for what they want and deserve; and we say more about doing that later in this section.
- In some cases, either wrong or inadequate criminal charges are brought leaving victims little or no hope of appropriate levels of compensation (if any) through the criminal courts even if persons are convicted.
- A court cannot make a compensation order unless the defendant has the means to pay it.
- Defendants should not be required to pay compensation if it requires sale of an asset where there may be difficulty in selling the asset.
- An order the payment of which would require the sale of a family home may not be made.
- A defendant will often have dissipated his assets or spent them on living expenses before the conclusion of a criminal trial and / or before enforcement of any compensation order against the fraudster.
- The criminal courts are not entitled to freeze wrongdoers' assets during the currency of the criminal case to secure assets for a potential compensation order. The freezing of assets will only occur if the court issues a restraint order designed to secure assets to meet a potential confiscation order which may be made in due course (see more about those below).
- If police and prosecutors do not obtain restraint orders or are late obtaining restraint orders then assets will not have been secured.
- Even if a compensation order is made, the victim is reliant upon the Magistrates' Court's enforcement of that order (even if the order had been made by the Crown Court) and many defendants string out payments or try to avoid making payments altogether.
- The courts have no power to bankrupt a defendant who refuses to pay a compensation order.
- The Magistrates' Court's strongest enforcement tool – the threat of imprisoning a person who fails to pay a compensation order – is actually a double-edged

sword. This is because a person who serves such a sentence would no longer have to pay the compensation order.

- International enforcement of compensation orders is complex and uncertain as enforcement has to be through official requests which would have to be made by the Magistrates' Court to overseas authorities and courts (▷ *Section 7.5.5, Enforcing E & W criminal compensation orders overseas*).

None of this is meant to try and put you off the criminal justice system. It can and has worked very well for some victims of fraud. It also offers you the opportunity to see wrongdoers sent to prison or otherwise punished if that is important to you. We just feel that it is necessary to give you some realities about the system and will give you a few more throughout this section.

Signpost

Most victims do not seek help from lawyers when making complaints to the police. But some do and in fraud cases this can make a big difference to the likely outcome, particularly in relation to criminal court awards of compensation or restitution. ▷ *Section 2*

6.7.2 Restitution orders

The power of the criminal courts to make restitution awards to victims is contained in a statute, the Powers of Criminal Courts (Sentencing) Act 2000. Section 148 of the Act empowers a criminal court to make a restitution order after a person has been convicted of a criminal offence of theft, blackmail or fraud or where such an offence is taken into consideration in determining his sentence. Significantly, criminal court restitution is not available in the case of a conviction for bribery.

In essence, the criminal courts are able to order that "goods" (defined as including money and intangible property, such as rights to credit balances in bank accounts, but not land) be restored to victims. The three powers available to the criminal courts are:

- the court may order anyone having possession or control of the stolen or fraudulently extracted goods to restore them to any person entitled to recover them from him;
- the court may order any other goods which represent (directly or indirectly) the goods stolen or fraudulently extracted from the victim to be restored by the convicted offender to the victim; and
- the court may order that the convicted offender pay a sum of money from any money taken from his possession on his apprehension.

The second of these powers is potentially the most useful to victims of fraud. This is because most victims lose money and most offenders move that money or "invest" or spend it on other goods which then "represent" the original money.

This power allows victims to ask for restitution of those other goods. It can be used for the return of money in bank accounts, shares, cars and other "goods" which the offender has in his possession or under his control. Unfortunately, it does not allow for restitution of land if that is what the victim's money has been spent on.

Just what can be said to "represent" an asset which was originally stolen or extracted by fraud is not spelled out by the law and the criminal courts have developed no case law to help us interpret the court's statutory power. It is, we think, likely that the criminal courts would utilise thinking from the civil courts, in particular the way in which the civil courts will, in proprietary claims, allow a victim to trace and seek restitution of assets from one form to another (▷ *Section 5.11, Proprietary claims*).

The fact that a court has multiple powers does not mean that victims can obtain multiple orders restoring more than they lost in the first place. You'll remember the civil courts have the same approach on this (▷ *Section 5.14, Overlapping and alternative claims*).

The first of the powers, in which the court can order the return of stolen or fraudulently extracted "goods" (including money), is not limited to restoration from the convicted offender. If he has passed the goods on to another person, then the court can also order that other person to restore them to the victim.

Signpost

It is critical that you are aware of, and that you evaluate, all of your choices as early as possible. A failure in this regard is often not the fault of the victim but it is frequently the biggest cause of problems and regret later on. ▷ *Section 2*

In contrast to compensation proceedings, victims do have the right to apply to court for a restitution order, meaning that they (and their lawyers) have the right to address the court to ask for restitution. This is a very significant and important right, which gives the victim a real opportunity to directly influence the court's decision-making in relation to reparation for the victim.

When considering making a restitution order, the court can (and can only) make an order based on the information it received in the form of the evidence that was deployed during the trial of the offender or which was prepared for that use.

This means that the court cannot receive new evidence after the conclusion of the trial and so victims must ensure that all relevant evidence as to what property needs to be restored and who possesses or controls that property is used or available to the court and to the accused person before or during the trial.

Enforcement of a restitution order is not straightforward. Contempt of court proceedings do allow the court to punish or threaten punishment in order to coerce the fraudster into complying with the order. The punishment can be a prison sentence of up to two years, a fine or the sequestration of assets held by the wrongdoer.

Signpost

When things work well with the police and the CPS, they work very well. Both organisations have substantial state-funded resources which can be used well. In addition, both have very strong legal powers which are rightly feared by wrongdoers. ▷ *Section 2*

6.7.3 Seeking compensation and restitution

Your lawyers will advise you on the best time to make your request for compensation and / or application for restitution. You will need to start thinking about your needs and wishes as soon as you engage with the police at the outset of making a criminal complaint.

As a victim, you have every right to expect the police to make themselves aware of your needs and wishes for financial reparation. They ought to know whether you intend to bring civil proceedings to run in parallel with their criminal case. The police also ought to be interested in knowing whether you would like the criminal court to award you compensation or restitution.

We have used "ought" here because the reality is that police understanding and appreciation of victims' needs and wishes for financial reparation is patchy and inconsistent. Some officers have a decent grasp of the issues, whilst others barely understand the victim's needs and opportunities. Unfortunately, there have been and will continue to be cases where victim's needs for financial reparation are not adequately appreciated by the police.

Worse still, there is a risk that the police will have other priorities, not least because they operate under targets to obtain financial orders – known as "confiscation orders" – for the benefit of the state rather than victims. Indeed, it may well be a policy of the police force that would deal with your case to favour prosecuting cases that give them the opportunity to obtain confiscation or forfeiture orders in favour of the state (see more about that below in relation to police priorities). That problem was highlighted by an academic study in which one fraud officer quoted a neighbouring police force:[14]

> "...we'll only do the ones where we don't have an identified victim, because, we get to keep the money, if you've got a victim and the victim is going to get the money, then, we're not interested."

If you do wish to pursue the possibility of compensation or restitution through the criminal courts, then your lawyer will be able to help manage this aspect for you in contact with the police and prosecutors. We think that lawyers can and do make a real difference for victims:

- Firstly, lawyers can be assertive on behalf of victims whilst still leaving the police-victim relationship on good terms.
- Secondly, lawyers can liaise with police and prosecutors to try and steer the police investigation to meet the financial reparation needs of the victim and with the hope of avoiding the possibility that the incorrect criminal charges are brought.
- Thirdly, lawyers can answer questions posed by the police and prosecutors in relation to the victim's rights and needs.
- Fourthly, lawyers can pull together a good case for compensation or restitution, including the evidence which supports it and at the same time explain that case in the simplest possible terms to maximise its chance of success.

---

14 Button, M., Lewis, C., Shepherd, D., Brooks, G. and Wakefield, A., *Fraud and punishment: enhancing deterrence through more effective sanctions* (2012, Portsmouth: UoP).

You will have to ensure that the evidence on which you base your case for compensation or restitution is made available to the police and prosecutors and that they make that evidence available to the wrongdoer and the criminal court.

Obviously, any request or application you make for compensation or restitution will be pending any trial of the accused and contingent on conviction. And so, you will need to be sure that you have supported the case for criminal liability as well as your case for financial reparation.

> **Signpost**
>
> It may be possible to hire lawyers under alternative "no-win-no-fee" or "no-win-low-fee" arrangements. It may also be possible to obtain funding from companies which specialise in litigation funding. ▷ *Section 3*

6.8 Structure of fraud policing in E & W

There was a time when a member of the public simply reported fraud to the local police or to the SFO. However, this has fundamentally changed. In response to the proliferation and scale of fraud threats, a national intelligence-led approach to policing fraud has emerged. The primary purpose of this approach is to identify and target specific threats, especially organised crime gangs. Different law enforcement authorities do different things. Here is a summary of the main authorities:

- *Action Fraud.*[15] Members of the public are now required to report fraud complaints to a national reporting centre, Action Fraud. This is a call centre-type service supervised by the City of London Police (CoLP). It passes on genuine fraud reports to the National Fraud Intelligence Bureau. The public can call the police, but they will almost always be re-directed to Action Fraud.
- *National Fraud Intelligence Bureau (NFIB).*[16] The NFIB also sits within the CoLP. It assesses the reports processed by Action Fraud and selects cases for action by the appropriate police force. It prioritises more serious cases and those involving crime gangs.
- *Police forces.* Nowadays, frauds are investigated by police Economic Crime Units (ECUs), which used to be called Fraud Squads. The great majority of the case load comes from the NFIB. The police will nearly always re-direct reports to Action Fraud. The police will respond to the public under exceptional circumstances, when a report complies with so-called "call for service" criteria. In practice this means the police will only respond to direct reports if the fraudster is in the act of committing the crime and intervention is required, the victim is vulnerable and needs support, or the case is blindingly obvious with a known suspect.
- *National Crime Agency (NCA).*[17] The NCA was set up to be the UK's equivalent of the FBI in America. It gathers intelligence from multiple sources, including the NFIB, to target serious and organised crime. It is staffed by police officers,

---

15 www.actionfraud.police.uk.

16 www.cityoflondon.police.uk/advice-and-support/fraud-and-economic-crime/nfib/Pages/default.aspx.

17 www.nationalcrimeagency.gov.uk.

shares intelligence with police forces, co-ordinates high profile cases and conducts its own operations.

- *National Cyber Crime Unit (NCCU)* is a unit within the NCA that provides support to serious cyber crime investigations led by the NCA and police forces.[18]
- *Serious Fraud Office (SFO).*[19] The SFO works with the other agencies, but only handles the most serious cases. The public can report their cases directly to the SFO.

6.9 Making a criminal complaint

A victim wishing to report a fraud needs to make out the complaint in the right format and emphasise the right things in order to secure the interest of law enforcement. This is not easy because victims are rarely aware of the key criteria and important triggers that the agencies are looking for. The government has developed a national policy which governs what the relevant authorities do, how they should act and how they should prioritise cases.

There are essentially two routes for complainants. One to the Serious Fraud Office. The other to the Police. As its name implies, the Serious Fraud Office only handles a few high value, significant public interest cases. Unless you have an exceptionally serious case, you are extremely unlikely to arouse the SFO's interest.

The most common route is to the police, except you do not report directly to the police. Complainants are now required to report frauds, including cyber-enabled frauds, to Action Fraud, a call centre supervised by the City of London Police (see above).

As the first gatekeeper, the handlers at Action Fraud consider complaints and pass those with merits onto the NFIB, which then filters and passes cases to local constabularies.

The official guidance for the police in deciding to take up a case is contained within the Home Office Circular 47/2004 (see below). This Circular is now so old that its ongoing value is questionable. The fact that it has not been updated has been strongly criticised by the UK's Fraud Advisory Panel,[20] calling for new clear, transparent criteria to be applied consistently by all police forces in the UK.

Given that the Circular remains in force and remains an important cornerstone to police decision-making regarding fraud, we will now take a more detailed look at what it says.

---

18 www.nationalcrimeagency.gov.uk/about-us/what-we-do/national-cyber-crime-unit.

19 www.sfo.gov.uk.

20 In a letter addressed to the City of London Police and copied to the Home Office. This letter can be retrieved at: www.fraudadvisorypanel.org/wp-content/uploads/2017/03/Policing-Priorities-for-Fraud-Investigations-Final-Web-Copy-08Feb17.pdf. The Fraud Advisory Panel is an independent charity whose members are within the community of anti-fraud specialists.

6.10 Home Office Circular 47/2004: Policing priorities for fraud cases

Home Office Circular 47/2004[21] was prepared by the Home Office and addressed to all Chief Police Officers in England and Wales. Below are the most important parts, which we quote in full.

> "The decision on whether to investigate an allegation of fraud, and on the resources to be devoted to any investigation, rests solely with the police. The police will only investigate in circumstances where there are good grounds to believe that a criminal offence has been committed. In some cases, some form of preliminary inquiry may assist the police in determining whether the case is suitable for a full investigation. In making this decision, the police will have regard to the resources available, government and local policing priorities, and the competing priorities of other fraud and criminal cases already under investigation as well as the priorities set out below."

The police will need co-operation and support from victims at all stages of investigation and prosecution. Victims will need to identify and preserve original documents and provide them to the police if necessary.

6.10.1 Higher priority cases[22]

- Frauds involving substantial sums of money. Cases meeting the substantial acceptance criteria of the SFO may be referred directly to the SFO, either by the victim or the police.
- Frauds having a significant impact on the victim(s). A negligible loss to a large company, for example, could be catastrophic for a private individual or small business.
- Frauds affecting particularly vulnerable victims (e.g. the elderly, people with disabilities, businesses providing key services in difficult circumstances) or in distinct communities.
- Frauds giving rise to significant public concern (possibly highlighted by a high degree of press interest).
- Frauds committed by, or knowingly facilitated by, professional advisers (e.g. lawyers, accountants, merchant bankers).
- Frauds likely to undermine confidence in leading UK institutions or otherwise undermine the economy.
- Frauds committed by members of Boards or other senior managers.
- Frauds where law enforcement action could have a material deterrent effect.
- Frauds which indicate a risk of more substantial/extensive fraud occurring.
- Cases where the victim has devoted significant resources to fraud prevention or has been willing to participate in appropriate crime prevention partnerships or otherwise assist the police.
- Frauds which it has been agreed should be a current law enforcement priority.

---

21 http://webarchive.nationalarchives.gov.uk/20130309162227; www.homeoffice.gov.uk/about-us/corporate-publications-strategy/home-office-circulars/circulars-2004/047-2004.

22 As set out in Home Office Circular 47/2004 and quoted here in full.

6.10.2 Lower priority cases[23]

- Cases where the victim's motive for making the complaint appears to be malicious, primarily focused on recovering monies owed, or designed to distract attention from the complainant's own involvement in the fraud. (Such cases might nevertheless merit investigation, particularly where there are other victims involved.)
- Cases where victims are not prepared to co-operate fully with investigation and prosecution, although the police will always consider carefully how to assist victims and witnesses who have concerns about safety.
- Frauds more suitable for investigation by another enforcement or regulatory agency.
- Cases where another police force has decided not to investigate other than for geographical reasons.
- Frauds that have already been investigated by the police or other enforcement agency or that have been the subject of regulatory proceedings, unless significant new evidence has come to light or the previous investigation had a narrow remit that did not address all the relevant issues.
- Cases where the existence of other proceedings might have a detrimental effect on a criminal investigation and subsequent prosecution.
- Frauds where the victim's conduct has contributed to the loss, in particular where the police have previously given guidance or warnings to victims about fraud risks that have not been acted upon.
- Frauds which took place a long time ago (probably more than two years) unless there are exceptional circumstances.
- Frauds where the likely eventual outcome, in terms of length of sentence and / or financial penalty, is not sufficient to justify the likely cost and effort of the investigation.

It is vital to understand what higher "priority" cases are, just as it is to understand what are viewed as cases which are not. You will want, of course, to have your case recognised as a priority.

Signpost

It may be possible to hire lawyers under alternative "no-win-no-fee" or "no-win-low-fee" arrangements. It may also be possible to obtain funding from companies which specialise in litigation funding. ⊳ *Section 3*

Getting your case recognised as a higher priority means trying to tick off as many of the priority criteria as you can, although some interpretation is required because some of the criteria are loosely defined.

Whatever criteria you may or not be able to meet there is one higher priority criterion that many business-victims of fraud are able to meet: that the fraud was

23 Referred to in Home Office Circular 47/2004 as "Cases where a more cautious approach might be appropriate" and quoted here in full.

"committed by members of Boards or other senior managers", given that a great number of frauds on businesses are inside jobs of some sort. If this is a feature of your case, you should highlight the fact to the police, referring them to the Home Office Circular.

6.11 Reporting a fraud to Action Fraud

You can report a fraud by telephone or using Action Fraud's online system. Your case may then be passed onto the NFIB. Here's how the Action Fraud website describes the work of the NFIB.[24]

> "When you report a fraud to Action Fraud, you are given a police crime reference number (Beginning NFRC) and your case is referred on to the National Fraud Intelligence Bureau (NFIB).
>
> - The reports are assessed and analysed by NFIB experts.
> - Data matching allows reports from different parts of the country to be linked through analysis, identifying the criminals behind the scams.
> - Crime information is sent to local forces for investigation.
>
> Not every report results in an investigation, but every report helps to build a clear picture of fraud within the UK. This contributes to making the UK a more hostile place for fraudsters to operate in and helps to keep other potential victims safe."

This last paragraph reflects one of the main functions of the NFIB. It gathers data to analyse trends and hotspots. It uses the information to identify emerging threats to the public, typically prolific criminal gangs, and directs the police accordingly. The Government has published a detailed guide to the workings of the NFIB.[25] But perhaps of most use to a victim of fraud is the *Action Fraud & National Fraud Intelligence Bureau User Guide* (April 2013).[26] The guide states that:

> "Within NFIB, the Crime Command reviews reports of fraud from victims and develops actionable packages for police forces and other law enforcement agencies. By absorbing fraud data from a range of cross sector partners they are able to enhance reports of fraud, identifying the most prolific and the most harmful fraudsters and their methods.
>
> If enforcement is viable the NFIB, will present a comprehensive case to the most appropriate police force or organisation to investigate. NFIB are not responsible for subsequent investigation but only the assessment of the report and the dissemination to other police forces, if suitable. Where enforcement is not a viable outcome, other disruption or intelligence activity is considered."

As you read these words, you are, we are sure, glaring at the word "viable". If not, you should be. The key to having your case investigated at all is that it is recognised by NFIB as "viable". So, what does this word mean?

---

24 www.actionfraud.police.uk/about-us/the-national-fraud-intelligence-bureau-process.
25 www.gov.uk/government/uploads/system/uploads/attachment_data/file; 118482/general-guide-nfib.pdf.
26 www.whatdotheyknow.com/request/187748/response/466202/attach/4/User%20Guide.pdf.

The User Guide goes on:

> "All reports of crime are scored according to the viability criteria at a network level. The system therefore automatically produces a daily queue of crime networks (which can range from one crime to thousands) ranked for viability."

And offers this advice to victims:

> "Scoring relies upon the data quality from the reporting person. It is of paramount importance that those reporting make use of the structured data fields, explicitly providing the suspects bank account, telephone number, address, registration, web address, full details etc. where available. This is fundamental both to the linking of harm as well as the scoring, and the identification of entities for disruption. If you are in any doubt then call the contact centre that can either put the report on for you or give you guidance."

Confused? You should be. None of this is clear. And if it's not clear to us it may not be all that clear to Action Fraud, the NFIB and other police forces either.

What is clear is that Action Fraud and the NFIB are deluged in reports and that your case may struggle to get the attention that it deserves. Here are some sobering statistics:[27]

- 264,056 genuine fraud reports were recorded by Action Fraud in the year to March 2017. 62% of reports are typically from businesses.
- 65,659 cases were passed to police forces for action.
- 8,214 resulted in some form of judicial outcome.
- 6,400 persons were charged.
- 5,382 were sentenced at court.[28]
- 1,132 persons were imprisoned.

The key message from these figures is that the overall attrition rate to charges for fraud is 98%. This means that the chance that the average complaint will lead to a criminal sentence is about 1 in 50. The attrition rate to imprisonment is 99.6%, so the chance that the average case will lead to a fraudster being imprisoned is 1 in 250.

You will note that just 25% of reports turn into cases for "action", which means investigation. If your case is not deemed viable for further immediate investigation, you'll receive the following kind of letter (or something similar) from Action Fraud:[29]

> "Dear [Victim]
>
> NFRC000000000000
>
> I'm sorry to hear you've been a victim of crime. Thank you for taking the time to report to Action Fraud.
>
> All Action Fraud reports are passed to the National Fraud Intelligence Bureau and we review every crime to identify investigative leads and opportunities to

---

27 www.actionfraud.police.uk/data; www.actionfraud.police.uk/cms/wp-content/uploads/2018/08/National-Fraud.pdf.

28 Based on sentencing and custodial rates for fraud in 2017 (www.gov.uk/government/statistics/criminal-justice-system-statistics-quarterly-september-2017).

29 Words in use by Action Fraud in December 2016.

disrupt criminal activity. We have reviewed your report and I regret to inform you that we have not identified any leads that would result in a successful criminal investigation therefore your report has not been sent to a local police force or other enforcement organisation to commence an investigation at this time.

Please be assured that we have not closed your report and it will continue to be reviewed against new information received from Action Fraud reports and other intelligence sources. If it is linked to an investigative opportunity in the future we will contact you."

Hopefully you won't get one of these kinds of letters but will instead be told that you case is to be further investigated by either the police or the Serious Fraud Office. Let's now then look at investigations by the police and the Serious Fraud Office, starting with the police.

6.12 Police investigations

6.12.1 Will the police investigate?

A fraud lawyer: "We have an under-resourced police service in the UK and as such they are not always able to commit the necessary man-power to investigating fraud. Where there is a police investigation (or an investigation by the Serious Fraud Office or HMRC) there is a risk that there will be confiscations or restraints of assets, which might prevent recovery by a victim taking the civil approach. I have worked with clients to exhaust civil recoveries and then compiled a portfolio of information which is provided to the police once we've run out of options. Whilst the police report isn't likely to help the client make further recoveries, it sometimes makes them feel they've done their civic duty."

From the above, you will now understand that it could be unlikely that your case will even reach the police. If it does hit their in-tray, the next question is: will they take it on? There are 43 police forces in England and Wales. They vary in size and resources and have different priorities which depend to a great extent on the attitudes and perceptions of the current Chief Constable and the elected Police and Crime Commissioner. If you are thinking of asking the police to investigate your case, you must understand how you can make your case enough of a priority to get taken on. What are the police's priorities?

The priorities set by the Home Office (▷ *Section 6.10, Home Office Circular 47/2004: Policing priorities for fraud cases*) are a good starting point but you should search the internet for other local policing priorities in the areas in which the main suspect resides and in which your business operates.

Take, for example, the priorities set out by Greater Manchester Police in their *Fraud Recording, Allocation and Investigation Procedure March 2013*,[30] which sets out the

30 https://meetings.gmpcc.org.uk/documents/s5705/GMP%20fraud%20recording%20allocation%20and%20investigation%20procedure%20-%20march%202013%20final.pdf.

expanded list of its priorities with their own additional criteria for "Higher priority cases" and "Lower priority cases".

In order to qualify for the higher priority status, the Greater Manchester Police look for the following additional features in cases:

- Strong positive lines of enquiry are immediately apparent.
- Clear opportunities to identify and restrain assets from the criminals with the aim of pursuing confiscation or forfeiture proceedings.

Pausing for a moment to think about these, here's what we think they mean:

- *"Strong positive lines of enquiry are immediately apparent"*. If you make it really easy for the police then you have a greater chance of having your case investigated. But if your case looks tricky, time consuming and uncertain, it will not be prioritised.
- *"Clear opportunities to identify and restrain assets from the criminals with the aim of pursuing confiscation or forfeiture proceedings"*. This criterion tells police to prioritise the cases that will lead to confiscation or forfeiture. Remember confiscation and forfeiture are procedures by which the police and prosecutors can ask courts to deprive offenders of assets, in favour of the state. At face value that means that the state gets the assets and not you. If that sounds unfair, it certainly would be if it trumped your entitlement to reparation.
- Confiscation or forfeiture can be effective tools on behalf of society as a whole, but so too is getting them to pay compensation to victims. Indeed, the two things need not be incompatible since the court can simultaneously make confiscation and confiscation orders and direct that the victim is first in the queue for payment.[31]

The Greater Manchester Police categorise cases as low priority when they exhibit the following features:

- Bring the case to a conclusion and would adversely impact upon our ability to investigate other crime.
- Frauds where the likely eventual outcome, in terms of length of sentence and / or financial penalty, is not sufficient to justify the likely cost and effort of the investigation.
- Available resources will not permit an immediate and expeditious investigation.
- Delays to the investigation will be caused by the location of key evidence elsewhere.

These criteria reveal the principal driver for police decisions – resource. Unfortunately, fraud is a low operational priority. Of the 122,407 full-time officers working in England and Wales in 2018, just 798 (0.7%) were assigned to the Economic Crime Units (ECUs).[32] Of these, 559 worked in 36 forces outside of London. Five forces do

31 It is a statutory requirement that compensation orders take priority over confiscation orders. The position regarding restitution orders is not so straightforward as statute does not mandate the relationship between confiscation and restitution orders. However, it is inconceivable that a victim who is entitled to a restitution order should lose out to a confiscation order and the courts would almost certainly strive to protect the victim against this happening.

32 Home Office (2018). *Police workforce, England and Wales, 31 March 2018*. Available at: www.gov.uk/government/statistics/police-workforce-england-and-wales-31-march-2018.

not have any officers dedicated to fraud. For those forces that do have ECUs, their priority may not be you. And when they do take on cases, resource shuffling can cause frustrating delays:

> "Although I discovered the theft and fraud, it has affected me as if it had happened to me. The past 18 months have been a wave of emotions. Extreme highs when we get another chunk back, and extreme lows when I have to reproduce the same evidence only in a different format for the police because a new officer has taken the case and likes it presented in a different way, to despair at times when [*offender*] is bailed for another two months."

Not only are the police seriously under-resourced when it comes to fraud, not all police forces even have policies on fraud investigation. This is what Avon and Somerset Police said in an answer published (in 2015) in response to a Freedom of Information request:

> "**Question**
>
> Q1. Please tell me whether Avon and Somerset police have any policy or have issued any guidance to officers relating to the investigation of fraud and if so give me a copy of it.
>
> Q2. If not governed by the above, tell me whether Avon and Somerset police consider the investigation of fraud a police matter
>
> **Answer**
>
> Q1. The requested information is not held as there is no specific force level policy regarding the investigation of fraud. However the Home Office Circular 47/2004 – Priorities for the Investigation of fraud cases is taken into account when Avon & Somerset Constabulary decides whether to accept a fraud case for investigation.
>
> Q2. All frauds are reported through Action Fraud. Cases are assessed by the National Fraud Intelligence Bureau and allocated to the relevant force if there are investigative lines of enquiry. If a criminal investigation is justified then it is a police matter – However, once again the Home Office Circular 47/2004 – Priorities for the Investigation of fraud cases is taken into account when Avon & Somerset Constabulary decides whether to accept a fraud case for investigation."

Considering the paucity of police and prosecutors who specialise in fraud, the multiple reasons set out in the official protocols for avoiding investigations, it is hardly surprising that one cyber fraud victim's experience of fraud reporting and the response of the police is, unfortunately, all too common:

> "The police are hopelessly unresponsive … their fraud reporting system is automated … they are light years away from being able to catch cyber fraud, let alone even understand what's happening on a timely basis. The only call I received was to offer psychological support."

It is also important to stress that the police do not respond to reports of fraud with blue flashing lights. Whatever victims may feel, frauds are not emergencies. They can take months to respond to reports, if at all, with little or no communication. Unfortunately, these delays can frustrate alternative forms of justice and leave the victim powerless. One fraud lawyer frequently grapples with the results of such delays:

> "The criticism I receive of the police time and time again from many victims is that they believe the investigation is taking place and let the months pass before coming to see me."

In the vast majority of cases victims would be far better served by a rapid rejection so that they can either come to terms with the impact on their lives or pursue an alternative strategy.

6.12.2 Police powers of investigation

The police have very considerable routine powers of investigation. The main powers are:[33]

- *Production orders.* The police can ask a court to make a production order against any individual holding relevant documents. In fraud cases, these orders are regularly made against banks requiring them to hand over bank statements; against telephone companies requiring them to hand over call and text logs; and can also require lawyers[34] and accountants to hand over their files.
- *Search and seizure.* The police can search premises (including cars) to look for and seize relevant evidence, including evidence stored on computers and phones. They can search not only suspects' premises but other premises as well. In the case of premises which do not belong to a suspect, the police would have to obtain a court warrant allowing the search.
- *Arrest and questioning of suspects.* The police can arrest and detain for questioning any person who they have reasonable grounds to suspect has committed an offence.

When the police conclude that a prosecution should be brought, they prepare charges (usually on the advice of the CPS) which are then brought (or "laid") against a wrongdoer, who then becomes a "defendant" to criminal proceedings in the criminal courts.

6.13 Serious Fraud Office investigations

The Serious Fraud Office (SFO) is responsible for investigating and prosecuting serious fraud, bribery and corruption cases. Its powers of prosecution differentiate the SFO from the police, which passes cases to the CPS. The SFO accepts complaints directly from businesses and members of the public as well as referrals from police forces, but only takes up the most serious, high value public interest cases.[35] In 2016, it succeeded in bringing 13 convictions in 7 cases.[36]

---

33 A full list and analysis of all police powers is beyond the scope of this guide.

34 But not documents which are properly covered by legal privilege (a subject beyond the scope of this guide).

35 www.sfo.gov.uk/contact-us/reporting-serious-fraud-bribery-corruption.

36 SFO (2015). *Annual Report 2016–17*. Available at: www.sfo.gov.uk/publications/corporate-information/annual-reports-accounts.

In considering whether to take on a case, the SFO applies a Statement of Principle, which includes the following criteria:

- the apparent criminality undermines the UK's commercial or financial interests in general and in the City of London in particular;
- the actual or potential financial loss involved is high;
- actual or potential economic harm is significant;
- there is a significant public interest element; and
- the case is of a new species of fraud.

The SFO is staffed by lawyers, accountants and investigators and also works with police forces to form teams dealing with its small number of cases. In addition to the routine powers of investigation which police have, the SFO can also compel any person holding relevant information or documents about a fraud to attend the offices of the SFO and:

- answer questions in a recorded interview; and
- hand over relevant documents.

These compulsion powers make the SFO's investigations very potent and wide-reaching in their scope. When it decides that a prosecution should be brought, it prepares charges and lays them against the defendant to the criminal proceedings.

If the SFO does take up your case, then you will of course need to have a dialogue with them about the kind of financial reparations which they may be able to obtain for you. They do apply for and obtain compensation orders alongside confiscation orders.

Signpost

Even if you think that you have caught the fraudster red-handed, you may find that he digs in for a fight, especially when the police are involved and the wrongdoer's liberty is at stake. Sometimes fraudsters confess in the early stages but then retract their admissions and raise defences when the full ramifications become apparent. ⊳ *Section 2*

When compensation and confiscation orders are made in the same case, the compensation order takes precedence. This is because a court will direct that any money realised from the offender and his assets must first be used to satisfy the criminal compensation order (i.e. go to the victim) and only surplus amounts can be used to satisfy the confiscation order (i.e. go to the state).

Figure 6.1 lays out some statistics on compensation orders and confiscation orders published by the SFO.[37]

37 www.sfo.gov.uk/about-us.

Figure 6.1: Confiscation and compensation orders obtained by the SFO (£GBP)

Year	Confiscation orders	Compensation included in confiscation	Compensation in stand-alone orders	Civil recovery orders
2017–18	276,000	0	0	0
2016–17	14,332,000	13,969,000	11,003,000	0
2015–16	3,388,000	121,000	0	0
2014–15	22,720,000	3,014,000	2,443,000	521,000
2013–14	2,869,000	2,869,000	0	7,000
2012–13	38,880,000	7,002,000	5,025,000	1,960,000
2011–12	1,896,000	232,000	150,000	16,224,000
2010–11	28,631,000	25,929,000	224,000	7,028,000

What do these figures tell us? *Figure 6.2* rearranges the figures according to whether orders were obtained in favour of victims (compensation orders)[38] or in favour of the state (confiscation and civil recovery orders).[39]

Figure 6.2: Comparison of compensation and confiscation (£GBP)

Year	Total compensation orders for the benefit of victims[40]	Total confiscation and civil recovery orders for the benefit of the state
2017–18	0	276,000
2016–17	24,972,000	14,332,000
2015–16	121,000	3,388,000
2014–15	5,457,000	23,241,000
2013–14	2,869,000	2,876,000
2012–13	12,027,000	40,840,000
2011–12	382,000	18,093,000
2010–11	26,153,000	35,383,000
Totals	**71,981,000**	**138,429,000**

The figures clearly show that the total amount of financial orders obtained by the SFO for the benefit of the state is more than double the total amount obtained for the benefit of victims of fraud.

Over the same period of time (2010–17) the financial orders which were actually enforced gave rise to payments of £78,806,000 to the government and £38,000,000

38 The SFO appear to have obtained no restitution orders for victims.

39 Civil recovery orders are orders forfeiting assets to the state, made by civil courts at the request of a prosecutor. They are for the benefit of the state and monies realised go to the state and not to victims.

40 Confiscation orders plus civil recovery orders.

returned to the victims. The state received over double the amount paid to victims at an overall recovery rate of 55%.

This pattern is reflected across all prosecution services for all types of offences. In 2017, the state collected £201 million for itself through confiscation and forfeiture orders. £60 million of this money was used to fund the asset recovery work of law enforcement agencies through the so-called Asset Recovery Incentivisation Scheme (ARIS).[41] The state thus profited to the tune of £140 million. In contrast, victims received just £30 million in compensation.

The data speaks for itself. It does appear wrong that the state's coffers are benefiting more than the victims. There may be reasons for this but it is hard to imagine that they are good reasons, and it is hard to see why victims should be encouraged by these figures.

6.14 Crown Prosecution Service and prosecutions

The Crown Prosecution Service (CPS) is headed by the Director of Public Prosecutions, is headquartered in London and operates in 13 different CPS "Areas". It prosecutes most kinds of crimes, including fraud, cyber crimes and bribery.

The CPS does not investigate cases at any stage but it can and does advise police forces and other agencies on which charges should be brought in any particular case. It acts independently of the police and according to its own internal legal guidance[42] and the Code for Crown Prosecutors.[43]

The Code for Crown Prosecutors sets out the basic principles to be followed by prosecutors when deciding whether to prosecute and what charges to prosecute. The Code stipulates a two-stage test: evidential and public interest.

> **Signpost**
>
> Given that you will be in an enduring relationship with your lawyers, you will need to do your bit to ensure that the relationship succeeds in order to maximise the chances of success. ⊳ *Section 3*

Evidential test

Prosecutors must be satisfied that there is sufficient evidence to provide a realistic prospect of conviction against each suspect on each charge. They must consider what the defence case may be, and how it is likely to affect the prospects of conviction. A case which does not pass the evidential stage must not proceed, no matter how serious or sensitive it may be.

41 https://assets.publishing.service.gov.uk/government/uploads/system/uploads/attachment_data/file/739567/asset-recovery-financial-years-2013-to-2018-hosb1818.pdf.
42 www.cps.gov.uk/legal/index.html.
43 www.cps.gov.uk/publication/code-crown-prosecutors.

Public interest test

If the case passes the evidential test, the prosecutor must then decide whether it is in the interests of justice to bring the prosecution. While the public interest will vary from case to case, broadly speaking the more serious an alleged offence the more likely it will be that a prosecution is needed in the public interest.

The CPS website contains a lot of links to helpful guidance and resources for victims of crime and witnesses to criminal cases.[44]

6.15 The Code of Practice for Victims of Crime

Issued by the Ministry of Justice in October 2015, the Code of Practice for Victims of Crime[45] broadly reflects the European Union's Victims' Directive in relation to victims' rights but it does not incorporate all aspects of the EU law,[46] whilst retaining the Directive's limitations[47] (⊳ *Section 7.5.3, The Victims' Directive*).

The Code sets out a number of rights which are said to be guaranteed to the victims of crime. That said, there is a notable distinction made in the rights given to individual (human) victims of crime and to legal persons (incorporated businesses), with business victims being given fewer rights.

It should also be noted that the Code is just a code. It is not legislation and provides no rights which can be enforced by victims, a point explicitly set out in the statute which created the Code.

Signpost

Speed is almost always vital in fraud cases in order to contain the situation, prevent further losses and stop the fraudster from dissipating your money. ⊳ *Section 3*

6.16 What if the authorities decline to investigate or decide to drop a case?

What are you rights and remedies if either the police decide not to investigate your case or a prosecutor decides not to bring a prosecution?

Ultimately, you have the right to bring a legal case against the police or prosecutor, known as a judicial review. This is a civil case, which you would have to bring in the High Court, in which you would be asking the court to overturn the decision with which you disagree.

---

44 See www.cps.gov.uk/victims-witnesses.

45 See https://assets.publishing.service.gov.uk/government/uploads/system/uploads/attachment_data/file/476900/code-of-practice-for-victims-of-crime.PDF.

46 The UK Government chose to not directly transpose the EU Victims' Directive into UK legislation.

47 Directive 2012/29/EU, retrieved from http://eur-lex.europa.eu/legal-content/EN/TXT/PDF/?uri=CELEX:32012L0029&from=EN.

You can also ask the police or prosecutor to review and change a decision under the "Victim Right to Review" scheme (and, if you are eligible to do so, you must do so before mounting a judicial review). The Victim Right to Review scheme applies where:

- The police have investigated but decided against brining criminal charges or have decided against referring a case to the CPS.
- The CPS have reviewed a case and advised the police that charges should not be brought.
- The SFO has investigated a case and decided against bringing charges.

If you do wish to request such a "Review" then you must do so within three months of being notified of the decision not to bring criminal charges.

If you are unhappy with the way in which the police or CPS are dealing with your case or indeed unhappy about a decision not to prosecute, then it would be sensible to take legal advice. The law in this area is quite complex and the police and prosecutors are given a wide margin of discretion in their decision making. This means challenges can be difficult.

> **Signpost**
>
> One consequence of the criminal disclosure rules is that the police may gather materials which you regard as both confidential and irrelevant and deliver copies to the accused. The sensitive information may also be revealed to the public through the course of the criminal trial. ⊳ *Section 2*

6.17 Engaging with the police and prosecutors

If your case is taken up then there are some things you need to think about to maximise the chances of a happy outcome for you. Here goes:

- Remember that you could be in for a very long haul. Some criminal cases take many years from the start of an investigation to the end of a criminal trial. You should manage your own expectations accordingly. If you are thinking that leaving the police to deal with your case will mean that they do all the hard work, think again: you will need to do a lot to support their investigation and prosecution.
- You will need to cultivate a really good relationship with both police and prosecutors. You'll see a lot more of the police but there is no reason why you cannot seek a meeting with the main prosecutors involved in your case to ask them questions and find out more about their approach to your case.

> **Signpost**
>
> Whatever the pressures may be, investigations must be conducted in an ethical manner. You do not want to give the police or prosecutors cause to drop your case on the grounds that evidence is inadmissible in court. Similarly you do not want to damage your credibility as a witness and victim. ⊳ *Section 1*

- You will probably want to ensure that the police and prosecutor apply for a restraint order to freeze the assets of the accused wrongdoer as soon as possible. This can be done during the investigation and for you the sooner it is done the better.
- Beware though; the restraint order is a court order that can only be made if the prosecutor intends to seek a confiscation order (for the benefit of the state). As we have set out above, this can be consistent with you also being awarded compensation, as payment of compensation orders (to you) will be given priority over payment of confiscation order (to the state) but there are risks in relying on the state to freeze assets and there is the risk that the state will eventually scoop up the frozen assets and you will get none.
- You will have to make your own judgement, assisted by your own lawyers, about the likelihood that you can obtain a satisfactory amount of compensation or restitution from the wrongdoer through the criminal courts, bearing in mind the possibility that the accused will be acquitted rather than convicted and bearing in mind that, even if convicted, the criminal court may not order any, or any satisfactory, amount of reparations for you.
- If you – and your lawyers – are not extremely confident that you can and will get what you deserve in financial reparations from the criminal case then you should at least consider the possibility of bringing a civil claim parallel to the criminal investigation and prosecution. This will allow you to obtain your own freezing order over the wrongdoer's assets and allow you to assert your own full claim to the assets held by the wrongdoer.
- Good police officers and prosecutors understand the need for victims to bring their own civil claims alongside criminal action. This should not put them off investigating or prosecuting a case and, managed well, the parallel proceedings may even offer some advantages to the public authorities.
- If the police or prosecutors assigned to your case are negative about the fact that you have brought or want to bring civil proceedings at the same time as expecting investigation and prosecution by them, then you can educate them about your needs and rights; perhaps best done by a lawyer who can not only point our your basic rights and needs but also tell them about the potential upsides for parallel cases.

Signpost

In fraud cases the identity of the victim is not always clear cut, for example where there is a group of companies and a parent or holding company, and sometimes there are multiple victims. ▷ *Section 5*

6.18 The steps leading to trial in the criminal court

In order to progress your case to trial, a number of basic stages will have to be dealt with and the court has a duty to actively manage your case to make sure that it progresses in good order. Here are the most basic stages which are typical in a fraud case.

> **Signpost**
>
> The police and prosecutor will not be able to advise you on or help you with your civil-court claim. Helping you to get financial reparations before the civil courts is not part of their job description or public duties. ⊳ *Section 2*

6.18.1 Plea and trial preparation hearing (PTPH)

The first main hearing of an accused is the so-called "PTPH". This is the first hearing at which the defendant must indicate his plea to the court – "not guilty" or "guilty" – and the judge then gives further directions, often including that there will be a further preparatory hearing. If the plea is "not guilty", then the court will set the pre-trial steps to be taken by the prosecutor and the accused. If the plea is "guilty", then the judge will set a date for the sentence of the defendant.

6.18.2 Prosecution witness statements

The prosecutor is obliged to provide to a defendant all witness statements taken from witnesses whose evidence the prosecutor intends to rely. These statements need to be comprehensive and to cross-refer to important documents (called "exhibits") which the prosecutor intends to rely on to prove its case. The exhibits need to be served with the witness statements.

6.18.3 Standard prosecution document disclosure

The prosecutor is obliged to disclose all documents which may either undermine its own case or assist the defendant's case, whether or not the prosecutor intends to rely on those documents at the trial of the accused.

6.18.4 Defence case statement

A defendant must provide the court and the prosecutor with a statement outlining the main points he will raise in his defence. If a defendant refuses to provide such a statement, he or she would not be punished by the court but the fact that he has failed to provide a statement will be made known to the jury in the trial of the defendant, who may then draw an adverse inference from the failure.

6.18.5 Additional prosecution disclosure

If the defendant has provided a defence case statement, the prosecutor will then have to review its disclosure, in the light of the defence revealed by the defence case statement, to ensure that any further relevant documents are identified and disclosed to the defendant.

6.18.6 Further case management hearing

It is common in fraud cases for there to be a further case management hearing before the commencement of trial. This is to ensure that pre-trial steps have been observed and to give the prosecutor and defendant a chance to make any applications of importance concerning management of the forthcoming trial. In some cases, these kinds of hearings are elevated to the status of so-called "Preparatory Hearings" which are, legally, then part of the trial itself, even though they are hearings before a judge alone and the jury in the case has yet to be "sworn in".

> **Signpost**
>
> The police or prosecutor may try to dissuade you from mounting a civil claim or ask you to wait until they have finished prosecuting the case. They may ask you to stay (suspend) live proceedings until the conclusion of the criminal case. This is usually not good advice. ⊳ *Section 2*

6.19 Criminal trial

The trial of the case against the wrongdoer-defendant would be presided over by a judge. Just one judge. There would also be a jury of 12 people (randomly selected for jury service) who are "sworn in" to try the case.[48] The judge and jury listen to all the evidence in the case. They also listen to the arguments and speeches of the advocates in the case. In a trial, there are set times when witnesses are called into court for questioning and there are set times when the advocates argue the cases of their respective clients.

As we set out earlier in this guide (⊳ *Section 2.7, Complain to the police*), to succeed with a criminal case, the prosecutor must be able to show beyond all reasonable doubt that the accused person is guilty of the crimes of which he or she is charged. Another way of describing the required standard of proof is that the jury will have to be "sure" of the guilt of the accused. This is a significantly higher standard than that for determining liability in the civil courts (⊳ *Section 2.9, Civil court claims*).

Here is a simple view of what a trial will typically look like in the prosecution against a wrongdoer-defendant:

- Prosecutor makes a speech telling the judge and jury what the case is about, goes through the key documents in the case and tells the judge and jury which witnesses are coming to court to give oral evidence.
- Prosecutor introduces ("calls") in turn each of the prosecution's witnesses, taking them through their evidence (this is called the "examination in chief" of witnesses).
- Defendant's advocate questions ("cross-examines") each of the prosecution's witnesses in turn.
- Prosecutor may question ("re-examine") each of the prosecution's witnesses just in relation to anything new which has arisen from the defence advocate's questioning.

48 We describe here the usual trial format for serious cases in the Crown Court. Some very minor cases are dealt with in the Magistrates' Court and, if so, are dealt with by either a single professional judge or by a panel of three "lay" magistrates who are supported by a legally qualified clerk of the court.

- Defence advocate may make a speech (in this case, called "submissions") to the judge (not the jury) that the prosecution have not proved their case to the standard required for the defendant to have to "answer" that case. If successful, the judge would direct the jury to return a "not guilty" verdict and the trial would come to an end.
- Defendant's advocate may make a speech telling the judge and jury what the case is about from the defence perspective, including introducing defence witnesses and documentation (but such an opening speech is not commonly made).
- Defendant's advocate introduces ("calls") in turn each of the defendant's witnesses, taking them through their evidence – the "examination in chief" of defence witnesses.
- Prosecutor questions ("cross-examines") each of the defendant's witnesses after each is introduced.
- Defendant's advocate may question ("re-examine") each of the defendant's witnesses just in relation to anything new which has arisen from the prosecutor's questioning.
- Prosecutor makes a closing speech, explaining the evidence that has been heard and considered and putting that together with the relevant legal principles to say why it is that the prosecutor's case has been successful in showing that the defendant engaged in the wrongdoing and should be convicted.
- Defendant's advocate makes a closing speech, explaining the evidence and legal principles and saying why it is that the prosecutor has failed to show that the defendant is guilty.
- Judge sums up the case to the jury, explaining the key points of the evidence and the relevant legal principles which must govern the jury's decision-making.
- Jury deliberate on the case and reach a verdict – either not guilty or guilty – on each of the charges against the defendant.
- If the defendant is found guilty, the judge will set a date for the sentencing of the defendant (usually three weeks after the defendant was found guilty) and at that later hearing the judge will sentence the defendant (typically) to imprisonment, to pay a fine, or both.
- Either at or after the sentence hearing or at a later date (perhaps when deciding confiscation), the judge will decide what (if any) compensation or restitution awards to make in favour of the victim.
- The judge will also deal with confiscation proceedings which may be at a final hearing at which the judge receives evidence concerning confiscation and decides whether to make a confiscation order and the correct amount of any such order.

Signpost

The combination of the burden of proof, the standard of proof and the procedural rules, especially the disclosure rules, mean that criminal investigations and trial preparation can take many months, if not years. It also means that criminal trials can be complex and lengthy, sometimes lasting many months. Trials have to proceed at a speed which juries are able to cope with. ▷ *Section 2*

6.20 Conclusions

This has been one of the longest sections in this guide. We hope that it has shown the possibilities for obtaining financial reparations through the criminal courts but also exposed the weakness of the criminal justice system as a route to such reparation for victims of fraud.

As long as police and prosecutor's resources are stretched and as long as the numbers of cases of fraud are as high as they are, there will remain a glaring gap between what public bodies could achieve and what they do achieve for victims of fraud, whether commercial fraud or cyber-enabled fraud. But resources are not the only problem.

As we have seen from the discussion of compensation and restitution awards, something is going wrong even when public prosecutors are successful in prosecuting fraud. The total value of confiscation orders (for the benefit of the state) is out-pacing the total value of compensation orders (for the benefit of victims). Whatever the reasons may be for this, in the context of fraud cases in which there will always be victims of fraud, the disparity between these kinds of orders looks wrong.

Finally, the effective voice of victims in the criminal courts is extremely limited. Victims are not muzzled, but in many cases they are not able to stand up for themselves (or have a lawyer do that for them). One would hope that, in the future, all victims will not only be better informed about their rights but also have an easy route to being able to assert those rights in the criminal courts.

International cases and enforcement

7.1 In this section

- Making criminal complaints
- Bringing civil claims
- Evidence gathering
- Freezing and seizing assets
- Enforcing judgments and awards

7.2 Introduction

A fraud lawyer: "Identify the practical and legal limitations of any key jurisdiction at the outset as well as procedural norms at odds with your own jurisdiction. Remember what you consider to be unusual, another jurisdiction may consider the norm."

This section is about international cases. It focuses on international issues from an English and Welsh perspective. By this we mean cases where victims are from outside the United Kingdom and need help in England and Wales; and cases where English or Welsh victims need to take action outside of the United Kingdom. This section is not about intra-UK cases[1] and much of the discussion addresses the needs of victims based outside of the UK.

Before we continue, we need to say a word or two about the split between the civil and criminal justice systems in England and Wales ("E & W" for short). English and Welsh courts are very firmly divided between the civil justice trial courts (High Court and the County Courts) and the criminal justice courts (the Crown Court and the Magistrates' Courts). Apart from seeking certain sorts of reparations in the criminal courts (⊳ *Section 6.7, Compensation orders and restitution orders*), you will not be able to bring civil claims within the criminal justice courts.

If you are a victim from another European country, you may find it strange that you cannot bring civil claims in the criminal courts in England and Wales because you will be familiar with the right to do so in your home country.

Most other European countries, and indeed many other countries in the world that have what is known as the "civil law" or "codified" approach to law, allow victims

1 The laws of the three parts / legal jurisdictions of the United Kingdom (that is, England and Wales, Northern Ireland and Scotland) are all but identical in many respects but differences between them do exist. And there are various laws and rules that apply to intra-UK investigations and court cases which cross the boundaries of the three jurisdictions. A discussion of the differences in the relevant laws of the separate parts of the UK is beyond the scope of this guide. Nor does this guide deal with cases that spread across the borders of the three UK jurisdictions.

to bring their civil claims in criminal courts alongside the criminal charges that are levied against alleged wrongdoers. A victim does so as a "civil party" (or in French, the "*partie civile*") in the criminal court proceedings.

This form of parallel criminal and civil justice can be time-saving and very effective for victims. As we have said, it is not available in England and Wales.

A fraud lawyer: "Discovering fraud is a shocking event for clients and raises very complicated issues. Clients need highly skilled lawyers in criminal law, corporate law; and, sometimes, even forensic accountants. But hope always remains because the law can provide good solutions for businesses that have become the victim of fraud."

The other difference between the "common law" legal systems in England and Wales and "civil law" systems, such as those in continental Europe, is in the procedures that govern court proceedings. Here's a quick summary:

- The English and Welsh courts, both civil and criminal, work on the "adversarial" approach. The parties in the case have the main responsibility to choose how to present their cases, including evidence-gathering and choosing what evidence is presented to the court. The adversarial approach gives the parties to the litigation greater choices and responsibilities in how a case is presented.
- By contrast, civil law systems tend to have what is known as the "inquisitorial" approach. In these countries, judges play a much bigger role in deciding what evidence is gathered and presented to the court. This has the advantage that the judge can decide what evidence is most important. It can also mean lower bills from lawyers, as the lawyers have less work to do.
- Many clients like the choices that the adversarial approach provides. This greater freedom does, however, come at a price: judges only tend to get really involved in the substance of the case at the final trial of the case, and the legal bills tend to be higher because of the greater amount of work that has to be done by lawyers to present a case.

It is important for non-lawyer readers to appreciate that the term "civil law" in other countries is used to describe their whole justice systems, both civil and criminal, and so it should not be confused with the meaning given to the "civil law" branch of the "common law" system in England and Wales, the branch which deals with "civil claims" (⊳ *Section 5, Civil court claims*).

Signpost

Being conned can be a longer, more emotional experience than, say, a burglary. A burglary is visible and obvious. You are quickly into the anger phase, you call the police and your insurer deals with it. A fraud often means someone you trusted has let you down. ⊳ *Section 1*

7.3 Choosing lawyers for international work

A fraud lawyer: "It is essential to find the right advisor as quick as possible, and this is especially important in fraud cases, in which the right advice is very complex, and the first steps the victim takes could lead to irreversible mistakes. Finding the right lawyer/firm, expert in both criminal and commercial law, can be vital. The first task is to freeze every asset as soon as possible, otherwise a potential win in Court can turn into a valueless victory."

We need to give you a health warning. International laws and their application can be difficult to understand and international cases present many strategic issues to think about.

It is, we think, essential for victims with international cases to get advice from lawyers who routinely carry out international work. It is not in your interests to hire lawyers who have little or no experience of international fraud and coordinating international cases (▷ *Section 3, Choosing, using and paying for lawyers*).

A fraud lawyer: "Always choose the international team personally. Collective experience of a firm is seldom fully shared. Much more depends on the experience of the individual lawyers involved."

Having read *Section 3*, you will be aware that the legal profession in England and Wales is split. Nevertheless, here is a quick reminder. Barristers are usually self-employed within groupings of barristers called "Chambers" and do most of the court advocacy, explaining cases to the courts. Most solicitors work in "law firms". They mainly do the case management and investigative work; they cannot undertake trial preparation or court advocacy. A solicitor will almost certainly advise you to engage a barrister. You may be able to save money by only using a "public access" barrister. You can appoint barristers and solicitors in the following ways:[2]

Signpost

Barristers tend to spend more time than solicitors in court, advocating (or "pleading") cases on behalf of clients. ▷ *Section 3*

7.3.1 Solicitor

You can appoint (instruct) any solicitor in England and Wales and he or she is entitled to then instruct a barrister on your behalf and is also entitled to conduct litigation on your behalf.

2 There are numerous professional conduct rules and restrictions which apply to both professions and which are beyond the scope of this guide.

7.3.2 Barrister

You can appoint (instruct) any barrister by asking another lawyer (a UK solicitor, a barrister in a law firm or a non-UK lawyer) to instruct that barrister to carry out work on your behalf. You can also hire the barrister directly yourself if he or she is licensed to take so-called "public access" work. Unless that public access barrister is also licensed to "conduct" litigation on your behalf, he or she would not be able to do certain things such as "serving" claims on defendants, which would have to be done by process servers.

> A fraud lawyer: "In case of an international fraud, clients need an international legal team, a united group of lawyers who work harmoniously with each other. It really helps if the lawyers already know each other and already understand the basics of each other's legal systems."

Much of what we say in *Section 3* about finding and selecting the right lawyers applies not only to English and Welsh lawyers but also to lawyers outside the UK. When choosing lawyers outside the UK, you may be able to access country specific guides to lawyers which are the product of research and peer reviews. The main UK guides also provide some information about lawyers in other countries.

> A fraud lawyer: "Realise that litigating in a common law jurisdiction like the UK is very different from litigating on the continent. Even if your legal partner in continental Europe speaks perfect English you may still end up 'lost in translation' as a result."

7.4 Victims who are outside the United Kingdom

7.4.1 Why might you need help in E & W?

If you are a victim from outside the United Kingdom, you may need help in England and Wales when:

- part of the wrongdoing occurred in England and Wales;
- your business suffered harm within England and Wales; and / or
- your monies or other assets have been (fraudulently) transferred to or brought to England and Wales.

In these cases, many of the options, court powers, advantages and disadvantages and opportunities and concerns that we have discussed in *Sections 1 to 6* will be applicable. In particular:

- You should consider the kinds of options open to victims in general in England and Wales (▷ *Section 2, Objectives and options*).
- You should consider whether it would be better to bring civil proceedings in England and Wales or to make a complaint to the police. Many of the advantages and disadvantages discussed in *Section 2* will be germane.

There are also some particular considerations which are unique to you as foreign victim:

- Are you eligible to bring civil court proceedings in England and Wales to ask the English court to determine claims against wrongdoers?
- You should think about whether the civil court powers for securing assets will be attractive and indeed of greater use than the kinds of powers available in your home country (▷ *Section 4, Tracing and securing assets in the civil courts*).
- You will want to consider whether you may be able to obtain higher levels of compensation or better civil court remedies in England and Wales (▷ *Section 5, Civil court claims*) than in your home country.
- Would it be possible to get help from within England and Wales to help investigate and build a case which may be brought in your home country?
- If you bring a civil claim in your home courts, can you ask the English and Welsh court to help you identify wrongdoers, trace and freeze assets in England and Wales? And even freeze assets in other countries as well?
- If you obtain judgment in a civil claim in your home country, will those courts ask the English and Welsh courts to enforce that judgment?
- What help can you expect or hope will be given to a police force or criminal court in your home country if it asks the UK authorities for assistance? Can assets be frozen in England and Wales in support of prosecutions in another country?

These are the questions (and others) which are the main focus of this section, as it relates to victims who are outside the UK.

Signpost

Victims who have a restitution claim have the right to address the criminal court (themselves or through a lawyer) when seeking a restitution order. Very few victims and lawyers are aware of their rights to claim restitution through the criminal courts. ▷ *Section 6*

7.4.2 Making a criminal complaint in E & W

We have devoted a whole section to criminal complaints in the UK (▷ *Section 6, Criminal investigations and criminal court prosecutions*).

The police in the UK are obliged to treat you with the same respect and courtesy as they would a victim who is resident in the UK and follow the same procedures. The last point is particularly important for you to note: you should experience the same speed of service or indeed delays that any other victim would experience.

If you are thinking of involving the police and prosecutors in an international case then you should be warned that law enforcement agencies have budgetary constraints and are very wary of getting involved in difficult and elusive international cases. You also need to know that cross-border cases can be very slow due to the rigorous procedures that the police and prosecutors must follow.

What is different for non-UK victims is that there may well be a need for UK police and prosecutors to ask for assistance from the authorities in your home country. If that is necessary, then they will need to make a formal request for assistance. We deal with that later in this section.

> **Signpost**
>
> Although you will be involved in making the complaint and the police will need your help to build a case against the fraudsters, you will have very limited rights of participation in the criminal investigation process. You will also have very limited rights in relation to the criminal prosecution process which would be conducted by lawyers of the CPS or perhaps the SFO. ▷ *Section 2*

7.4.3 Evidence gathering in E & W for foreign criminal cases

Statute laws enable UK authorities to help the police and prosecuting authorities of other countries with investigating crimes, including evidence gathering. In appropriate European Union cases, UK and other EU authorities can combine to create a "joint investigation team".

The UK authorities can[3] provide help in cases in which a crime is reasonably suspected and being investigated or any case where charges have been brought and proceedings are underway. The powers which can be exercised are:

- Power to search premises and seize relevant materials, including documents held electronically on computers and other electronic devices. Evidence can then be sent to the overseas authority that requested the help.
- Power to compel persons to attend court to give a deposition on oath before a judge and to produce documents to the court. This can be done in private rather than in public. The deposition and documents can then be sent to the overseas authority that requested the help.
- Power to compel persons to attend court to give live evidence via a videoconference or teleconference link to the foreign court.
- Power to the UK's Serious Fraud Office, in serious or complex fraud cases, to compel persons to answer relevant questions and to produce relevant documents.

In addition, the so-called "European Investigation Order" ("EIO"), created by the EU Member States,[4] is available as a means of requesting and indeed requiring help from UK authorities. It came into effect on 22 May 2017 and given effect under UK law on 31 July 2017.[5] The main features of the EIO are these:

- An EIO can only be issued by a judge or other competent authority in an EU Member State.
- It is a judicial decision requiring one or more specific investigative measures carried out in another EU Member State.

3 Crime (International Co-operation) Act 2003.
4 European Union's Directive 2014/41/EU.
5 Criminal Justice (European Investigation Order) Regulations 2017.

- A Member State which receives an EIO must recognise and "execute" it in accordance with the Directive.

When in receipt of an EIO, the competent authorities in England and Wales are obliged to do a number of things requested of them (with very limited exceptions):

- Provide evidence and information which they already possess.
- Provide information contained in police databases.
- Take the necessary steps to obtain identification of persons holding specified telephone numbers or IP addresses.
- Deploy the same non-coercive investigation powers as would be available in a domestic case. In England and Wales, this would mean that police officers can go about making inquiries of witnesses, just as they would in domestic cases, and then make that evidence available.
- Carry out covert surveillance and investigations and provide their results.
- Carry out telephone interceptions and provide their results.
- Convene hearings for the purposes of receiving evidence from persons; including from relevant witnesses, experts, suspects, accused persons and third parties.
- Obtain and provide details of bank accounts held by persons the subject of criminal proceedings.
- Obtain and provide details of specified banking transactions.
- Prevent the destruction, disposal or removal of specified items of evidence.

Signpost

The very fact that you have brought criminal proceedings may make the wrongdoer and his associates fight harder than they would had you just brought a civil claim. ⊳ *Section 2*

English and Welsh courts are also able to act on foreign requests (made through official channels) for help to investigate financial transactions in relation to serious crimes[6] as well as whether a person has benefited from crime and the whereabouts of that benefit.[7] For this purpose, the courts have some very specific and useful powers for information and documents to be obtained by English / Welsh authorities to be sent to the overseas requesting authority:

- *Customer information orders*: requiring financial institutions to hand over information they hold about specified customers;[8]
- *Account monitoring orders*: requiring financial institutions to provide ongoing information about activities in accounts for specified periods of time;[9]
- *Production orders*: requiring persons to hand over relevant documents or give access to materials;[10]

6 Crime (International Co-operation) Act 2003 ("CICA" for short).
7 Proceeds of Crime Act 2002 (External Investigations) Order 2013 ("POCA External Investigations Order").
8 Both CICA and the POCA External Investigations Order.
9 Both CICA and the POCA External Investigations Order.
10 Both CICA and the POCA External Investigations Order.

- *Search and seizure warrants*;[11] and
- *Disclosure orders*: requiring specified persons to answer relevant questions, provide relevant information and provide relevant documents.[12]

Finally, English and Welsh courts have the power (following a request through official channels)[13] to make orders for:

- searches of premises and seizure of relevant evidence (or, as an alternative in some cases, to order the handing over of material by a production order); and
- the freezing of that evidence pending its transfer to the overseas requesting country for use in overseas proceedings.

7.4.4 Restraining assets in E & W in support of foreign criminal cases

A further statutory scheme[14] (we will call it the "POCA External Orders Order") enables the English and Welsh courts to search premises and seize and restrain (freeze) assets in support of foreign criminal court proceedings. This is to give effect to so-called foreign "external orders", which are orders for the recovery of "specified property" or a "specified sum of money", which are based on findings that person(s) have obtained property by or in connection with crime. This sounds great. However, as we next look at, these procedures are preludes to the enforcement of foreign court orders which do not necessarily end up with victims receiving compensation.

Signpost

The situation for victims is particularly confusing because of the split legal regimes which they have to consider. We are talking here about the fact that there is a civil-court system of law and a criminal-court system of law, each with its own structures, complexities and legal language. ▻ *Section 2*

7.4.5 Enforcing foreign criminal court orders in E & W

The POCA External Orders Order allows English and Welsh courts to order that "specified property" or "specified sums of money" be realised from property held by persons in England and Wales. The English / Welsh court must be satisfied that the foreign court order was made "consequent" to a conviction or convictions and not subject to any appeal.

The problem with the External Orders Order is that, even if it is wide enough to allow for the enforcement of foreign compensation orders, the Order itself requires that any sums realised be paid to the government of the United Kingdom and not to any victims. This is subject only to standing or ad hoc "asset sharing" agreements which the United Kingdom has or can reach with other countries. This is not an easy

11 POCA External Investigations Order.
12 POCA External Investigations Order.
13 CICA.
14 Proceeds of Crime Act 2002 (External Orders) Order 2005.

route to compensation for victims and indeed carries such considerable risks that it is best avoided.

Thankfully, within the European Union, there is another route to enforcement of compensation awards. That is because awards of financial reparation by criminal courts in most other EU countries are granted to victims because of their status as civil parties in the relevant criminal proceedings and as such are treated as civil court judgments that are enforceable under what are called the "European Regimes" for the enforcement of civil-court judgments[15] about which we say more below.

We say *most* other countries, as Ireland is a known exception. The Irish legal system, like the English system, does not allow for civil party status for victims within criminal proceedings and so the same approach cannot be taken to the enforcement of compensation awards by the Irish courts. Instead, enforcement of Irish criminal court "compensation" awards must be through another European Union law[16] on the application of the principle of mutual recognition to financial penalties.

Unfortunately, it may be difficult or impossible to enforce financial reparation awards the criminal courts of countries *outside of the European Union*. If they are in fact civil judgments, it may be possible to enforce them as civil judgments (▷ *Section 7.4.9, Enforcing foreign civil court judgments in E & W*).

7.4.6 When can you bring civil claims in E & W?

We are talking here about the right to bring a "substantive claim" in England and Wales. We mean the kind of substantive claim which will require a court to decide whether certain persons have committed wrongs and are liable to pay compensation or otherwise account to you the victim for their wrongdoing. This is not the same as bringing a claim or court procedure merely to enforce a judgment obtained in another country, for example in your home country. We come on to deal with that further below.

Whether you have a right to bring a case before the English and Welsh courts depends on whether you can show that the English and Welsh courts have "jurisdiction" to try the case.

Questions about civil court "jurisdiction" are, in legal terms, questions of private international law (also known as conflict of laws). Private international law can be very difficult, even for lawyers and judges who have to understand and apply it and so this guide is not the place to give a detailed private international law analysis. However, we can give some useful guidance to help victims understand the main points that have to be considered.

The guidance we can give on "jurisdiction" has to be in two parts. Firstly, there are a number of rules established by European Union law.[17] These must always be considered first. If those EU rules do not apply, then the private international law

15 Regulation (EU) 1215/2012 and the Lugano Convention on jurisdiction and the recognition and enforcement of judgments in civil and commercial matters, signed on 30 October 2007, which entered into force on 1 January 2010.

16 Council Framework Decision 2005/214/JHA.

17 In one form or another, this EU approach is highly likely to remain in place even after the United Kingdom has left the European Union.

which will determine whether a claim can be brought in England and Wales is what we will call the "traditional" regime and we'll say more about that below.

7.4.6.1 European regimes for establishing "jurisdiction" for civil claims

European Union law dictates a certain kind of approach to jurisdiction by civil courts. This is to provide a harmonious approach within the European Union. An almost identical approach is taken by the laws which apply as between the EU Member States[18] and the European Free Trade Association countries, Iceland, Norway and Switzerland, which have entered into a relevant treaty with the EU countries.[19]

Here are the basics in terms of eligibility to bring claims in England and Wales under the European regimes.

The "domicile" rule

If an alleged wrongdoer is domiciled in England and Wales, the general rule is that victims should bring their claims against the wrongdoer in England and Wales. This rule applies whether the wrongdoer is an individual (natural person) or a legal person (company or other legal entity). It means that as a general rule you will have no problem bringing a claim in England and Wales against a wrongdoer who is domiciled in England and Wales. But the converse is, of course, also the case: if the wrongdoer is domiciled in another EU Member State then you are, as a general rule, expected to bring your claim in that other Member State. Whether a person is domiciled in England and Wales is itself an issue based on both the facts and the correct legal interpretation of what is meant by domiciled.

"Special jurisdiction" exceptions

Special jurisdiction exceptions are based on the nature of the claim: you can bring a claim in England and Wales, contrary to the usual domicile rule, if you can establish a special jurisdiction ground for doing so based on the nature of your claim. These special jurisdiction grounds include rules about contract claims, tort claims, unjust enrichment (also called restitution) claims and claims concerning pre-existing trusts (⊳*Section 5, Civil court claims*). The interpretation of the various special jurisdiction rules has been the subject of many cases both in the European Court of Justice as well as in national courts. Specialist fraud lawyers can advise on how these apply to fraud claims.

The "anchoring" rule

One of the most important special jurisdiction exceptions to the domicile rule is what we shall call the anchoring rule. This rule allows you to bring a claim in England and Wales against an EU national who is not domiciled in England and Wales, *if*, in the same case, you also bring a claim against another person who is domiciled in England and Wales.

---

18 Regulation (EU) 1215/2012.

19 Lugano Convention on jurisdiction and the recognition and enforcement of judgments in civil and commercial matters, signed on 30 October 2007, which entered into force on 1 January 2010.

The above rules *permit* you to bring a claim in England and Wales. They do not require you to do so. At the same time, the converse application of the same rules may also give you the freedom to bring a claim in your home country. This may be because the wrongdoer is domiciled in your home country or because one of the other special jurisdiction rules allows you to sue in your home state.

> **Signpost**
>
> You must remain professional. Whatever the temptations, you must maintain your integrity and honesty. Any lack of probity will be exposed and undermine your case. A prosecutor will be far less likely to proceed with the case. The civil courts may dismiss your claim and make you pay the defendant's costs. ⊳ *Section 1*

The "jurisdiction agreement" rule

The courts of England and Wales can hear any case where the parties had previously agreed by way of a contract that the English and Welsh courts should determine any dispute between them, either exclusively or non-exclusively. The exception is when an agreement is "null and void" under English and Welsh law. English and Welsh law upholds jurisdiction agreements, even where a victim asserts that a contract containing a jurisdiction agreement should be declared void or voidable, unless the jurisdiction agreement itself is found to be null and void. Jurisdiction agreements are typically made before a dispute arises as a term in a commercial contract, but they can be made after the dispute has arisen. There are detailed principles as to how such agreements should be interpreted which are beyond the scope of this guide.

> **Signpost**
>
> The freezing injunction is very wide in its scope. It is designed to catch not only the assets physically possessed by a wrongdoer (cash, car and other personal items) but also assets held by others, including banks and other financial institutions, friends and associates and so called "nominees". ⊳ *Section 5*

The "barring" rules

Other EU rules bar a claim being brought in England and Wales. Here are the basics of what we shall call the barring rules:

- Parties who have contractually agreed that disputes should be determined exclusively in another EU Member State will not, as a rule, be able to bring a claim in England and Wales.
- An attempt to bring a claim in England and Wales will also be barred if proceedings between the victim and the wrongdoer have already commenced in another EU Member State.
- Attempted claims in England and Wales may (as opposed to "will") also be barred where "related" litigation has already commenced in another EU Member State.

- Attempted claims in England and Wales which have as their object a claim to ownership of a real property (houses etc) will also be barred (although this does not prevent a so-called proprietary *tracing* claim into real property – ⊳ *Section 5.11, Proprietary claims*).

7.4.6.2 The "traditional" regime for establishing jurisdiction for civil claims

The traditional regime for establishing jurisdiction to bring a claim, comprise a collection of "common law" rules long-established by the English and Welsh courts. These rules have, to a large extent, now been codified in the Civil Procedure Rules which apply in the English and Welsh courts.

The traditional rules apply to all cases to which the European regimes' rules do not apply. The most frequent reason for application of the traditional rules is that the wrongdoer who is to be sued is not domiciled in any EU Member State or EFTA state.

In compliance with the "Hague Convention on Choice of Agreements",[20] the courts must hear cases in which the parties have agreed that England and Wales is the appropriate jurisdiction. Conversely, the E & W courts will not hear a case arising from a contractual agreement which stipulates that another country's courts should deal exclusively with any dispute. These principles invariably apply whether or not the agreed jurisdiction is a signatory to the Hague Convention. The relevant law in these cases is beyond the scope of this guide.

Here's a short guide to when the English and Welsh courts have a *discretion* to accept jurisdiction to deal with and determine a claim – these are often referred to as "gateways" for grounding jurisdiction:

- The wrongdoer is present in England and Wales when the claim is instigated and served on that person. If the wrongdoer is a human, then this could be because he or she is temporarily in England and Wales. A company is "present" in England and Wales if it has a branch in or carries on business in England and Wales.
- The claim is against more than one wrongdoer, one of whom has been or will be served with a claim in England and Wales. This means that as long as you have one "anchor" wrongdoer over whom jurisdiction can be grounded, then you will also be entitled to sue others in the same court. This is an important and very useful ground.
- Jurisdiction based on the nature of the claim. There are rules which allow you to bring a claim in England and Wales depending on the kind of claim you are brining. Importantly for fraud claims, there are rules for contract claims, tort claims, unjust enrichment (aka restitution) claims, claims about pre-existing trusts, and proprietary tracing claims. The contract claims rules include rules that the English Court will have jurisdiction if the parties stipulated this in a relevant agreement and that this will apply even if the claim asserts that the relevant agreement was and is void unless the jurisdiction agreement clause itself is separately found to be void.

---

20 The Convention on Choice of Court Agreements concluded on 30 June 2005 at the Hague, which is given effect in England and Wales by the Civil Jurisdiction and Judgments Act 1982 (as amended). Fully ratified parties are currently: all the EU Member States, Mexico, Montenegro and Singapore.

- Assuming that you can establish one of the above "gateways", the English and Welsh court may still not allow your claim to be determined in England and Wales. This is because the court has a discretion as to whether to accept jurisdiction, taking into account whether England and Wales is the most suitable country in which to determine your claim, or indeed, whether the courts of another country would be more suitable. The general principle is that the court must consider where the case can be most suitably tried in the interests of all parties to it and in the interests of justice generally.
- In deciding which country's courts are most suitable for the case to be determined, the English and Welsh courts consider a range of factors, including: the convenience and expense to the parties of each of the potential alternatives (for example, witness locations); which country would allow proceedings against all potential wrongdoers in one set of proceedings (which is a good thing); which country's law will apply to the dispute; the residence and place of business of each party; the nature of the dispute and questions of local knowledge; whether proceedings between the same parties or between related parties have already commenced in another country.

Signpost

Civil courts hear applications in secret and prepare court orders which can be unleashed on an unsuspecting target and / or on his banks and other asset holders. ▻ *Section 4*

7.4.6.3 Forum shopping in civil claims

A fraud lawyer: "It is common, in cases of financial offences, to have criminal and civil proceedings simultaneously pending. The availability of a combined criminal and civil process in some jurisdictions may be attractive to victims. There is of course the general principle that victims cannot initiate and simultaneously pursue the same civil case in different countries. They have to chose which country they wish to be the place to bring the lead case. So if the victims decide to make a civil claim within the criminal proceedings in one country, that will become the lead place for their civil claim and other than bringing supportive proceedings in other countries it would not generally be possible or desirable to mount the same claim elsewhere."

You may find that you can effectively choose whether to bring a claim in England and Wales or bring a claim in your home country. If this is the case then you will be able to engage in what lawyers call "forum shopping" for the best legal forum to bring your claims. Whether England and Wales will be the right forum for you, is a matter of judgment for you based on a comparison of your options and the advice you receive from your lawyers – perhaps both from English and Welsh lawyers and lawyers in other places. You may also find that your options are limited and that only one place is open to you to bring a claim.

7.4.7 Freezing assets in E & W in support of foreign civil cases

A fraud lawyer: "Getting the strategy right in an international asset tracing case is critical. If assets are not locked down at the outset or the efforts to recover get bogged down in procedural wrangling, the claimant can end up throwing good money after bad."

Any victim of fraud is entitled to use his own resources to informally investigate the fraud and the whereabouts of his money in England and Wales. This can mean hiring private investigators and lawyers to make enquiries and analyse facts and so on. Many points we discuss in *Section 1.7, Professional investigators* should help.

A victim from outside the UK is also able to get help from the English and Welsh civil courts. The points discussed in *Section 4* should help you understand the powers of the civil courts to help you identify wrongdoers and trace money as well as freeze assets and seize evidence.

You may be able to get help from the English and Welsh courts even if you are bringing your main claims in a court in your home country. The English and Welsh court can and will even issue a freezing order which has reach beyond England and Wales, if this is appropriate.

But you should know that, if you are bringing your main claim in another country, the English and Welsh courts will consider a number of things before making invasive provisional protective orders. To take freezing orders as an example, the courts must carefully exercise a discretion as to whether to make them in support of foreign proceedings. The court's considerations will include:

- The location of assets to be frozen, in particular whether assets are in England and Wales.
- The location of wrongdoers who are holding the assets to be frozen, in particular whether they are in England and Wales.
- Exercising caution before granting a freezing order, particularly when asked to issue one in support of a foreign court claim.
- Not being timid about granting an injunction in support of foreign proceedings if they are justified in fraud cases and indeed doing so unless it is "inexpedient" to make an injunction.
- If the foreign court has itself refused to grant a freezing injunction, being "slow" to do so, but there may still be circumstances when it is appropriate to do so.
- Being cautious about making orders which overlap with orders made in other foreign courts because overlapping orders increase costs and court time to all parties and can be oppressive to those who are made the subject of them.
- What power, if any, the English and Welsh court would have to enforce its order if it were disobeyed by the alleged wrongdoer.

Signpost

The civil courts are able to empower claimants by making orders which assist investigations and the preparation of cases. These orders cover investigating the identity of the fraudsters and what has become of the money or other property you have lost, obtaining evidence from the defendant and other parties such as banks. ⊳ *Section 2*

7.4.8 Evidence gathering in E & W in support of foreign civil cases

There are two legal regimes in England and Wales that govern formal evidence gathering. They are:

- the so-called "Evidence Regulation",[21] which governs all requests for evidence gathering from other EU Member States;[22] and
- a statutory regime,[23] which provides that evidence gathering assistance may be given in response to all other countries' requests.

Under the Evidence Regulation, you or your lawyers[24] would have to request that the court dealing with your case send a request for evidence direct to the High Court in England and Wales, specifying from whom the evidence is sought and the nature of the evidence sought. The English / Welsh High Court would then "execute" the request, by compelling the relevant persons to attend court to give testimony and produce relevant documents. If required by the requesting court, the English / Welsh court would allow the use of videoconferencing or teleconferencing for the relevant evidence to be given and transmitted live to the requesting court.

Under the Evidence Regulation, a requesting foreign court can also be ask to and must be allowed to convene itself in England and Wales for the purposes of directly receiving evidence in England and Wales but in this case it can only do so if the persons whose evidence is sought are willing to cooperate and give their evidence voluntarily, as the foreign court would have no power to compel their attendance.

Under the statutory scheme for dealing with requests from other countries,[25] on receiving a request from overseas, the English and Welsh High Court is empowered to organise and order:

- the examination of witnesses, either orally or in writing;
- the production of documents;
- the inspection, photographing, preservation, custody or detention of any property; and
- the taking of samples of any property and the carrying out of any experiments on or with any property.

21 Council Regulation 1206/2001/EC.
22 But not Denmark, which has not accepted the Evidence Regulation into its national law.
23 Evidence (Proceedings in Other Jurisdictions) Act 1975.
24 This would probably be best done by your home country lawyer but can also be done by an English / Welsh qualified lawyer.
25 Evidence (Proceedings in Other Jurisdictions) Act 1975.

7.4.9 Enforcing foreign civil judgments in E & W

7.4.9.1 Enforcing EU and EFTA civil court judgments in E & W

Judgments of courts in other EU and EFTA Member States are generally enforceable in England and Wales.[26] It does not matter what form the judgment takes and so the judgment could be for the payment of a sum of money, or it could be that the wrongdoer hands over a particular asset to the victim.

Under no circumstances can the substantive correctness of the foreign court judgment be questioned. There are only limited reasons why EU / EFTA court judgments cannot be enforced in England and Wales, the most important of which are:

- if the judgment was obtained in the absence of the person subject to it and he has not been given an opportunity to challenge it in the foreign court;
- if the judgment is irreconcilable with a judgment of a court in the United Kingdom in relation to the same parties; or
- if the judgment offends one of the so-called exclusive jurisdiction rules, for example the rule that a claim can only be brought and judgment can only be given in relation to ownership of land in the courts of the jurisdiction where the land is sited.

7.4.9.2 Enforcing civil court judgments of "Commonwealth" countries in E & W

The English and Welsh High Court is *empowered* to enforce *money* judgments (i.e. judgments requiring payment of a sum of money and not, for example, requiring the handing over of particular assets) emanating from certain other designated countries and territories, which broadly speaking we shall call "Commonwealth" countries and territories because most of the countries and territories in this list are also members of the Commonwealth.[27] The current list of countries whose judgments can be enforced, in alphabetical order, is:

Anguilla, Antigua and Barbuda, Bahamas, Barbados, Belize, Bermuda, Botswana, British Indian Ocean Territory, British Virgin Islands, Cayman Islands, Christmas Island, Cocos (Keeling) Island, Republic of Cyprus, Dominica, Falkland Islands, Fiji, The Gambia, Ghana, Grenada, Guyana, Hong Kong, Jamaica, Kenya, Kiribati, Lesotho, Malawi, Malaysia, Malta, Mauritius, Montserrat, Newfoundland, New Zealand, Nigeria, Territory of Norfolk Island, Papua New Guinea, St Christopher and Nevis, St Helena, St Lucia, St Vincent and the Grenadines, Saskatchewan, Seychelles, Sierra Leone, Singapore, Solomon Islands, Sovereign Base Areas of Akrotiri and Dhekelia in Cyprus, Sri Lanka, Swaziland, Tanzania, Trinidad and Tobago, Turks and Caicos Islands, Tuvalu, Uganda, Zambia, Zimbabwe.

The English and Welsh court cannot and will not, however, enforce a judgment from any one of these countries or territories in certain situations. Most importantly:

- the judgment debtor was neither ordinarily resident in nor carrying on business within the jurisdiction of the original court;

---

26 Regulation (EU) 1215/2012; and the Lugano Convention on jurisdiction and the recognition and enforcement of judgments in civil and commercial matters.

27 The court's power derives from the Administration of Justice Act 1920.

- the judgment debtor was not duly served with the process of the original court and did not appear in the original court's proceedings;
- an appeal is pending or the judgment debtor is entitled to appeal and intends to appeal against the judgment;
- the judgment was obtained by fraud; or
- the judgment was in respect of a kind of claim which, for reasons of public policy or some other similar reason, could not have been entertained by the English and Welsh courts.

7.4.9.3 Enforcing civil court judgments in E & W under bi-lateral agreements

The English and Welsh High Court is also obliged to enforce *money* judgments (i.e. judgments requiring payment of a sum of money and not, for example, requiring the handing over of particular assets) of a number of other designated countries, with whom the United Kingdom has concluded treaties for the reciprocal enforcement of civil court judgments.[28] The countries / territories are:[29]

Australia, Canada, Guernsey, Isle of Man, Israel, Jersey, Suriname, Tonga.

In these countries / territories, the money judgments of foreign courts will qualify for enforcement, including judgments requiring interim payments of money, except in certain situations, including:

- the judgment debtor was not duly served with the process of the original court and did not appear in the original court's proceedings;
- an appeal is pending or the judgment debtor is entitled to appeal and intends to appeal against the judgment;
- the judgment was obtained by fraud;
- the enforcement of the judgment would be contrary to public policy in England and Wales; or
- the sum payable is the nature of a fine, penalty or tax.

7.4.9.4 Enforcing judgments under the Hague Convention on Choice of Court Agreements

The Hague Convention on Choice of Court Agreements requires signatory states, including England and Wales, to recognise and enforce a judgment of another signatory state whenever parties have agreed upon a specific jurisdiction (⊳ *Section 7.4.6.2, The "traditional" regime for establishing jurisdiction for civil claims*).[30] This requirement is subject to the limited specific exceptions set out in the Hague Convention, which are beyond the scope of this guide.

---

28 This is under the Foreign Judgments (Reciprocal Enforcement) Act 1933.

29 Some other European countries signed reciprocal agreements with the UK but those have now been superseded by EU law.

30 The Convention on Choice of Court Agreements concluded on 30 June 2005 at the Hague, which is given effect in England and Wales by the Civil Jurisdiction and Judgments Act 1982 (as amended). Fully ratified parties are (currently): all the EU Member States, Montenegro, Mexico and Singapore.

7.4.9.5 Enforcing other foreign civil court judgments in E & W

The position in relation to enforcement of judgments of courts which do not fall under the categories set out above is that they may be enforced under the so-called common law rules, which act as residual court powers of enforcement.

The basic position is that the English and Welsh courts will enforce judgments if certain criteria are met, including, most importantly, that the foreign court judgment:

- was issued by a court of competent jurisdiction;
- must be final and conclusive (i.e. not provisional or subject to an appeal);
- must be for a sum of money;
- in the case of non-money judgments, does not offend certain principles of private international law (notably, the English and Welsh court will not enforce foreign declarations as to ownership of personal property or real property which is sited in England and Wales at the time the declaration is made); and
- must not be in the nature of a fine, penalty or tax.

The English and Welsh court may also refuse to allow the enforcement of a foreign judgment, the most important grounds for refusal being:

- the foreign judgment or the court proceedings it stemmed from offends certain English and Welsh standards of justice;
- the person against whom the foreign judgment was made did not have an adequate opportunity to defend the case against him or her;
- the proceedings giving rise to the judgment were contrary to an agreement between the parties as to the correct forum for the resolution of the dispute between them and the person made the subject of the judgment did not nonetheless submit to the foreign court proceedings;
- the foreign judgment is irreconcilable with another judgment between the same parties (whether an English and Welsh judgment or other judgment); or
- the foreign judgment was obtained by fraudulent means.

7.5 UK-based victims seeking help from overseas jurisdictions

7.5.1 Some general guidance

> A fraud lawyer: "The common law and civil law legal systems are different. The legal cultures are therefore different as well. There are also broader cultural differences to take into account when dealing with cross-border cases. For this reason, the success of a case may depend not only on the competence of the lawyers from different countries who represent the same client but, quite crucially also, on their ability to understand and agree on the right strategies and approaches."

In this part of this section, we look at the options open to victims who are based in England and Wales but who may need to take action outside the UK. This may be because wrongdoing occurred in another country, because the victim suffered harm in another country or because money has been laundered in another country.

What we cannot do and do not attempt to do is give detailed guidance about what to expect under local laws outside the United Kingdom. Even though one of the authors of this guide is a qualified lawyer who is familiar with other legal systems, it is important to recognise that the laws of different countries are materially different and that local law advice is essential if a victim intends to bring action outside the United Kingdom.

What we can do, however, is give guidance on how to go about getting help and advice overseas and what to expect in very broad terms from some countries based on the fact that the United Kingdom is (currently) a member of the European Union, which regulates certain aspects of court proceedings within the EU, and based on the fact that the UK has signed various bi-lateral treaties with other countries, governing certain aspects of investigations and court cases.

Which overseas lawyers should you use? Your English / Welsh lawyer, assuming that he or she is experienced in international fraud cases, should be able to recommend good lawyers outside of the UK. If you want, you can also do some research on the internet, using international directories of lawyers which contain rankings and peer-reviews but beware that these may not be accurate.

> A fraud lawyer: "The differences between the common law and civil law systems often mean that certain obstacles need to be addressed at an early stage. This is the reason why it is of utmost importance to establish at the outset the strategy between the Non-UK and UK teams of lawyers retained by the victim of a fraud. When legal advisers from both countries enjoy a similar mind set, the client will often greatly benefit from the common understanding in the setting-up of the priorities."

7.5.2 Making a complaint to police and prosecution overseas

> A fraud lawyer: "Frequently, a victim's lawyers will need to do work to supplement and complement the evidence collected by the police in financial cases. For the evidence to really "speak", it is necessary to highlight the key and most relevant aspects of it, to put it into perspective and to ensure that its various elements are consistent with and cross-refer to documents and other pieces of evidence. Sometimes, evidence being prepared needs to be made more comprehensive; other times it needs to be simplified. It is often the case that the police do not have the time or skills to do this evidence-preparation work alone and will rely on the victim's lawyers to do much of the necessary work."

The exact mechanics and your exact rights, when it comes to making a complaint to police outside the UK, are of course a matter of law and practice in the relevant country. The response times and resources of the relevant foreign authorities are likely to vary from one country to the next, just as they will be different to those of the UK police and other prosecutors.

Probably the easiest countries to understand, and indeed to expect responsive help, fall into two categories:

- EU countries; and
- Common law countries, for example Australia and Canada.

In the case of other EU countries,[31] they too have accepted the European Investigation Order regime, which we have described above as well as other EU laws.

> **Signpost**
>
> Whichever route you choose to bring your case to court, you need to use the same kind of rigour when investigating the extent of your losses as you do investigating the fraud itself. And often the two things will be linked, as showing how much went to the wrongdoers helps you prove not only who was involved but how much you lost. ⊳ *Section 1*

7.5.3 The Victims' Directive

> A fraud lawyer: "Collaborating with the police is not an easy process. The relationship between lawyers and policemen is often tense and tainted by respective prejudices. However, good cooperation is essential in order to obtain effective results. An engaged and tenacious investigator can make a difference in a case as she/he has more flexibility than an investigating magistrate to adapt her/his actions to the specific situation. The problem, however, is that the police often work secretly without sharing the results of their investigations with the victims when more transparent dialogue would assist."

The EU law with most eye-catching appeal to victims of fraud is likely to be the so-called "Victims' Directive".[32] Sounds really promising, doesn't it? And it is indeed a significant and historic piece of law. But it has its limitations. The most significant limitation of all needs to be called out straightaway. That is that the Victims' Directive's rights apply only to victims who are *'natural'* persons, i.e. individuals, and not legal persons such as companies. Given that most businesses operate as companies, this qualification is a big limitation.

With that big limitation in mind, let's take a closer look at the Victims' Directive.

The Victims' Directive contains a number of provisions which require EU Member States to ensure that victims of crime (including fraud) are given timely information and support in relation to criminal complaints to the police and criminal investigations and prosecutions. Victims must be informed about any decision not to proceed with an investigation or not to prosecute an offender. Conversely, they must also be provided details of where and when offenders will be prosecuted, information about the state of criminal proceedings and the results of the prosecution.

The Victims' Directive requires victims to be given free and confidential "victim support services". This means free support, such as that provided by Victim

---

31 Apart from Denmark, which has opted out of various EU criminal justice laws.
32 Directive 2012/29/EU, adopted by all EU Member States except Denmark.

Support[33] in the UK and many other similar organisations throughout the EU, all of whom are supported by Victims Support Europe.[34] These organisations' priorities are the immediate and emotional needs of victims, such as how to avoid or manage contact with offenders and psychological support for victims. Their services are appropriate and necessary for all crimes. But these kinds of organisations do not provide strong practical and legal guidance for victims of fraud who want to obtain financial reparations.

Signpost

Frauds tend to involve repeated events. Once an offender has learnt how to commit a fraud and got away with it, they do it again, often accelerating their offending. Without intervention, the opportunistic offender turns into a habitual fraudster. Unfortunately this means the detected fraud is often just the tip of an iceberg. ⊳ *Section 1*

The Victims' Directive requires that all victims have the right to review a decision to not bring a prosecution, although the Directive clearly contemplates that this is dependent on national laws and priority is to be given to victims of "serious crimes". In our view, fraud, even a relatively modest value one, is a serious one but don't be surprised if police and prosecutors take a different view.

What about the rights of victims at the criminal trial of accused persons? Well, here the rights of victims become even more vague and imprecise in the Victims' Directive. In relation to criminal trials, the Directive requires that "victims may be heard during criminal proceedings and may provide evidence" in a way that accords with the procedural rules of the national legal system in the place of the criminal trial. In the UK and Ireland, this translates into very few rights, whereas in other countries the rights of victims are much greater.

What about victims' rights to financial reparations? At least in one respect the Victims' Directive is very clear, that "recoverable property which is seized in the course of criminal proceedings is returned to victims without delay" (subject only to the fact that it may be necessary to await the outcome of the trial if the property is required for the criminal proceedings). What is left vague by the Victims' Directive is the meaning of "recoverable property".

Is this restricted to stolen articles such as vehicles or paintings or does it also include property such as money in which, by operation of English / Welsh law, a victim has a proprietary claim (⊳ *Section 5.11, Proprietary claims*)? If the latter, who should decide whether the victim has a valid proprietary interest in the money? The police or the courts and, if the latter, which ones? The meaning of "seized" is also open to interpretation. Does it just mean property which the police have taken into their possession or does it also mean property which has been "frozen" by the courts in freezing injunctions and their foreign equivalents?

33 www.victimsupport.org.
34 www.victimsupport.eu.

Signpost

A freezing order issued in England and Wales may purport to have worldwide effect but if the wrongdoer holds assets in another country or territory you need to know that the English and Welsh courts' freezing injunctions may be of little effect unless and until you obtain a freezing injunction (or equivalent) in that other place. ▻ *Section 4*

The Victims' Directive is much less clear on rights to financial compensation for victims. The Directive requires only that criminal courts make a "decision on compensation by the offender, within a reasonable time". This clearly does not mean that victims must be awarded compensation. Furthermore the relevant provision is further qualified in that it allows criminal courts to make no decisions in relation to compensation "where national law provides for such a decision to be made in other legal proceedings", which means that criminal courts may be allowed to avoid making decisions on compensation if the civil courts would also have competence to deal with the question of compensation.

Finally, we need to mention the fact that the Victims' Directive stipulates that victims must be given "access to legal aid, where they have the status of parties to criminal proceedings". In the UK and Ireland they have no such status but, in many if not most other EU countries, they do have the status of parties (civil parties) and so this is a useful right. Just how useful depends on the applicable "access" conditions and on the legal spend granted to victims.

Ultimately, the rights of victims outside the UK depend very heavily on the national laws and the qualities of the justice system in the countries in which they report crimes and in which investigations and prosecutions are brought.

7.5.4 "Civil party" status

A fraud lawyer: "Criminal proceedings are an extremely useful way to move forward a civil case. Indeed, provided that the victim's lawyer has succeeded in triggering the opening of criminal proceedings with credible evidence from the victim, then the resources of the Public Prosecutor, therefore of the State, will be available to provide support the civil side of the case. The state's powers to gather evidence in support of the criminal allegations are much more powerful and incisive than those available to the victims themselves. And the costs of gathering this evidence are borne by the Public Prosecutor which means a huge saving of money for the victim. Parallel criminal and civil proceedings can have the effect of putting a lot of legitimate pressure on a wrongdoer to settle the civil liability elements of the case."

Some countries have very strong rights for victims, indeed much stronger rights than are accorded to victims in England and Wales. This is largely due to the fact that in many other countries victims play a major part in criminal investigations and prosecutions as the "civil party" (*partie civile*) within those processes.

Given this role, a civil party can influence the course of investigations; to see documents and information gathered in the criminal investigation; to demand certain charges are brought against offenders; to play an active role in the trial of accused persons; and finally, to ask for an be awarded compensation by the criminal court which can then be enforced as a civil judgment against the offender.

Although there are differences in the rights that come with "civil party" status according to the country in question, as a general rule the status gives victims hugely significant rights. These can include the right to disclosure of police files enables victims to get a clear understanding of how the fraud was perpetrated and of the gains made by a defendant. They can also include the right of victims to make their formal claims for compensation to the court that deals with the criminal case. And of course the right to participate in the trial to advance the victim's case for compensation and to defend the victim against unwarranted attacks from the wrongdoer.

7.5.5 Enforcing E & W criminal compensation orders overseas

It is possible to enforce English / Welsh criminal court *compensation* orders (▷ *Section 6.7.1, Compensation orders*) in most other EU Member States. This is under a specific EU law for this purpose.[35] The compensation order enforcement has to be requested by the relevant public authorities in the United Kingdom and then "executed" by the relevant authorities in the country where enforcement is sought.

It may be possible to enforce English / Welsh restitution awards (▷ *Section 6.7.2, Restitution orders*) under the same EU law but this is far from certain, given that the law refers to compensation and makes no reference to restitution.

It is not currently possible to directly enforce English / Welsh court compensation or restitution orders in countries which are not members of the European Union. It may be possible that English / Welsh confiscation orders can be enforced abroad and some of the proceeds returned to the UK under asset sharing agreements, which can then be made available to victims of fraud by the UK government. But such a route is at best very uncertain and risky for victims as well as being very complicated (▷ *Section 6.7.3, Seeking compensation and restitution*).

Signpost

Speed is almost always vital in fraud cases in order to contain the situation, prevent further losses and stop the fraudster from dissipating your money. ▷ *Section 3*

We should also stress that theoretical rights to expect public agencies in one country or another to apply laws quickly or at all do not mean that this will be the outcome.

35 Council Framework Decision 2005/214/JHA, on the application of the principle of mutual recognition to financial penalties.

7.5.6 Enforcing E & W civil judgments overseas

You will often be able to enforce an English / Welsh civil-court judgment in another country. Your lawyers would make the running to give effect to your right. Your right to do so depends, of course, on the country in which you seek enforcement.

If it is an EU or EFTA country, then you will be able to rely on the "European Regimes" for the enforcement of civil-court judgments.[36] We have already described these European Regimes in detail earlier in this section. As already discussed, you should be able to enforce any form of judgment, subject only to limited exceptions.

The really significant thing about the European Regimes is that they require all countries to enforce the exact form of order made by the court in the country in which the case was tried. This means, for example, that English / Welsh court "proprietary" orders have to be recognised and enforced in the other EU / EFTA states.

The position in relation to non-EU / EFTA countries is much less certain and much more complicated. We set out earlier the various obligations of the English / Welsh courts to recognise and enforce inbound judgments issued by courts in other countries. Similar (but not identical) approaches can be expected from the courts in other countries, particularly in countries with which the UK has concluded bi-lateral treaties for the enforcement of judgments (we have set out those countries above).

7.5.7 Bringing a civil claim outside the UK

We have already discussed the "European regimes" rules of civil-court "jurisdiction" which determine the country or countries in which you may be eligible to bring proceedings. We looked at this from the perspective of victims from outside the UK who may be considering bringing claims in England and Wales. In fact, the same sets of European rules apply to victims who are based in England and Wales. Those rules set out whether you can bring a civil claim in a particular EU or EFTA country. There is one additional rule, which may be of use to you.

The "civil party" rule

If you are intent on issuing a claim outside of the UK (and outside of Ireland) then there is one "special jurisdiction" rule which may help you, even if others do not. That is if you are eligible to bring a civil claim in a criminal court case as a "civil party" alongside the criminal court case. If criminal proceedings are to be brought and you have the right to become a "civil party", then that entitles your civil claim to be brought in your home country – if that is what you want.

---

36 Regulation (EU) 1215/2012 and the Lugano Convention on jurisdiction and the recognition and enforcement of judgments in civil and commercial matters, signed on 30 October 2007, which entered into force on 1 January 2010.

7.6 Drawing the threads together and some practical guidance

As this section has been rather long and complex, it is helpful to draw the various threads to together to identify the most important principles, points and guidance we can give, in a few bullet points:

- If your case is international in some way, don't expect to be able to develop a full strategy straightaway. This is because your strategy should be formed after taking advice from experienced lawyers, often in multiple countries.
- Recognise and accept that international laws and international cases are more difficult and expensive than ones which are neatly contained within one country. Don't make assumptions about what the laws or practices will be in another country.
- When taking advice from lawyers in multiple countries, first establish a lead lawyer in one country to co-ordinate the activities of the other lawyers. This will minimise duplication of efforts and help keep the whole project manageable, co-ordinated and focused.
- Listen very carefully to all the advice you receive, to decide what all your options are. Do not be surprised if you are advised to bring civil proceedings in one country but that it is better to make or bring a criminal complaint / case in another country.
- Don't be surprised if the advice you receive is less certain that you might hope for. International law can itself be uncertain and international cases raise difficult issues even for the most experienced of lawyers.
- If you do bring or support a criminal case in another country, beware that police and public prosecutors will play a significant role in that case, even if, as a "civil party", you have an important role in their investigation and in the criminal court case.
- If you do bring or support a criminal case in another country, beware that the criminal investigation / prosecution in that other country may take a long time to get going and indeed to complete.
- If you do bring or support multiple legal proceedings in different countries against the same wrongdoer, be very careful to ensure that the cases that you / your lawyers are articulating (in lawyers' lingo, "running") are consistent with each other.
- Be aware that courts do expect multiple proceedings across different countries but that judges want to see parties, even victims, co-ordinate the various cases in a way that does not duplicate or waste the efforts of the courts and which is not oppressive to the alleged wrongdoers.
- Don't be surprised if the wrongdoer in your case has tried to launder your / his money in different countries, using a variety of corporate structures, involving corporate service providers and even lawyers to help establish and run those structures.
- It can be very hard to find assets which have been moved around by fraudsters. Be open-minded and curious about the motives, methods and actions of the wrongdoer and keep following the money trail to locate your / his assets and find the fraudster.

- Whether and where you can find assets is likely to play a very big role in what you choose to do. It will heavily influence who you sue or prosecute and whether and where you bring action.
- Think very carefully about the legal costs you incur. Insist on realistic cost estimates and ask your lead lawyer to play an active role in managing overall costs of each of your lawyers.

7.7 Conclusions

This section has set out just some of the issues relating to international fraud cases. The appropriate processes are fundamentally affected by three simple variables: the location of the victim; the location of the perpetrator; and the location of the act.

The legal landscape of intersecting jurisdictions, law systems, framework agreements and conventions is very complex and seriously difficult to navigate. Doing it yourself is all but impossible and there are few lawyers with real expertise in all the relevant international law and practice.

Victims must ask themselves, "Is it worth it?". If it is a high value fraud and it is worth the gamble, they must find a lawyer with the right knowledge and experience, otherwise a lot more of their money will disappear chasing people and assets that are elusive.

Index

All references are to paragraph number.

www.ingramcontent.com/pod-product-compliance
Ingram Content Group UK Ltd.
Pitfield, Milton Keynes, MK11 3LW, UK
UKHW021037150926
475561UK00003B/158

9 781526 509147